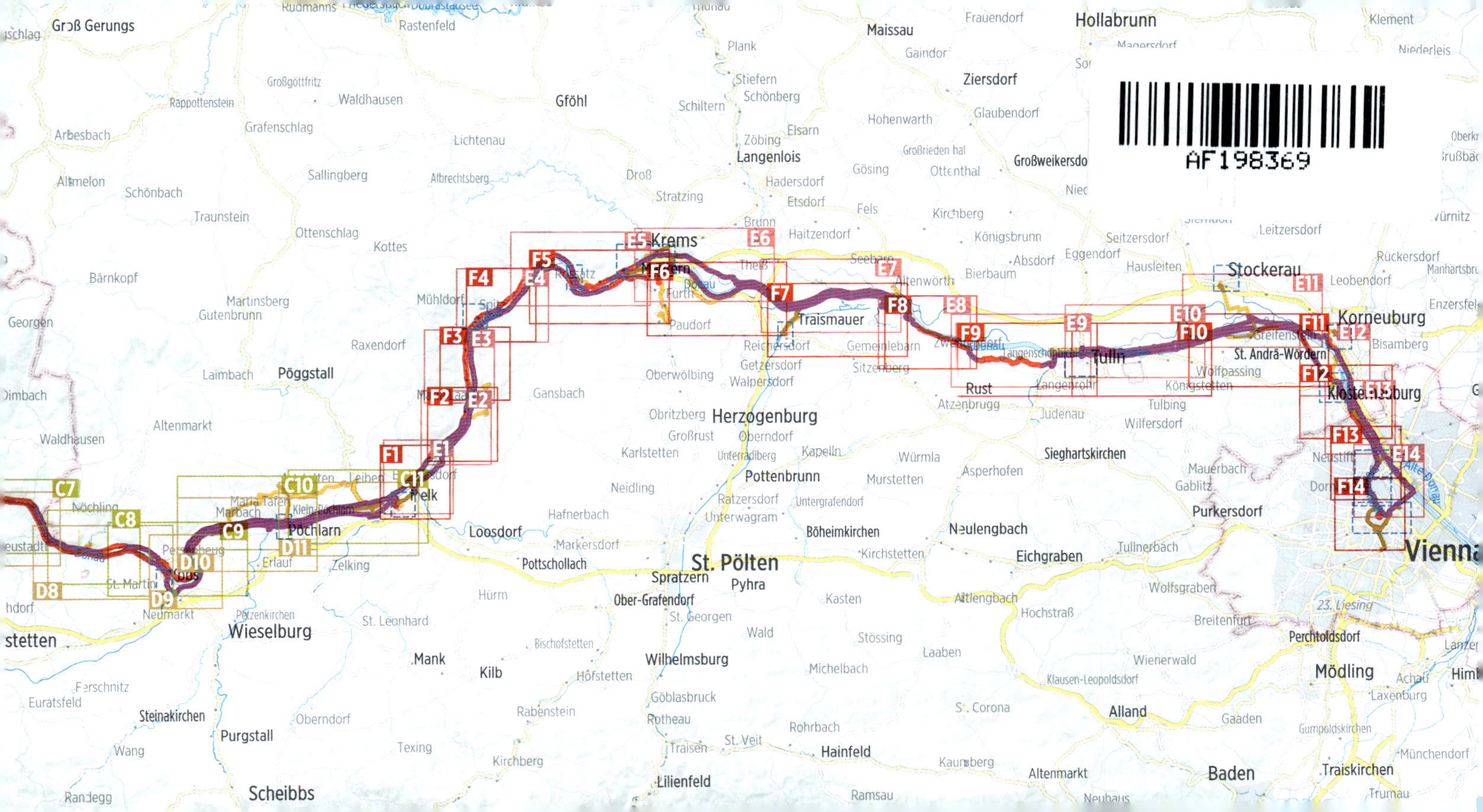

Groß Gerungs
Rudmanns
Rastenfeld
Thunau
Frauendorf
Hollabrunn
Klement
schlag
Niederleis
Maissau
Gaindor
Magersdorf
Ziersdorf
Sonn
Groß göttfritz
Waldhausen
Gföhl
Plank
Schönberg
Stiefern
Schiltern
Hohenwarth
Glaubendorf
Großweikersdo
Brußbad
Oberk
Rappottenstein
Grafenschlag
Lichtenau
Zöbing
Großrieden hal
Arbesbach
Langenlois
Elsarn
Gösing
Ottenthal
Rückersdorf
Leitzersdorf
Manhartsb
Altmelon
Schönbach
Sallingberg
Albrechtsberg
Droß
Hadersdorf
Fels
Kirchberg
Seitzersdorf
Würnitz
Traunstein
Kottes
Stratzing
Etsdorf
Königsbrunn
Absdorf
Eggendorf
Hausleiten
Stockerau
Leobendorf
E11
Ottenschlag
Brunn
Haitzendorf
E6
E5 Krems
Bärnkopf
F5
Enzersd
Martinsberg
E4
F4
Bierbaum
E7
Altenwörth
Seebarn
Georgen
Gutenbrunn
F6
ern
Theiß
F7
E8
E10
E9
Korneuburg
Mühldorf
Spitz
Furth
Paudorf
Traismauer
F8
E12
Gansbach
Reichersdorf
F9
Tulln
St. Andrä-Wördern
Bisamberg
Raxendorf
F3
E3
F2
E2
Pöggstall
Getzersdorf
Gemeinlebarn
Zwentendorf
Langenschönbichl
Wolfpassing
F10
Laimbach
Oberwölbing
Walpersdorf
Sitzenberg
Rust
Langenrohr
Königstetten
F11
E14
Obritzberg
Herzogenburg
Atzenbrugg
Judenau
Tulbing
F12
Dimbach
Großrust
Oberndorf
Wilfersdorf
Klosterneuburg
Waldhausen
Altmarkt
Karlstetten
Kapelln
Sieghartskirchen
Mauerbach
F13
C7
Nöchling
Karlstetten
Unterradlberg
Würmla
Murstetten
Gablitz
E14
C8
C10
Leiben
C11
Melk
Neidling
Ratzersdorf
Asperhofen
F14
Dorn
stetten
D8
C9
Pöchlarn
Loosdorf
Hafnerbach
Untergrafendorf
Böheimkirchen
Neulengbach
Purkersdorf
Vienna
D10
Marbach
Klein Pöchlarn
Markersdorf
Unterwagram
D11
Eichgraben
Tullnerbach
neustadt
St. Martin
Erlauf
Zelking
Pottschollach
St. Pölten
Kirchstetten
Wolfsgraben
Mödling
D9
Neumarkt
Pötzenkirchen
Hürm
Spratzern
Pyhra
Altlengbach
Hochstraß
Breitenfurt
23. Liesing
Perchtoldsdorf
Wieselburg
St. Leonhard
Ober-Grafendorf
St. Georgen
Kasten
Wald
Stössing
Laaben
Wienerwald
Klausen-Leopoldsdorf
Achau
Ferschnitz
Mank
Kilb
Bischofstetten
Höfstetten
Wilhelmsburg
Michelbach
Alland
Gaaden
Gumpoldskirchen
Laxenburg
Euratsfeld
Steinakirchen
Oberndorf
Rabenstein
Rotheau
St. Corona
Münchendorf
Wang
Purgstall
Texing
Kirchberg
Traisen
St. Veit
Hainfeld
Kaumberg
Altmarkt
Baden
Traiskirchen
Randegg
Scheibbs
Göblasbruck
Wilhelmsburg
Lilienfeld
Ramsau
Neuhaus
Trumau
Him



AF198369

*bikeline*®-Cycling guide
Danube Bike Trail | 2
© 2023, **Verlag Esterbauer GmbH**
A-3751 Rodingersdorf, Hauptstr. 31
Tel.: +43/2983/28982-0, Fax: -500
E-Mail: bikeline@esterbauer.com
www.esterbauer.com
9th revised edition, Summer 2023
**ISBN 978-3-7111-0169-3**
Please quote edition and ISBN number in all correspondence!

We wish to thank all the people who contributed to the production of this book.

**The *bikeline*-Team:** Birgit Albrecht-Walzer, Renata Andrejeva, Katrin Baumhauer, Beatrix Bauer, Michael Binder, Veronika Bock, Petra Bruckmüller, Roland Esterbauer, Dagmar Güldenpfennig, Gregor Münch, Mario Nakić, Karin Neichsner, Carmen Paradeiser, Amélie Pommier, Manuel Randa, Petra Schartner, Sonja Schleifer, Christina Steinbrecher, Christian Thoren, Isabella Tillich, Martin Trippmacher, Carina Winkelhofer, Martin Wischin, Wolfgang Zangerl

**Photo credits:** Cover: Mistervlad - stock.adobe.com; Agata Kadar - stock.adobe.com: 66; © Angela - Adobe Stock: 32; © Animaflora PicsStock - Adobe Stock: 44; Archiv: 18; © balakate - adobe stock.com: 100; © Christa Eder - Fotolia: 70; © Comofoto - stock.adobe.com: 154; ©Donau NÖ Tourismus/Wagensonner: 7; © EXTREMFOTOS - Fotolia: 139; © fotofrank - Fotolia: 14; © Freesurf - fotolia: 106; Gemeinde Haibach: 46; Gemeinde Wilhering, Antonio Bayer: 54; © Gina Sanders - fotolia: 88; Heidi Authried: 7, 28; © imagine.iT - fotolia: 98; © JFL Photography - Fotolia: 140; © Karin Wabro - Fotolia: 50; Krems Tourismus, Fotograf Gregor Semrad: 118, 120; © LianeM - fotolia: 114, 146; Marktgemeinde Wallsee-Sindelburg: 94; Michael Bernhrad: 110; © mdworschak - adobe stock.com: 134; MG Persenbeug-Gottsdorf: 76; Martin Wischin: 82; Passau Tourismus e. V.: 16; © Pecold - fotolia: 134; © photo 5000 - Fotolia: 158; Pixabay: 22, 26, 30, 40, 119, 142; Pöchlarn: 104; © salparadis - Fotolia: 113; ©serawood-fotolia: 116; Stadtgemeinde Tulln: 126; Stift Göttweig : 144; Tourismusverband Aschach: 48; Tourismusverband Linz, Röbl: 36; Tourismusverband Mauthausen: 67; Touristinfo Linz und Oberösterreich: 56, 58; TV Linz/Röbl: 85; TV St. Florian: 86; © WGD Donau Oberösterreich Tourismus GmbH-Hochhauser: 72; © Wolfgang - Adobe Stock.com: 74, 90; WTV, Gredler-Oxenbauer: 136; © Zechal - Fotolia: 62



Cover Design: martinveicht.de
Cartography created with axpand (www.axes-systems.com)

# bikeline

*What is bikeline?*

*We are a team of writers, cartographers, geographers and other staff united by our enthusiasm for cycling and touring. Our project first "got rolling" in 1987, when a group of Vienna cyclists came together to begin producing cycling maps. Today we are a highly successful publisher that offers a wide range of bikeline® books in five languages covering many European countries.*

*We need your help to keep our books up-to-date. Please write to us if you find errors or changes. We would also be grateful for experiences and impressions from your own cycling tours.*

*We look forward to your letters and e-mails (redaktion@esterbauer.com),*

*Your bikeline team*

# Preface

The Danube bicycle route between Passau and Vienna ranks as Europe's best-known and most-loved cycling route – and for good reason. No other section of the river offers as diverse a range of landscapes and cultural landmarks or as many historical sites. Tranquil valleys, fertile plains, and steep vineyards line the banks of one of Europe's great rivers, where pretty farms and glorious abbeys stand side-by-side. The loop of the Danube at Schlögen, the abbey at Melk, and the romantic Wachau wine-producing region are just some of the highlights along the 330 kilometer route.

This cycling guide includes detailed maps of the countryside and of many cities and towns, precise route descriptions, information about historic and cultural sites as well as background information and a comprehensive list of overnight accommodation. The one thing this guide cannot provide is fine cycling weather, but we hope you encounter nothing but sunshine and gentle tailwinds.

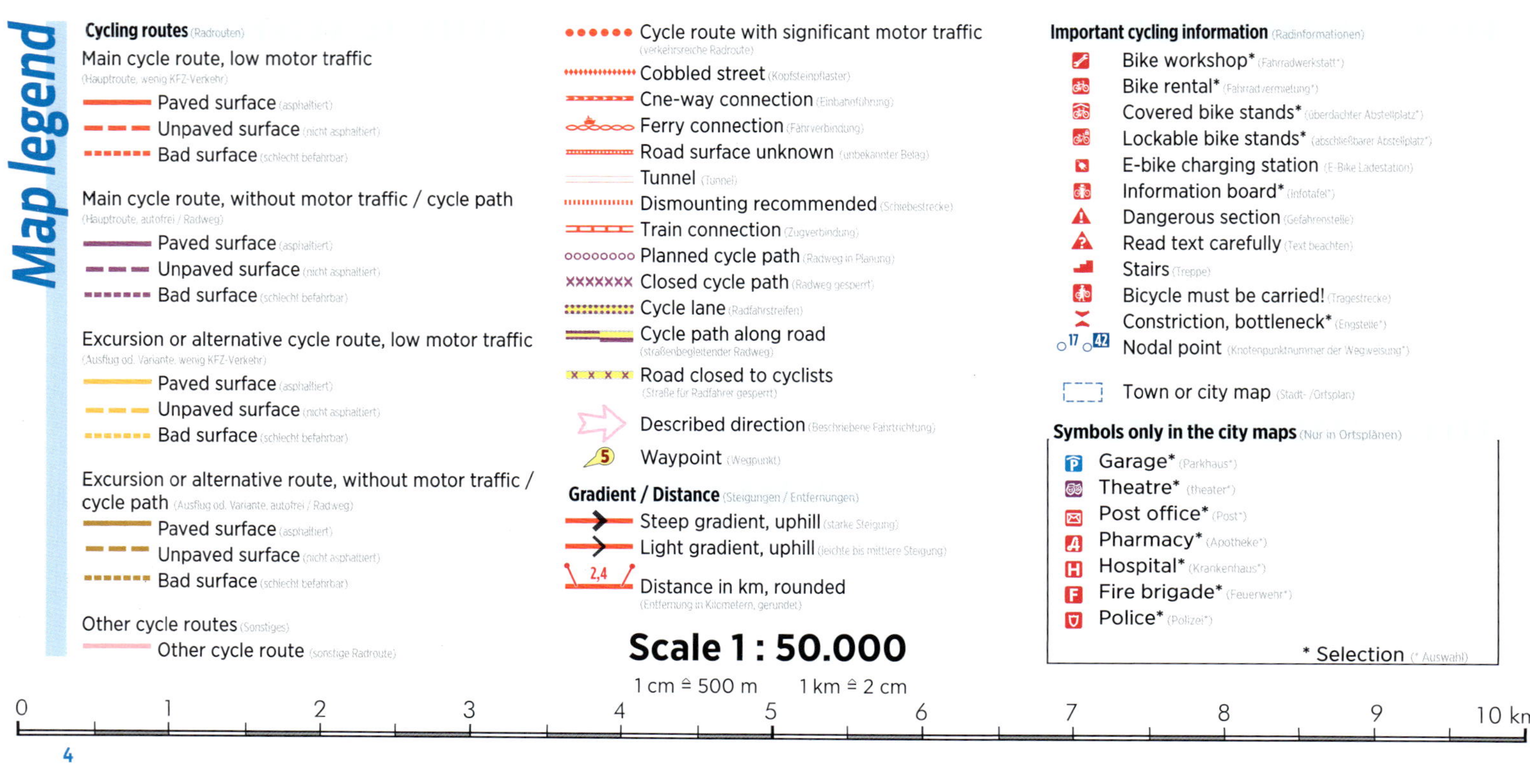

Map legend

Cycling routes (Radrouten)

Main cycle route, low motor traffic
(Hauptroute, wenig KFZ-Verkehr)
Paved surface (asphaltiert)
Unpaved surface (nicht asphaltiert)
Bad surface (schlecht befahrbar)

Main cycle route, without motor traffic / cycle path
(Hauptroute, autofrei / Radweg)
Paved surface (asphaltiert)
Unpaved surface (nicht asphaltiert)
Bad surface (schlecht befahrbar)

Excursion or alternative cycle route, low motor traffic
(Ausflug od. Variante, wenig KFZ-Verkehr)
Paved surface (asphaltiert)
Unpaved surface (nicht asphaltiert)
Bad surface (schlecht befahrbar)

Excursion or alternative route, without motor traffic /
cycle path (Ausflug od. Variante, autofrei / Radweg)
Paved surface (asphaltiert)
Unpaved surface (nicht asphaltiert)
Bad surface (schlecht befahrbar)

Other cycle routes (Sonstiges)
Other cycle route (sonstige Radroute)

Cycle route with significant motor traffic
(verkehrsreiche Radroute)
Cobbled street (Kopfsteinpflaster)
One-way connection (Einbahnführung)
Ferry connection (Fährverbindung)
Road surface unknown (unbekannter Belag)
Tunnel (Tunnel)
Dismounting recommended (Schiebestrecke)
Train connection (Zugverbindung)
Planned cycle path (Radweg in Planung)
Closed cycle path (Radweg gesperrt)
Cycle lane (Radfahrstreifen)
Cycle path along road (straßenbegleitender Radweg)
Road closed to cyclists (Straße für Radfahrer gesperrt)

Described direction (Beschriebene Fahrtrichtung)
Waypoint (Wegpunkt)

Gradient / Distance (Steigungen / Entfernungen)
Steep gradient, uphill (starke Steigung)
Light gradient, uphill (leichte bis mittlere Steigung)
Distance in km, rounded (Entfernung in Kilometern, gerundet)

Scale 1 : 50.000
1 cm ≙ 500 m     1 km ≙ 2 cm

Important cycling information (Radinformationen)
Bike workshop* (Fahrradwerkstatt*)
Bike rental* (Fahrradvermietung*)
Covered bike stands* (überdachter Abstellplatz*)
Lockable bike stands* (abschließbarer Abstellplatz*)
E-bike charging station (E-Bike Ladestation)
Information board* (Infotafel*)
Dangerous section (Gefahrenstelle)
Read text carefully (Text beachten)
Stairs (Treppe)
Bicycle must be carried! (Tragestrecke)
Constriction, bottleneck* (Engstelle*)
Nodal point (Knotenpunktnummer der Wegweisung*)

Town or city map (Stadt- /Ortsplan)

Symbols only in the city maps (Nur in Ortsplänen)
Garage* (Parkhaus*)
Theatre* (theater*)
Post office* (Post*)
Pharmacy* (Apotheke*)
Hospital* (Krankenhaus*)
Fire brigade* (Feuerwehr*)
Police* (Polizei*)

* Selection (* Auswahl)

0   1   2   3   4   5   6   7   8   9   10 km

## Sights of interest / Facilities (Sehenswertes / Einrichtungen)

- Church; Chapel (Kirche, Kapelle)
- Monastery/Convent (Kloster)
- Synagogue; Mosque (Synagoge, Moschee)
- Palace, Castle; Ruin (Schloss, Burg; Ruine)
- Tower; Lighthouse (Turm; Leuchtturm)
- Watermill; Windmill (Wassermühle; Windmühle)
- Power station (Kraftwerk)
- Mine; Cave (Bergwerk; Höhle)
- Airport, Monument (Flughafen, Denkmal)
- Other sight of interest (sonstige Sehenswürdigkeit)
- Museum (Museum)
- Excavations; Roman site (Ausgrabungen; röm. Objekte)
- Zoo; Nature info (Tierpark; Naturpark-Information)
- Nature reserve/Monument (Naturpark, -denkmal)
- Natural sight of interest (sonstige Natursehenswürdigkeit)
- Panoramic view* (Aussichtspunkt*)
- Tourist information; Restaurant (Tourist-Info; Gasthaus)
- Hotel, Guesthouse; Youth hostel (Hotel, Pension; Jugendherberge)
- Campground; Simple tent site* (Camping-; Lagerplatz*)
- Shopping facility*; Kiosk* (Einkaufsmöglichkeit*; Kiosk*)
- Picnic tables*; Covered stand* (Rastplatz*; Unterstand*)
- Outdoor pool; Indoor pool (Freibad; Hallenbad)
- Natural pool; Thermal baths; Waterpark* (Naturbad; Thermal-; Erlebnisbad*)
- Drinking fountain*; Parking lot* (Brunnen*; Parkplatz*)
- Schör ern Picturesque town (sehenswertes Ortsbild)
- Facilities available (Einrichtung im Ort vorhanden)

## Topographic information (Topographische Informationen)

- Church; Chapel (Kirche, Kapelle)
- Monastery/Convent (Kloster)
- Synagogue; Mosque (Synagoge, Moschee)
- Palace, Castle; Ruin (Schloss, Burg; Ruine)
- Tower; Lighthouse (Turm; Leuchtturm)
- Watermill; Windmill (Wassermühle; Windmühle)
- Power station, Solar power station (Kraftwerk)
- Mine; Cave (Bergwerk; Höhle)
- Monument; Burial mound (Denkmal; Hügelgrab)
- Airport; Airfield (Flughafen, Flugplatz)
- Windturbine (Windkraftanlage)
- TV/Radio tower (Funk- und Fernsehanlage)
- Transformer station (Umspannwerk, Trafostation)
- Wayside cross; Boundary stone (Wegkreuz; Grenzstein)
- Playing field, Stadium (Sportplatz, Stadion)
- Golf course; Tennis courts (Golfplatz; Tennisplatz)
- Boat landing; Sluice/lock (Schiffsanleger; Schleuse)
- Natural spring; Wastewater treatment plant (Quelle; Kläranlage)
- International border crossing (Staatsgrenze; Übergang)
- State border (Landesgrenze)
- District border (Kreis-, Bezirksgrenze)
- Nature reserve, National park (Naturschutzgebiet, Naturpark, Nationalpark)
- Prohibited zone (Truppenübungsplatz, Sperrgebiet)
- Contour line 100m/50m (Höhenlinie 100m/50m)

## Topographic information (roads)

- Motorway/Freeway; Expressway (Autobahn; Schnellstr.)
- Highway (Fernverkehrsstraße)
- Main road (Hauptstraße)
- Secondary main road (untergeordnete Hauptstraße)
- Secondary road; Access road (Nebenstraße, Fahrweg)
- Track; Ferry (Weg; Fähre)
- Road planned/under construction (geplant/in Bau)
- Railway/station; S-train station (Eisenbahn/Bahnhof, S-Bahnhof)
- Railway disused; planned (Eisenbahn stillgelegt; geplant)
- Narrow gauge railway (Schmalspurbahn)
- Mountain railway; Cable car (Bergbahn; Seilbahn)
- Forest; Park (Wald; Parkanlage)
- Marsh/Bog; Heath (Sumpf; Heide)
- Vineyards; Allotment gardens* (Weinbau; Gärten*)
- Quarry; Open cast mine* (Steinbruch; Tagebau*)
- Cemetery; Dunes/Beach (Friedhof; Düne, Strand)
- Tidal flats; Glacier (Watt; Gletscher)
- Rock; Cliff; Scree (Felsen; Geröll)
- Greenhouse; Plantation (Gewächshäuser; Plantage)
- Commercial/Industrial area (Gewerbe-, Industriegebiet)
- Urban area; Public building (Siedlung; öffentl. Gebäude)
- Defensive wall/Wall (Stadtmauer; Mauer)
- Embankment, Dike (Damm, Deich)
- Canal (Kanal)
- River/Dam/Lake (Fluss/Staumauer/See)

# Contents


3 Preface
4 Map legend
7 Danube Bike Trail
13 About this book

15 **Passau to Linz along the north bank** 98.6 km
30 Route via Walding (16 km)

38 **Passau to Linz along the south bank** 95.9 km

60 **Linz to Emmersdorf along the north bank** 106.9 km
66 Mauthausen memorial (5.4 km)
68 Via Clam Castle to Grein (13,7 km)
78 To Maria Taferl (18,6 km)

84 **Linz to Melk along the south bank** 117.3 km
86 Excursion to St. Florian (16 km)
88 To the ferry
94 Alternative route over Wallsee (2 km)

108 **Emmersdorf to Vienna along the north bank** 120.6 km
130 Stockerau Excursion

137 **Melk to Vienna along the south bank** 116.9 km
144 To Göttweig Abbey (11 km)
157 To the main railway station (2,1 km)

166 Overnight accommodation
180 Geographical Index


# City maps


| | |
|---|---|
| Dürnstein | 117 |
| Enns | 91 |
| Klosterneuburg | 155 |
| Korneuburg | 132 |
| Krems | 121 |
| Linz | 59 |
| Linz-Urfahr | 37 |
| Melk | 107 |
| Ottensheim | 34 |
| Passau | 17 |
| Pöchlarn | 104 |
| Spitz | 112 |
| Steyregg | 62 |
| Stockerau | 130 |
| Traismauer | 148 |
| Tulln | 128 |
| Vienna (Centre) | 163 |
| Vienna (Danube Canal) | 161 |
| Vienna (North) | 160 |
| Ybbs | 100 |


## LIVE-UPDATES

On our web page we offer an online-service, that provides updated information and current changes concerning this cycling guide. This information is brought up-to-date regularly and enables you, in combination with the current edition of this book, to plan your trip in the best possible way. The Live-Update for this book is freely available on our web page while looking up the title or under:

www.esterbauer.com/danube-bike-trail-2

Have you noticed some changes or mistakes during your journey concerning the itinerary, the overnight accommodation or the tourist information along the route? Then you have the possibility to bring the bikeline-team up-to-date using the Update-section on our web page. We are looking forward to getting your information and say Thank You in the name of all cyclists.

The latest bikeline GPS-Track for this book is freely available under:

www.tracks.world/?dir=at/trk40ne452

# Danube Bike Trail

In the last decade the Danube bike trail has emerged as Europe's most important long-distance bicycle touring route. Its popularity is due primarily to the Danube's natural beauty and the wealth of cultural and historical sites that line its banks. But the large numbers of bicycle tourists visiting the Danube would not be possible without well-developed infrastructure and services. The Danube bike route has benefited from well-built posted bike trails and an extensive network of services oriented to meeting the needs of bicycle tourists. The following pages provide a few practical notes about how to use the book, and some tips on getting ready for the tour.

## Route statistics

Length of main route: 326 km

elev. m/km: ↗ 1.4 m $^{(467 m)}$ ↘ 1.8 m $^{(592 m)}$

cycle path: 63 % unpaved: 0 % busy road: 4 %

Sum of all routes: 889 km

## The Route

### Length

The total distance from the start in Passau to the final destination, Vienna, is about 330 kilometers (north shore 326 km, south shore 330 km). This figure does not include about 240 kilometers of side-trips and alternative routes.

### Surface quality and traffic

The Danube bicycle route is very comfortable to ride. Virtually the entire distance follows paved bicycle paths or lightly traveled public roads. For most of the distance, a bicycle route is present on both sides of the river.

### Signage

The Danube bicycle route is thoroughly signposted to show the way. In Austria, rectangular green signs are posted along the route and in most

places the route is clearly labelled the "Donauradweg." The signs are complemented by the logo of Eurovelo route no. 6. Other regional bicycle trails branch off from the main route. Excursions and alternative routes often follow their own signs, and are also described in this book.

### EuroVelo 6, Atlantic - Black Sea

The Danube Cycle Route is part of the EuroVelo 6 cycle route, which connects the Atlantic Ocean near Nantes with the Danube Delta in the Black Sea. You can travel almost the entire 4700-kilometer route with cycling travel guides from the bikeline series. You can find more information about Eurovelo 6 at https://de.eurovelo.com/ev6.

### Planning a tour

The descriptions of the 326/330 kilometer tour follow the river downstream, from west to east. This allows cyclists to take advantage of the prevailing winds and the river's downward slope (minimal though it may be).

The Danube usually has bicycle routes on both sides of the river. All of these routes are marked as part of the Danube bicycle route. Keep in mind when planning your route, that the hills along much of the way cause the south bank to be generally shadier than the north bank during the spring and autumn months. This book describes the routes on both sides of the river: the route on the northern, or left bank is described first, followed by the route on the southern, or right bank. The entire tour is divided into three sections: Passau to Linz, Linz to Melk, and Melk to Vienna. The two sides of the river are identified as the left and the right sides, as seen when look-ing downstream. In the maps you can find the Danube's kilometers for your orientation (| 1925).

The division of the tour into six sections is in-tended to aid tourists' general orientation and does not necessarily suggest one-day stages. If you intend to include museum visits and swimming stops along the way, we recommend planning at least a week for the entire distance. The book also includes descriptions of short excursions which offer an opportunity to extend the ride as desired.

If the tour turns out to take longer than expect-ed, there are **taxi companies** that also transport bicycles if the need arises. The contact details are listed under Bicycle Transport below. Rail lines also run along much of the Danube, giving riders the option of boarding a train to complete a stretch. Refer to the section Bike & Rail.

*Information*
Additional information is available from regional tourism offices:
**Tourismusverband Donau Oberösterreich**, Lindeng. 9, 4040 Linz, ☎ 0732/7277-800, info@donauregion.at, www.donauregion.at
**LAG Perg-Strudengau**, Schlossberg 1/12, 4391 Waldhausen im Strudengau, ☎ 07260/45255, info@pergstrudengau.at, www.region-strudengau.at
**Oberösterreich Tourismus GmbH**, Freistädterstr. 119, 4041 Linz, ☎ 0732/7277-100, tourismus@oberoesterreich.at, www.oberoesterreich-tourismus.at

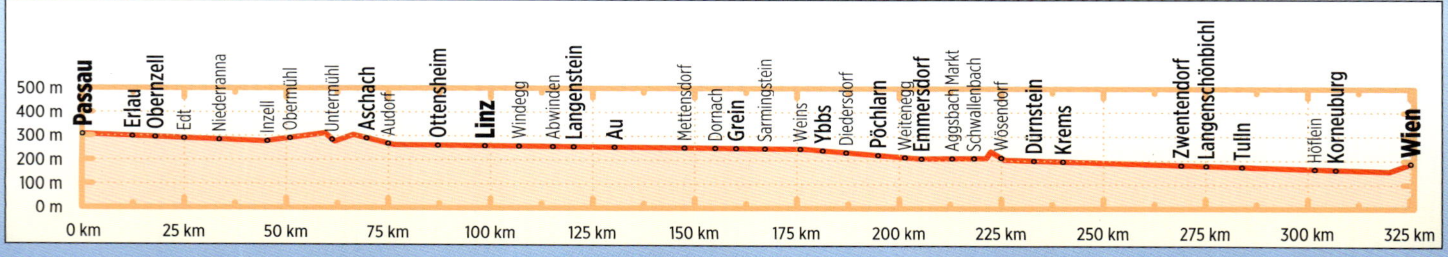

**Donau Niederösterreich Tourismus GmbH**, Schlossg. 3, 3620 Spitz/Donau, ☏ 02713/30060-60, urlaub@donau.com, www.donau.com

**Regionalbüro Tullner Donauraum-Wagram**, Minoritenpl. 2, A-3430 Tulln, ☏ 02272/67566-0, tullner-donauraum@donau.com, www.tullnerdonauraum.com

**Niederösterreich Information**, ☏ 02742/9000-9000, info@noe.co.at, www.niederoesterreich.at

**Tourist Information Wien**, Albertinaplatz/Maysedergasse, 1010 Wien, ☏ 01/24555, info@wien.info, www.wien.info

*International telephone codes:*
Germany 0049
Austria 0043

*Arrival & Departure by rail*
Due to the constantly changing prices and conditions for transport of a bicycle by rail we suggest that you inform yourself about your personal rail travel at the following addresses.
**Reise Service Deutsche Bahn (German Rail):** ☏ 030/2970, daily 0-24 hours. Information about train schedules, prices in Germany and other countries, tickets and reservations. www.bahn.de/bahnundbike (only in German)

**Österreichische Bundesbahnen:**
**ÖBB Kundenservice (customer service)** ☏ 05/1717 (Austria-wide at local rate), Mon-Sun 6am-2pm, www.oebb.at, www.oebb.at/en/reiseplanung-services/im-zug/fahrrad-mitnahme

**Schweizer Bundesbahnen:**
**Rail-Service** ☏ 0041/848446688 (CHF 0,08/Min.), Mo-So 0-24 Uhr, www.sbb.ch, www.sbb.ch/en/timetable/travel-advice/bicycles.html

*Bicycle shipping*
**Deutsche Bahn AG** (within Germany): If you are arriving and departing by Deutsche Bahn, you can use the DB luggage service. However, e-bike shipping is not possible. Your bike will be shipped door-to-door to the agreed destination if you are in possession of an appropriate rail ticket. The bicycle must be packed and remain rollable and steerable, weight max. 31.5 kilograms. Bicycle packing can be booked free of charge. Information and current prices can be found at www.gepaeckservice-bahn.de.
With the **ÖBB Haus-Haus-Gepäck service**, you can also have your bicycle collected from home and transported to your destination in Austria, South Tyrol and Germany, max. weight 30 kg. Information at www.oebb.at/de/reiseplanung-services/vor-ihrer-reise/haus-haus-gepaeck.

**(Return) transports incl. bicycles:**
**Taxi Ecker Sabine,** Edholz 49, 4115 Kleinzell im Mühlkreis, ☏ 0676/840073400, taxi@sabine-ecker.at, www.sabine-ecker.at/taxi/

**Taxi-Sitz,** A-3380 Pöchlarn, ☏ 0043/(0)676 525 63 40, www.taxi-sitz.at, info@taxi-sitz.at.

**Taxi Eilmannsberger,** Pasching 2, A-4085 Waldkirchen, Pasching 2, ☏ 0043/7718/7372, 0043/664/2132940, office@eiltaxi.at, www.eiltaxi.at

**Schönhofer,** Hauptstr. 5, A-4360 Grein, ☏ 0043/7268/72044, office@schoenhofer-on-tour.com, www.schoenhofer-on-tour.com

**Kofferbutler,** www.kofferbutler.com/gepaeckservice/radreisen

**Bikebus Klosterneuburg**: From May to September there is the possibility to return to Passau by bike bus from Klosterneuburg every Thursday and Sunday. More detailed information at www.klosterneuburg.at/en/Klosterneuburg_-_Passau or (in German) https://

stadtmarketing-klosterneuburg.at/radbus-nach-passau.

*Arrival and departure by car*
If you are travelling to Passau by car, you can park your car in various long-term parking spaces. You can find more information on the following websites: https://globus-group.de/de/leistungen-passau, ✆ 0049/(0)851 989000168 www.parkplatz-passau.de, ✆ 0049/(0)851/50015. https://stoegbauer-garage.jimdo.com/parken/, ✆ 0049/(0)851/ 5609880

*Bike & Rail*
All major centres along the Danube are connected by regular train services, which you can use to skip longer sections of the route when desired. Only parts of the route are accompanied by a railway line through the smaller centres, the most notable of these being the historic **Wachaubahn**, which services the 34 km stretch through the Wachau. It runs from Krems to Emmersdorf and back at weekends during the summer. Information under ✆ 02742/360990-1000, info@niederoesterreich-bahnen.at, www.wachaubahn.at.

**ÖBB** (Österreichische Bundesbahnen) offers the "Einfach-Raus-Radticket" for small groups of 2 - 5 persons on local trains. For more information, please contact ÖBB at ✆ 05/1717 or Donau Niederösterreich at www.donau.com/de/donau-niederoesterreich/infos-service/anreise/fahrradmitnahme-in-oebb-zuegen/ or directly at the ticket office of major railway stations.

*Bike & ship along the danube*
Travelling by ship can make a charming addition to a tour along the Danube. The route Passau-Engelhartszell-Brandstatt-Linz and back, as well as Passau-Vienna is served by the regular ships of the following shipping company:
**Wurm & Noé**, Höllg. 26, D-94032 Passau, ✆ 0049/851/929292 or Untere Donaulände 1, A-4020 Linz, ✆ 0043/732/783607, info@donauschiffahrt.eu, www.donauschiffahrt.eu
Within the Wachau, the ships of **Brandner Schiffahrt GmbH**, Ufer 15, 3313 Wallsee, ✆ 07433/2590-21, schiffahrt@brandner.at, www.brandner.at operate.
Between Melk and Krems, the ships of **DDSG Blue Danube Schiffahrt GmbH**, ✆ 01/58880, info@ddsg-blue-danube.at, www.ddsg-blue-danube.at also operate.

*Bike & Info*
Information points have been installed along the Danube Bike Trail especially for bicycle tourists. These provide information about available tourism services and landmarks in the region, and can help arrange overnight accommodation. In addition, there are many other tourism information sites and a growing number of electronic boards that show accommodation and assist with reservations.

*E-bike charging stations*
Charging stations for your e-bike are regularly available along the Danube Cycle Path. You can find detailed information on this website: www.donauregion.at/e-bike-ladestationen.html

*Donau.Erlebnis-Card*
In Upper Austria, this card gives you a 50% discount on many sights in the region. This applies from one overnight stay along the Upper Austrian Danube. Ask your accommodation provider for more information.

*Niederösterreich Card (Lower Austria Card)*
With the Niederösterreich-Card, which is available online in 2023 for 65,- Euro, also as an app, you have free admission to numerous

excursion destinations in the Danube region or in the whole of Lower Austria and at selected sights in Vienna. In addition, you can cycle free of charge for a whole day on the nextbike. All information under ℓ 01/5350505, www.niederoesterreich-card.at

## Overnight accommodation

Because the Danube River and adjacent regions are so popular with (bicycle) tourists, pensions and hotels may not always have rooms available during the peak season. This is especially true for the relatively sparsely populated stretch between Passau and Aschach. For this reason some hotels that are not directly on the Danube, and in the Nibelungengau between Ybbs and Melk, have set up shuttles that pick up bicycle tourists from the trail. Accommodation may also be hard to find between Tulln and Vienna. It is always a good idea to reserve rooms in advance. In general, during the peak season we recommend reserving rooms one to two days in advance. A comprehensive list of overnight accommodation is provided at the end of this book. We have endeavoured to put together the largest possible choice of providers for you. The following internet addresses of accommodation providers, who also provide alternative types of accommodation, are recommended for those who are looking for alternatives:

**ADFC-Dachgeber** works on the principle of reciprocal benefit: Here you find offers of private accommodation for cycling enthusiasts by cycling enthusiasts. More under www.dachgeber.de.

The **Bett+Bike** logo defines cyclist friendly accommodation providers in Germany only. More information under www.bettundbike.de Find a youth hostel through **Hostelling International**, www.jugendherberge.at or **Österreichischer Jugendherbergsverband (ÖJHV)**, www.oejhv.at.

Also the **Naturfreunde** offer an alternative form of accommodation with their Naturfreunde Houses. More under: www.naturfreunde-haeuser.net.

You will find just the **camping ground** you are looking for under www.campsite.at or www.campingplatz.de.

## Seasons

The best time to travel along the Danube is between May and September. However, the period from the end of March to mid-April is also attractive, as this is the time of the apricot blossom in the Wachau, as well as October, the time of the grape harvest.

Weather in the Danube river valley is influenced primarily by the systems moving into the continent from the Atlantic Ocean. One result is that the prevailing winds generally blow from west to east, and can be strengthened by the river valley's west-east orientation. Bicycle tourists starting in Passau can generally expect pleasant tailwinds, though the winds can occasionally turn and come from the east. Further east, the weather is increasingly affected by the continental-pannonian climate, which can bring longer periods of stable good weather.

## Bicycle tours with children

The Danube Cycle Route is characterized, among other things, by the fact that it runs almost entirely on asphalt paths and has virtually no gradients. In addition, the route runs almost exclusively on cycle paths or on low-traffic country roads. You can always avoid busy stretches of road on the other bank. The Danube Cycle Path is therefore highly recommended for children over the age of 8. In Austria, children under the age of 12 are required to wear a bicycle helmet.

## Bicycle & Public Transport & Parking in Vienna

**Underground**: Mon-Fri 9 a.m.-3 p.m. and from 6.30 p.m., Sat/Sun/Fri all day. The blue sign with the bicycle symbol indicates those underground cars in which you may take your bicycle. The transport is free of charge with all tickets. Information also at blog.wienerlinien.at/fahrrad_ubahn

**Schnellbahn**: In trains marked with a bicycle symbol in the timetables, you can take your bicycle with you without a reservation and depending on the availability of seats. An ÖBB bike ticket is required. Information at www.oebb.at/de/reiseplanung-services/im-zug/fahrradmitnahme

**Bicycle garage**: You can safely park your bicycle in a total of 3 covered and locked bicycle garages in Vienna (Hauptbahnhof, Kennedybrücke, Liesing). Exact address and costs at www.fahrradwien.at/tipps-und-regeln/radgaragen.

## Bike rental

**Renta a bike Fahrradverleih**, Bahnhofstr. 29, D-94032 Passau, ℂ +49(0)151/12834224, anfrage.verleih-passau@bikeambulanz.de, www.rent-a-bike.store

## Bicycle tour operators

**Eurobike**, Mühlstr. 20, A-5162 Obertrum am See, ℂ 0043/6219/60866, Fax: 8272, Infohotline: ℂ 0800/0706333 (free of charge from Germany, Austria and Switzerland) office@eurobike.at, www.eurobike.at

**Pedalo**, Kickendorf 1a, A-4710 Grieskirchen, ℂ 0800/2400999 (free of charge from Germany, Austria and Switzerland), otherwise ℂ 0043/7248/635840, info@pedalo.com, www.pedalo.com

**Austria Radreisen**, J.-Haydn-Str. 8, A-4780 Schärding, ℂ 0043/7712/55110, office@austria-radreisen.at, www.austria-radreisen.at

**Rückenwind Reisen GmbH,** Am Patentbusch 14, D-26125 Oldenburg, ℂ 0800/5889717 (free of charge from Germany, Austria and Switzerland), otherwise ℂ 0049/441/485970, info@rueckenwind.de, www.rueckenwind.de

**Pedalo Radtours,** Westerburgerstr. 6, D-94032 Passau, ℂ 0049/851/32124, info@pedaloradtours.de, www.pedaloradtours.de

**Velociped Fahrradreisen**, Alte Kasseler Str. 43, D-35039 Marburg, ℂ 0049/6421/886890, info@velociped.de, www.velociped.de

**Oberösterreich Touristik GmbH,** Freistädter Str. 119, A-4041 Linz, ℂ 0043/732/7277-260, info@touristik.at, www.touristik.at

**Augustus Tours e. K.**, Turnerweg 6, D-01097 Dresden, ℂ 0049/351/56348-28, aktiv@augustustours.de, www.augustustours.de

**Rad & Reisen GmbH**, Schickg. 9, A-1220 Wien, ℂ 0800/0700570 (free of charge from Germany, Austria and Switzerland), otherwise ℂ 0043/1/4053873, office@radreisen.at, www.radreisen.at

**Donau Touristik GmbH,** Ledererg. 4-12, A-4010 Linz, ℂ 0043/732/2080, free service phone number from Germany: ℂ 0800/1001147, office@donautouristik.com, www.donaureisen.at

# About this book

This cycling guide contains all the information you need for your cycling vacation along the Danube from Passau to Vienna: Precise maps, a detailed description of the route, a comprehensive list of overnight accommodation, numerous detail maps of cities and towns, and information about the most significant sights.

And all that information comes with our **bikeline guarantee**: The route described in this book has been tested and evaluated in person by one of our editors! To assure that the book is as up-to-date as possible, we welcome corrections submitted by readers and local officials or businesses. We cannot, however, always check and confirm such changes before deadline.

## The maps

The detail maps are produced in a scale of 1:50,000 (1 centimeter = 500 meters). In addition to exactly describing the route, these maps also provide information about roadway quality (paved or unpaved), climbs (gentle or steep), distances, as well as available cultural and culinary highlights.

Even with the most precise map, consulting the written description of the route may be necessary at times. Locations where the route is difficult to follow are shown by the ⚠ symbol on the maps, the same symbol can then be found in the written description where the route is explained in detail.

Note that the recommended main route is always shown in red or purple; alternative and excursion routes in orange. The individual symbols used in the maps are described in the legend on pages 4 and 5.

## Height and distance profile

The detailed route altitude profiles at the beginning of each section provide a graphic depiction of elevations along the route, the total length as well as waypoints and the location of towns and cities along the way. The waypoints enable a direct reference to the maps and route description. The altitude profile does not show every individual small hill and dip, but only the major changes in elevation. On the detail maps smaller gradients are shown by arrows that point uphill.

## The text

The maps are supplemented by a written text that describes the route starting in Passau and proceeding down the Danube to Vienna. Key phrases about the route description are indicated with the ⁓ symbol.

Many distinctive or important positions along the route are marked as waypoints with consecutive numbers **1**, **2**, **3**, ..... and, to help with navigation, are to be found with the same symbol in the maps.



**TIP** Text printed in purple indicates that you must make a decision about how your tour shall continue. For instance, there may be an alternative route that is not included in the tour description, or a turn-off to another location.

**EXCURSION** These also indicate excursion suggestions, interesting sights or recreational facilities that are not directly on the main route.

Furthermore, the names of important **villages**, towns and cities are printed in bold type. If a location or community has important points

Danube valley

of interest, addresses, telephone numbers and opening times are listed under the headline with the name of the place.

*Descriptions of the larger towns and cities, as well as historic, cultural and natural landmarks help round out the travel experience. These paragraphs are printed in italics to distinguish them from the route description.*

### Opening hours · Categories

- Opening hours
- freely accessible
- daily
- frequently (5-6 days/week)
- average (3-4 days/week)
- rare (up to 2 days/week)
- after tel. request

This information is valid during the cycling season and serves as a guide. The daily opening hours can be found via the web link.

### Weblink

In the location data block at the respective tourist entry there is a six-digit number and a letter combination after the @ symbol, e.g. @ abc123. Entering this weblink ID on our website www.esterbauer.com will take you directly to the corresponding website and thus replace the tedious entry of long web addresses.

### Accommodation and service directory

On the last pages of this cycle tour book you will find a list of overnight accommodations in almost every place along the route, from simple campsites to 5-star hotels. You will also find extensive information about bike workshops and bike rental stations.

### With the e-bike

More and more cyclists are now riding an e-bike. Basically, the requirements are the same, even if longer stages and more climbs can be covered. Since the performance of non-motorised cyclists also varies greatly, we have not specified stage lengths in the past.

Narrow passages, stairs or carrying points that are difficult to overcome due to the weight of the e-bike are marked on the maps and alternatives are indicated where possible.

We deliberately refrain from systematically recording official charging stations, as the "unofficial" charging stations (sockets) are disproportionately more frequent. Do not forget the charging cable.

# Passau to Linz along the north bank



**m/km:** ⬈ **2.8** (275m) ⬊ **3.2** (312m)  cycle path: 46 %  unpaved: 0 %  busy road: 1 %

Departing the three-rivers city Passau, the Danube flows through the densely-wooded slopes of the narrow valley between the Bavarian Forest and the Sauwald until it reaches the Danube's loop at Schlögen. Here the Danube's path is blocked by a granite mountain, forcing the river to flow back on itself in a very sharp S-curve. The valley begins to widen at Aschach as the Danube enters the fertile plains of the Eferdinger Basin. Our destination for this stage is the steel-making city of Linz, with cultural offerings that belie the city's industrial reputation.

The route along the left bank from Passau to Linz is almost completely signposted. It follows bicycle trails and paths as well as minor public roads. There are no significant inclines. In the Schlögener Schlinge between Au and Inzell, the topography does not allow a continuous cycle path on the north bank. This section of the path can be bridged with a ferry ride.

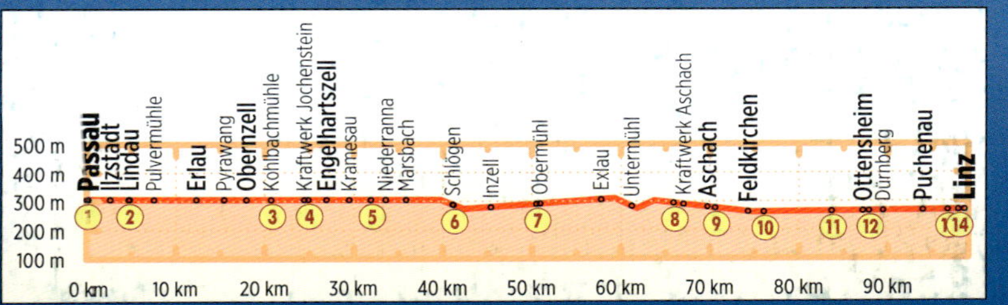

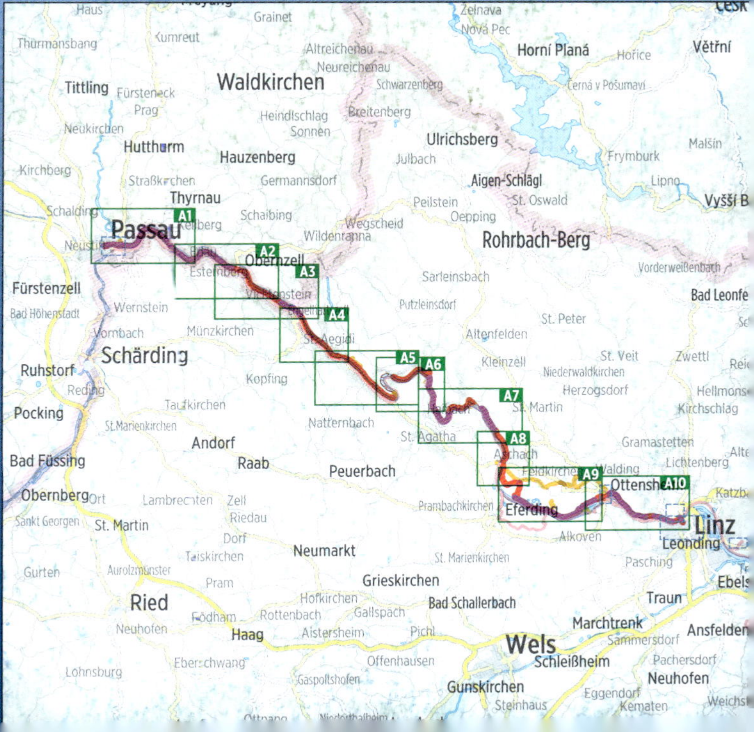

**1** The cycle tour starts at Passau's main railway station ~ follow the cycle sign "Zum Donauradweg" to the left into **Magalettigasse** ~ turn right into the cycle path ~ at the end of the path turn left under Regensburger Straße to the Danube ~ turn right and always along the bank towards Passau's city centre ~ go straight on to the next bridge, the **Luitpoldbrücke**. The north bank variant crosses the Danube.

At Römerplatz in front of Luitpoldbrücke, the route for the south bank variant branches off to the right into **Lukas-Kern-Straße** through the old town.

## Passau ⓓ

prefix: 0851

ⓘ **Tourist-Information (Tourist information)**, Rathauspl. 2, ✆ 396610, @ fap284en

ⓘ **Tourist-Information (Tourist information)**, Bahnhofstr. 28, ✆ 396610, @ enr843en

⛴ **Donauschifffahrt Wurm & Noé (Danube shipping society Wurm & Noé)**, Höllg. 26, ✆ 929292 ⊜ Three river tours from March to October, daily scheduled service to Engelhartszell, Schlögen and Linz from April to October. @ duh285en

🏛 **Dackelmuseum**, Große Messerg. 1, ✆ 30439 ⑦ Humorous and informative exhibition about the cultural history of the Dachshund. @ byt625en

🏛 **Glasmuseum Passau (Glass museum)**, Schrottg. 2, ✆ 35071 ⑦ The world's largest collection of glass from Bavaria, Bohemia, Austria and Silesia from 1620 - 1950 gives an overview of four centuries of European glass history. @ ugd368en

🏛 **MMK - Museum Moderner Kunst (Museum of Modern Art)**, Bräug. 17, ✆ 3838790 ⊜ Alternating international exhibitions of 20th and 21st c. art presented in one of the most handsome old buildings in Passau. @ dlq537en

🏛 **Museum am Dom (Museum at the Cathedral)**, Residenzpl. 8, ✆ 393-3331 ⊜ In the Cathedral Treasury and Diocesan Museum, valuable exhibits bear witness to the history of what was once the largest bishopric in the Holy Roman Empire. @ goo213en

🏛 **Oberhausmuseum**, Oberhaus 125, ✆ 396800, ✆ 396812 ⑦ Historical city museum with exhibitions on city history; Böhmerwaldmuseum, firebrigade museum etc., viewing tower. Shuttle bus from the town hall. @ gbu153en

⛪ **Dom St. Stephan (St. Stephan's Cathedral)**, ✆ 3930. Its roots go back to the early Middle Ages. The cathedral received its Baroque form when it was rebuilt by Italian builders after the city fire of 1662. The nave is the largest Italian-Baroque, ecclesiastical space north of the Alps. The cathedral houses the world's largest church organ, with 17,974 pipes, 233 stops and 4 Glockenspiele (chimes). @ vrx157en

⛪ **Universitätskirche St. Nikola (St. Nicolai university church)**, Innstr. ⑦ The interior of the former collegiate church of the monastery of St. Nicholas combines Gothic and Baroque styles with a variety of modern elements. One of the oldest buildings in Passau is the Romanesque crypt of the church from the 11th century. ⓦ asq156en

- **Kloster Niedernburg (Niedernburg convent)**, Klosterwinkel 1, ☎ 955980. On the eastern tip of the city, established in 740 and active until 2013, the monastery church houses the late gothic grave of Gisela, who joined the Benedictine Abbey as Queen of Hungary in 1045, dying in 1065. The convent contains 800 year old, Romanesque frescos. ⓦ ghl547en

- **Veste Niederhaus (Fortress)**, Ferdinand-Wagner-Str. 1, ☎ 396800. It was probably built in the 14th c. in front of the upper house. In the 17th c. it served as prison, later as workhouse. Today it is privately owned.

- **Veste Oberhaus (Fortress)**, Oberhaus 125 ⓐ Besides cathedral and pilgrimage church Mariahilf, the fortress is one of the three urbanistic dominants of the city. It is one of the largest preserved castles in Europe and was founded in 1219. ⓦ xje244en

- **Stadttheater (town theatre)**, Gottfried-Schäffer-Str. 2-4, ☎ 9291913. The former prince-bishop's opera house from 1783 is today the only preserved early classicist theater building in Bavaria. ⓦ wcl444en

- **Neue Bischöfliche Residenz (New Episcopal Residence)**, Residenzpl. 8, ☎ 3930. Built in 1712-1730 for the prince-bishop in the Viennese, late-Baroque style. The Rococo stucco interior dates from 1768 and the late-Baroque, early-classical facade dates from 1770.

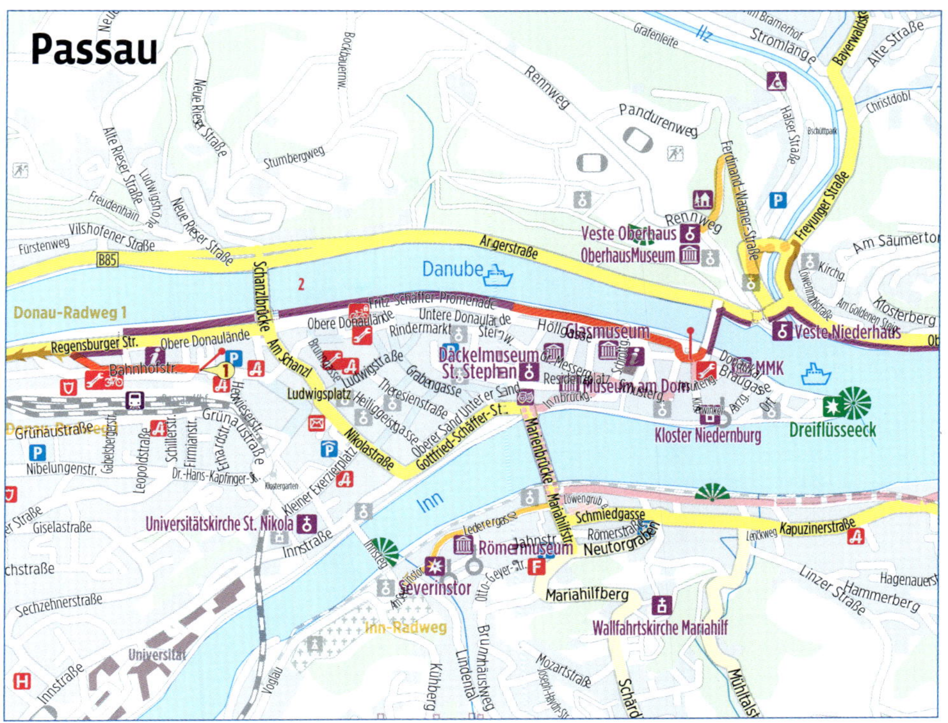

* **Rathaus (Town hall)**, Rathauspl. 2, ☎ 396610 ℂ In the town hall there are two representative chambers in baroque style with colossal paintings from the 19th c. Glockenspiel in the town hall tower: Mo-Su 10:30 am, 2 pm and 3:30 pm. @ mbt171en
* **Dreiflüsseeck (Three rivers confluence)**. The spot where the three rivers Inn, Danube and Ilz Rivers come together.
* **Passauer Erlebnisbad (Passau adventure bath)**, Messestr. 7, ☎ 560260. With outdoor and indoor swimming pools, sauna world and wellness area. @ efu285en

*Passau, the three-rivers city, occupies a dramatic narrow peninsula formed by the Danube and Inn rivers. The third river, the Ilz, joins the Danube from the north near the city's eastern tip. Passau's history extends back to around 500 years BC. The original Celtic settlement was succeeded by the Romans around the time of Christ. In 460 AD St. Severinus, also known as the Apostle to Noricum, established a monastery here. In the 6th century, the Bavarii took control of what was the last Roman outpost on German soil. Batavis became Bazzava which finally became Passau. In 1161, the emperor withdrew from Passau and presented the Niedernburg Abbey to the high monastery of Passau, which governed the city until 1803. In 1568 Austrian nobles filled the prince-bishop's seat until Napoleon restored the city to Bavarian rule.*

*Passau's cathedral has gone through numerous incarnations. In the 13th century it was rebuilt as a gothic church. In 1407, Hans Krumenauer was instructed to build a completely new cathedral. It and large parts of the city were destroyed in a great fire in 1662. Because the city could not afford to build a new church at the time, the Italian architect Carlo Lurago added a baroque long-church to surviving elements of the gothic choir and transept. Today the church's interior is regarded as the largest baroque church space north of the Alps. The church also has five organs which can be played simultaneously from a single main console. It is considered the largest church organ in the world.*

*The city lies to the west of the Dreiflüsseeck, the point of the peninsula at which the three rivers join to form the Danube as it enters Austria. To the south lies the Innstadt, with the Mariahilf pilgrimage church. The Ilzstadt to the north is dominated by the lower Veste Niederhaus and the upper Veste Oberhaus fortress that offers excellent views on the panorama. Across from the cathedral one can find the "Passau Tölpel, " or "idiot," jokingly considered the city's mascot. It is actually a fragment from a statue of St. Stephen, which fell from the cathedral's south tower and shattered during the fire of 1662.*

**Passau to Obernzell**     **17.6 km**

After crossing the Danube on the **Luitpold-brücke** turn right ～ proceed through the tunnel and across the Ilz.

A1
Limbach
Zwölfing
Oberilzmühle
Raßbach
Kinsing
Oberöd im Ilztal
Zwecking
ureuth
Zwecking
Eggersdorfer Teiche
Reut
Schleiferberg
St232
Wood oven bakery
Grafmühle
Eggersdorf
Ries
Zieglreuth
Satzbach
Fattendorf
Sandberg
Schmiedemuseum
Sieglgut
Erdbrüstbachl
St2319
Grubweg
Löwmühle
2,8
Kellberg
Sturmsölden
Sieglberg
B388
Stromlänge
Pulvermühle
Wolfersdorf
Hals
Aichet
Kernmühle
Buchsee
B12
Kuchlhof
Lindau
Wingersdorf
König-Max-Höhe
Passau
Untersölden
2222
B130
Kapfham
Hacklberg
Anger
Achleiten
Leithen
Ilzstadt
Obersölden
Parz
Veste Oberhaus
Schörgendorf
B85
Fritz-Schäffer-Promenade
2,6
2
Danube
Regensburger Str.
B388
5
Bahnhofstr.
Passau Hbf
St. Stephan
MMK
Danube
Faberhof
St. Nikola
i
Dreiflüsseeck
Hinding
Universitätskirche St. Nikola
Inn
Krautergrabenbach
Höllmühle
Inn Bike Trail
Römermuseum
Haibach
A2
Wallfahrtskirche Mariahilf
Rosenau
Freinberg
Edlhof
Innstadt
Neundling
Erlau
Hamberg
Lindenthal
Unterfreinberg
B130
Waging
Neusaming
Anzberg
19
Ingling
Rad
Saming
Unteresternberg
Schwendt

To reach the **Veste Oberhaus**, turn left after crossing the Ilz taking the next bridge to reach the road up the hill.

Stay right on the bicycle and pedestrian path next to the main road towards Obernzell **2** you pass below a railway bridge at Lindau past the **Löwmühle** and the **Kernmühle** further to Erlau.

## Erlau (Obernzell) Ⓓ

*The Donauleiten nature reserve stretches along the left bank of the Danube from Passau to the Austrian border at Jochenstein. Its six segments, with names like Fuchsberg, Fürstberg or Jochenstein together comprise 405 hectares. The steeply-rising slopes form the southern edge of the Bavarian forest. Over the eons the Danube has cut a path that is up to 300 metres deep through the mountain ridge, which is called the Sauwald on the Austrian side of the river. Most of the valley's slopes are covered with mixed woods broken occasionally by stark rock outcroppings.*

*The strong sunshine that the south-facing slopes are exposed to, has helped create an environment in which many rare, warmth-loving animals and plants thrive. The Danube's slopes, or Donauleiten, are noteworthy for the wide variety of plants from different geographical origins. For instance, many alpine and eastern-Alpine flora like cyclamen grow here, alongside broom-mugwort and knotty-grasslily from warmer, drier southern regions.*

*The Donauleiten's fauna is also distinguished by the presence of typical mountain dwelling animals as well as southern species. No German region has as many different reptiles: seven of the nine German species of lizards and snakes are found here, plus rare southern species like the emerald lizard and the Aesculapian viper, the largest and perhaps most beautiful snake found in Germany.*

In the small settlement of **Erlau**, cross the stream of the same name at river level just below the slope on to Obernzell.

## Obernzell Ⓓ

prefix: 08591

- **Tourist-Information (Tourist Info)**, Marktpl. 42, ☏ 9116119, @ qqw158en
- **Donaufähre Obernzell (Ferry Obernzell)**, Jochensteiner Str. 2, ☏ 8243, ⊙ Mid May to mid Sept., Mon–Fri 8:30 a.m.–4:30 p.m., Sat, Sun & Fri 9:30 a.m.–4:30 p.m.; mid Sept–mid May, Mon–Fri 8:30 a.m.–4:30 p.m. @ kab664en
- **Donauarche (River cruises)**, Jochensteinerstr. 1, ☏ 9394899, ☏ 0171/6157179. Trips take place between Obernzell, Jochenstein and Passau. @ rry752en
- **Keramikmuseum (Ceramics museum)**, Schloßpl. 1, ☏ 1066 ⊜ Branch museum of the Bavarian National Museum, shows an insight into the history of ceramics from the Neolithic Age to the present and an overview of the manufacturing processes up to industrial production. @ ibg541en
- **Marktkirche (Parish church)**, Marktpl., ☏ 1861. "Assumption of the Virgin Mary" was built in Rococo style. @ ing154en
- **Schloss (Palace)**, Schloßpl. 1, ☏ 1066 ⊜ Main attraction of the former second residence of the Passau bishops (16thc.) is the gala room in the style of the Passau Renaissance. @ pbs338en
- **Gasthof Alte Schiffspost (Inn)**, Marktpl. 1., ☏ 2560. The worth seeing putti reliefs of the building, which was built in 1805-1810, showing cheerful scenes of the preparation and tasting of wine, remind us of Obernzell's past as a wine town.
- **Schlossgarten (Palace gardens)**, Schloßpl., ☏ 91160 ㉔ A spacious recreational facility was built on the site of the former Münch leather factory and the existing castle garden. @ dfh178en
- **Freibad (Public outdoor pool)**, Am Hafen 1, ☏ 912263, @ igv165en

*Since the 13th century, graphite crucibles have been produced in Obernzell. Since 1516 a guild order existed, from 1613 the Oberzell masters*

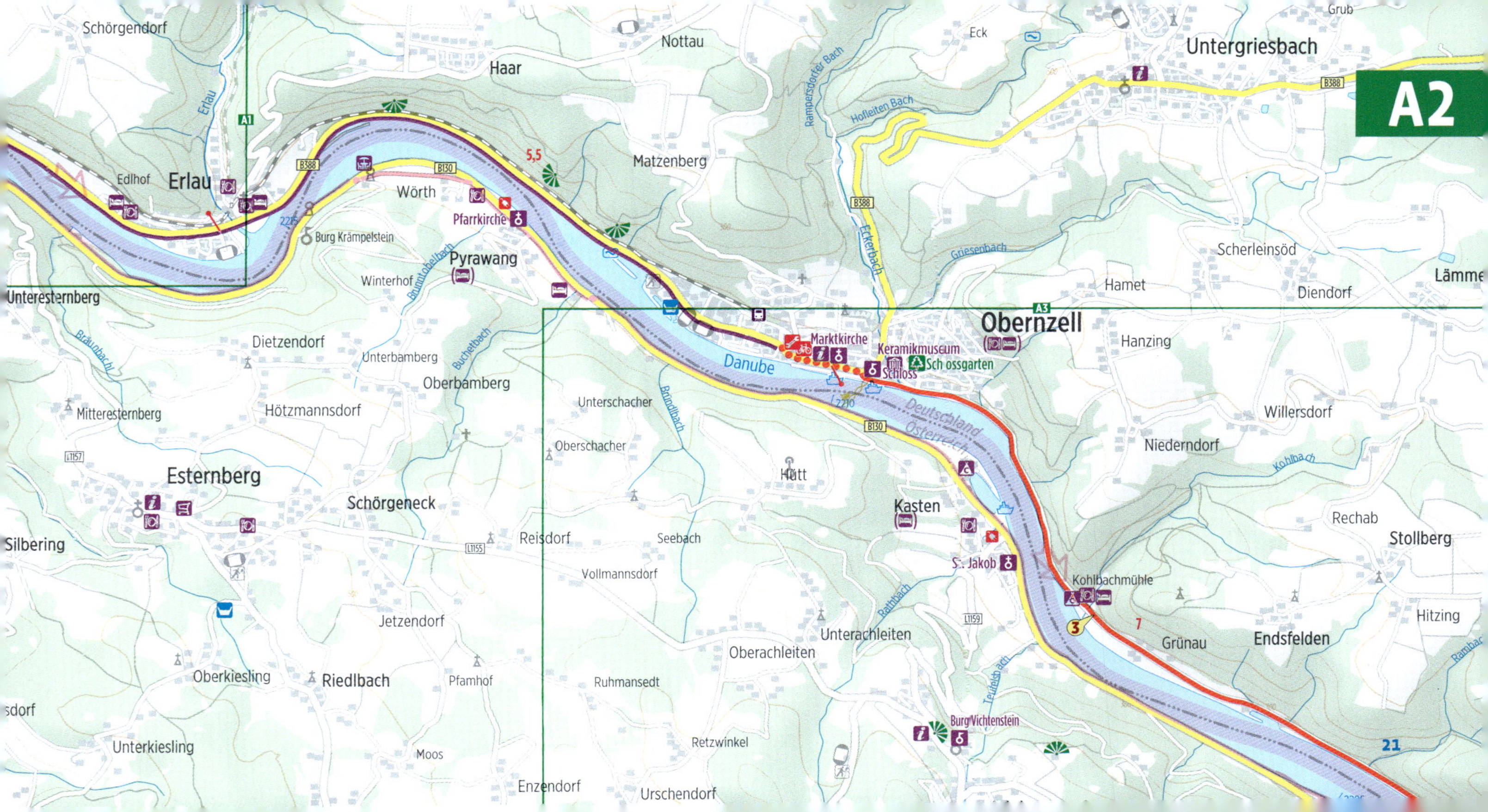

A2
Grub
Untergriesbach
Schörgendorf
Nottau
Eck
Haar
Rampersdorfer Bach
Hofleiten Bach
B388
5,5
Matzenberg
B388
Eckerbach
Scherleinsöd
Erlau
Edlhof
B388
B130
Wörth
Griesenbach
Pfarrkirche
Hamet
Diendorf
Burg Krämpelstein
Lämme
Unteresternberg
Winterhof
Pyrawang
Braunlobelbach
Obernzell
A3
Dietzendorf
Hanzing
Unterbamberg
Buchetbach
Danube
Marktkirche
Keramikmuseum
Sch ossgarten
Oberbamberg
Schloss
Unterschacher
Mitteresternberg
Hötzmannsdorf
Brändlbach
Willersdorf
Oberschacher
Niederndorf
L1157
Esternberg
Hütt
Deutschland
Österreich
B130
Kohlbach
Schörgeneck
Kasten
Rechab
Silbering
Reisdorf
Seebach
St. Jakob
Kohlbachmühle
Stollberg
L1155
Vollmannsdorf
Hitzing
Jetzendorf
Rathbach
L1159
3
7
Grünau
Endsfelden
Oberkiesling
Riedlbach
Pfamhof
Unterachleiten
Oberachleiten
dorf
Unterkiesling
Moos
Ruhmansedt
Retzwinkel
Burg Vichtenstein
Rambac
Enzendorf
Urschendorf
21

*received privileges which made the place a centre of trade with graphite.*

### Obernzell to Niederranna       15.4 km

Turn towards the river at the **palace** ～ pass the ferry ～ you follow the quiet road beside the Danube ～ **3** after 3 km you pass an inn with a campground.

*Vichtenstein Castle can be seen on the other side of the river. This mighty castle, which*

Power station Jochenstein

*dates back to the 12th century, stands in front of the 895-meter Haugstein, the tallest peak in the region.*

*Another 4 km further downstream you reach the barrage and the* **Haus am Strom** *at Jochenstein.*

### Jochenstein (Untergriesbach) ⓓ
prefix: 08591

ⓘ **Tourist-Information (Tourist information)**, Marktpl. 24, Untergriesbach, ✆ 08593/9009-0, @ lya643en

🏛 **Haus am Strom (House on the stream)**, Am Kraftwerk 4, ✆ 4629960 ⊜ The theme of the museum is water in all its facets. @ ddw234en

✳ **Nixenskulptur Isa (Nixie sculpture Isa)**, Uferstr. Sculpture made of granite and oak wood of the mermaid Isa, a sister of the Loreley of the Rhine. @ rcx774en

*From here one can see the legendary Jochensteinfelsen, a rock outcrop looming out of the river downstream of the sluice gates. It is the home of the Danube nixie Isa, one of the sisters of Loreley, the Rhine's famous nixie.*



At the power station you can cross the Danube during opening hours from 6 am to 10 pm. However, the path is tedious due to the many stairs and is not recommended for bicycles with luggage, despite pushing assistance. You should therefore take the Uferhäusl-Engelhartszell ferry or the Danube bridge at Niederranna.

**4** Turn right after the transformer station ～ follow the path along the fence towards the river ～ turn left on **Am Jochenstein** and ride through the village ～ keep right at the intersection and ride out of the village ～ follow the path to the Austrian border, where you cross the Dantlbach creek to depart Germany and enter Austria ～ the tour now follows the old towpath.



About 700 m further on the bicycle ferry transports cyclists across the river to Engelhartszell. Here you can visit Austria's only Trappist monastery. Ferry, ✆ 0664/9937026, Operates: daily from April/Oct 10:30-17 h, May/Sept 9:30-17:30 h, June 9-18 h, July/Aug 9-18:30 h. www.engelhartszell.at/Radfaehre.

### Engelhartszell see page 42

After the Engelhartszell bicycle ferry, the left bank route follows the well-built towpath once used by the horses that pulled ships upstream

### Kramesau (Neustift im Mühlkreis)

**5** Turn right towards Niederranna ～ in Niederranna turn right after the little church ～ follow the left curve of the street.

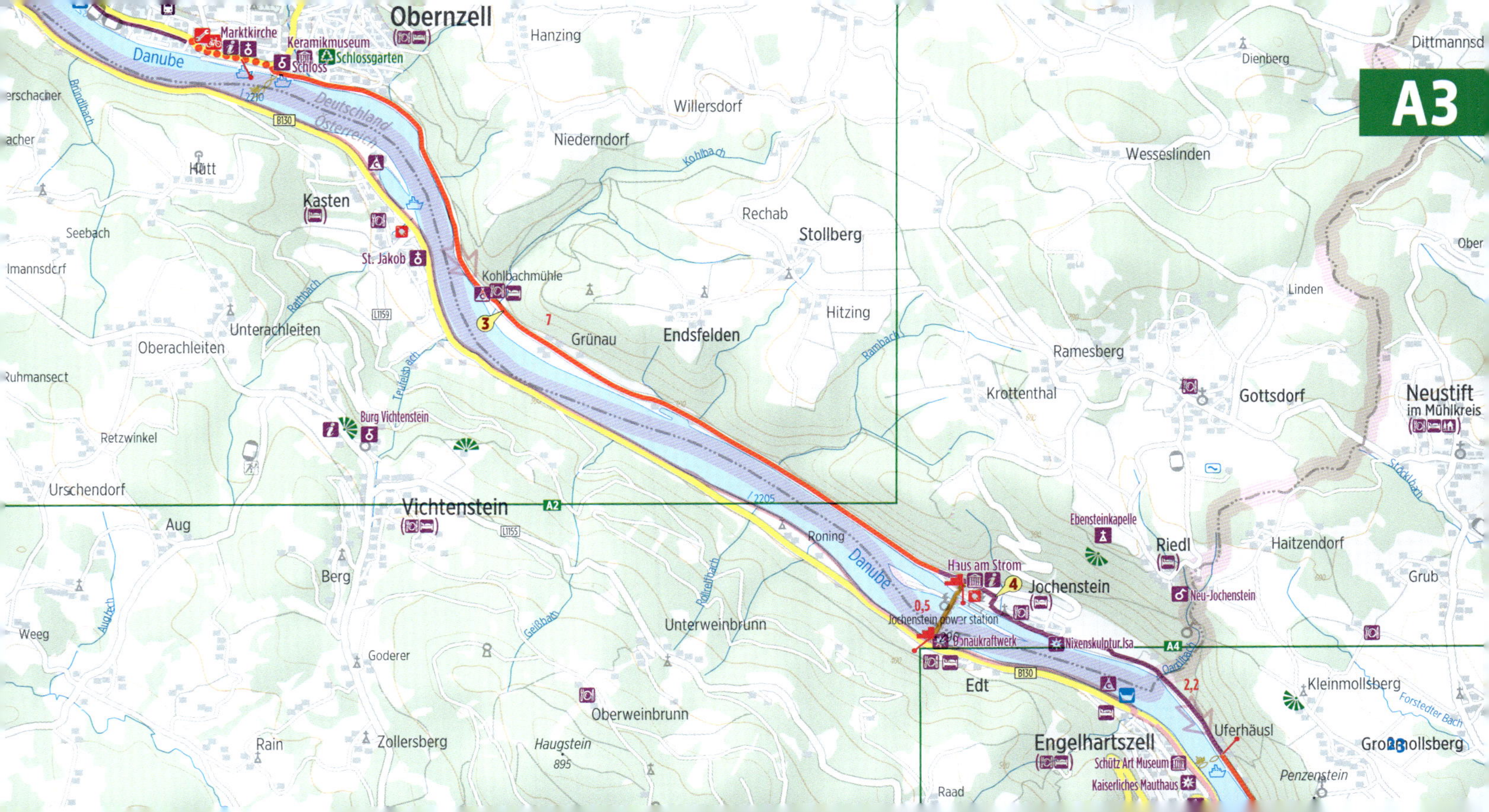
A3
Obernzell
Hanzing
Dittmannsd
Dienberg
Marktkirche
Keramikmuseum
Schlossgarten
Schloss
Danube
Deutschland
Österreich
B130
Willersdorf
Wesseslinden
Hütt
Niederndorf
Rechab
Ober
Kasten
Stollberg
Seebach
Linden
Imannsdorf
St. Jakob
Kohlbach
Kohlbachmühle
Hitzing
Unterachleiten
7
Grünau
Endsfelden
Ramesberg
Oberachleiten
Rambach
Ruhmansect
Krottenthal
Gottsdorf
Neustift
im Mühlkreis
Burg Vichtenstein
Retzwinkel
Urschendorf
Vichtenstein
A2
Aug
L1155
Ebensteinkapelle
Riedl
Haitzendorf
Roning
Danube
Berg
Neu-Jochenstein
Grub
Haus am Strom
Jochenstein
Weeg
0,5
Goderer
Jochenstein power station
Unterweinbrunn
Donaukraftwerk
Nixenskulptur.Isa
A4
Edt
B130
Kleinmollsberg
Oberweinbrunn
Rain
Zollersberg
Haugstein
895
Uferhäusl
Engelhartszell
Großmollsberg
Schütz Art Museum
Penzenstein
Kaiserliches Mauthaus
Raad

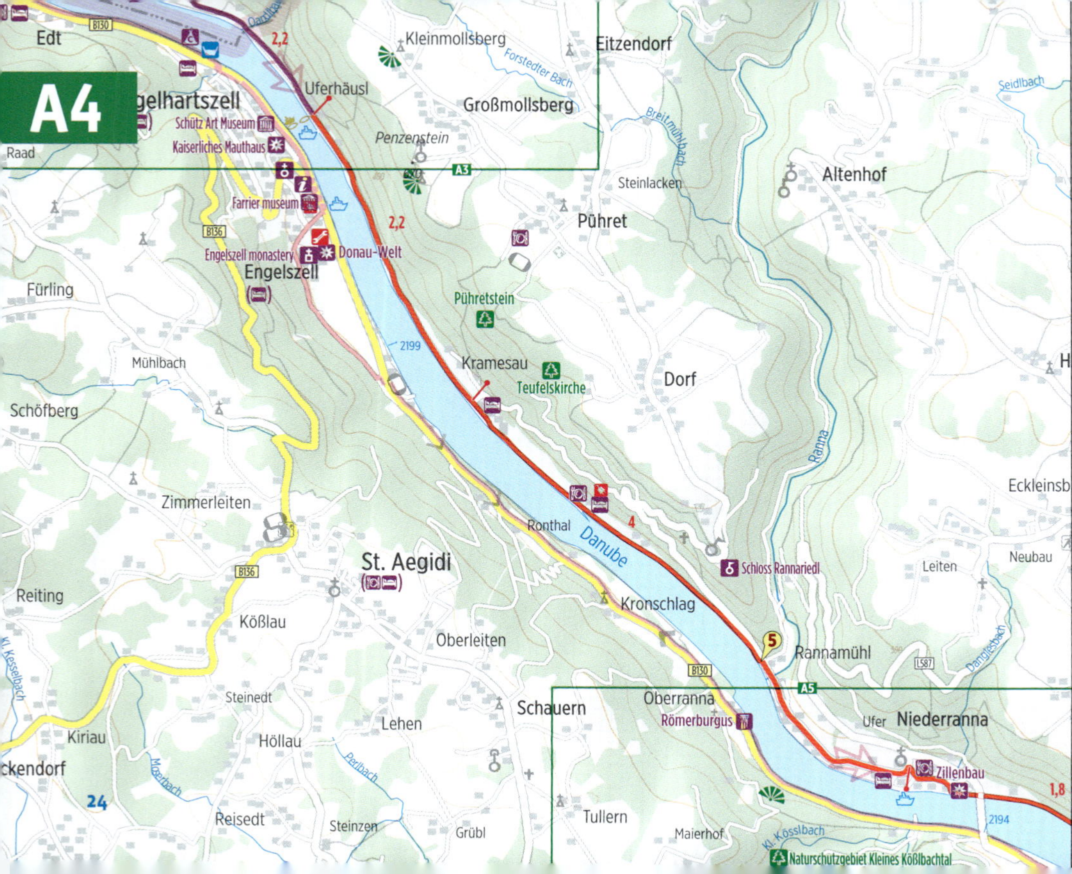




### Niederranna (Hofkirchen im Mühlkreis)
prefix: 07285

**Marktgemeindeamt Hofkirchen (Municipal office)**, Markt 8, Hofkirchen im Mühlkreis, ✆ 7011, @ kaw344en

**Schloss Rannariedl (Rannariedl castle)**, Rannariedl 1. Falkenstein property until 1357/58, after which it belonged, with interruptions, to the Passau prince bishops. The residential wing with courtyard dates to the 16th c. The tall keep is medieval. Across the road lies the ruin of the 12th c Oberburg Rannariedl. (private property) @ oub687en

**Zillenbau Königsdorfer (Barge builder)**, Niederranna 38, ✆ 508 © Besides Anton Witti from the neighboring village Freizell, Rudolf Königsdorfer is the last Zillenbauer in Austria. @ ocs636en

### Niederranna to Obermühl          16 km
Follow the street to the river bank    turn right and ride under the Danube bridge.



### Marsbach (Hofkirchen im Mühlkreis)
prefix: 07285

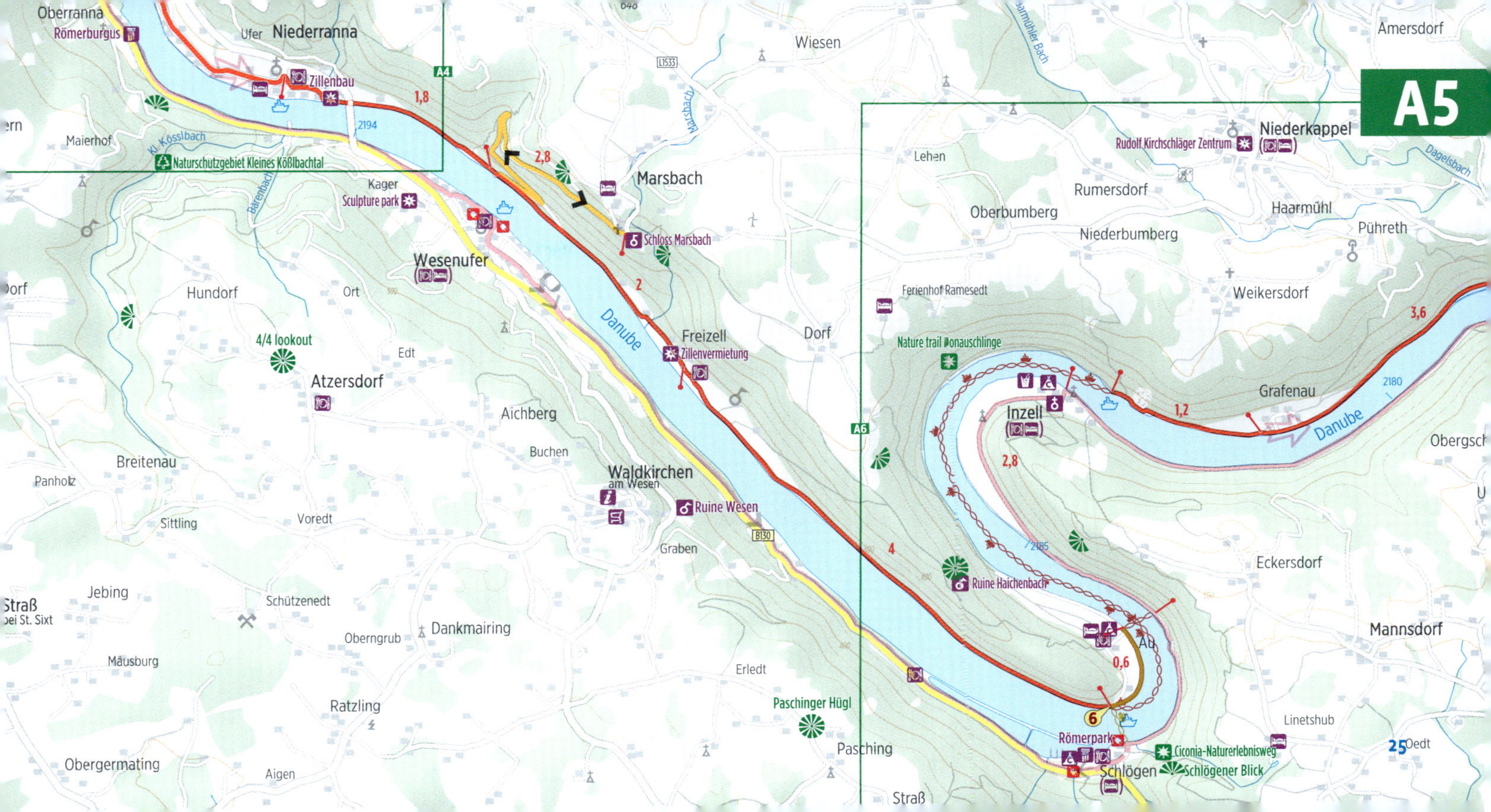

Oberranna
Römerburgus
Ufer
Niederranna
Zillenbau
A4
1,8
Amersdorf
Wiesen
648
L1533
Marsbach
Niederkappel
A5
Rudolf Kirchschläger Zentrum
Lehen
Maierhof
Kl. Kösslbach
Naturschutzgebiet Kleines Kößlbachtal
Kager
Sculpture park
2,8
Marsbach
Schloss Marsbach
2194
Bärenbach
Rumersdorf
Oberbumberg
Haarmühl
Pühreth
Niederbumberg
Weikersdorf
Wesenufer
Ort
2
Danube
Dorf
Ferienhof Ramesedt
Dorf
Hundorf
Edt
4/4 lookout
Freizell
Zillenvermietung
Nature trail Donauschlinge
3,6
Atzersdorf
Aichberg
Buchen
Inzell
Grafenau
2180
A6
Obergsch
Breitenau
Waldkirchen
am Wesen
2,8
Panholz
Sittling
Voredt
Ruine Wesen
B130
Ruine Haichenbach
2185
Eckersdorf
Straß
bei St. Sixt
Jebing
Schützenedt
Dankmairing
4
Mannsdorf
Mäusburg
Oberngrub
Erledt
Au
0,6
Linetshub
Ratzling
Paschinger Hügl
6
Römerpark
Ciconia-Naturerlebnisweg
Schlögener Blick
25 Oedt
Obergermating
Aigen
Pasching
Schlögen
Straß

*Danube near Schlögen*

**Marktgemeindeamt Hofkirchen (Municipal office)**, Markt 8, Hofkirchen im Mühlkreis, ☎ 7011, @ kaw344en

**Schloss Marsbach (Palace)**, Marsbach 1. The three-storey rectangular main building with a round tower is the oldest noble residence in the upper Mühlviertel, first mentioned in a document in 1075. Today it is privately owned and therefore unfortunately not open to visitors.

You pass Freizell.

### Freizell (Hofkirchen im Mühlkreis)

**Marktgemeindeamt Hofkirchen (Municipal office)**, Markt 8, Hofkirchen im Mühlkreis, ☎ 07285/7011, @ kaw344en

**Zillenvermietung Witti (Barge rental)**, Freizell 4, ☎ 07285/6390, ☎ 0664/4124504 ⑦d Not only are barges built here professionally, they can also be rented for a trip on the Danube. @ dow471en



### Dorf (Niederkappel)

**Burgruine Haichenbach (Castle ruins)**, Dorf 12 ㉔ First mentioned in a document in 1160, the castle fell into disrepair from 1529 onwards. Popularly known as "Kerschbaumer Schlössl", the viewing platform offers a dreamlike view of the Danube valley and the Danube gorge Schlögen. @ abk486en

The route follows a narrow road along the river to the ferry Au/Schlögen **6**.

You are now in the famous Schlögener Schlinge. Here the cycle path is interrupted and you have to use a ferry. You can travel through the loop with the longitudinal ferry/Donaubus or use the cross ferries.

### Au/Schlögen (Hofkirchen im Mühlkreis)

**Donaubus Au-Grafenau (Ferry)**, Au 4, ☎ 0699/11152578, ☺ May, June & Sept. 10am-6pm, July & Aug. 9.30am-7pm. The Donaubus takes you 5 km along the water through the natural spectacle Schlögener Schlinge and docks on the left bank near Grafenau. @ cru743en

**Querfähre Au-Inzell (Ferry)**, Au 1, ☎ 07285/6317, ☎ 0664/2801144, ☺ April, Sept. to Oct. 9am-6pm, May-Aug. 7.30am-8pm, @ qpt746en

**Radfähre Au-Schlögen (Au-Schlögen Cycling cross ferry)**, Schlögen 2, ☎ 07279/8212. From Au on the left side of the Danube, the cycle ferry Hotel Donauschlinge takes you to the right bank of the Danube, from where you can continue your journey through the Donauschlinge. @ exa225en

## Grafenau

From Grafenau, continue on the country road along the Danube to Obermühl

## Niederkappel

prefix: 07286

**Gemeindeamt (Municipal office)**, Hauptstr. 12, ☎ 8555, @ wdd354en

**Mühlviertler Dom (Mühlviertel Cathedral)**, Hauptstr. The Gothic church from 1404 was enlarged in 1890 according to plans by Raimund Jeblinger, master builder of the Linz cathedral. @ gpq455en

**Dr. Rudolf Kirchschläger-Gedenkzentrum (Rudolf Kirchschläger Centre)**, Hauptstr. 12, ☎ 8555, ☎ 0680/1192197 Ⓒ Memorial for Dr. Rudolf Kirchschläger, born here and popular former Federal President of Austria. @ dgk423en

**Freibad (Public outdoor pool)**, Schulstr. 8, ☎ 8555, ☎ 0680/2347227, @ byx577en

## Obermühl (Kirchberg ob der Donau)

prefix: 07286

**Gemeindeamt (Municipal office)**, Ortspl. 5, ☎ 07282/4601, @ omi638en

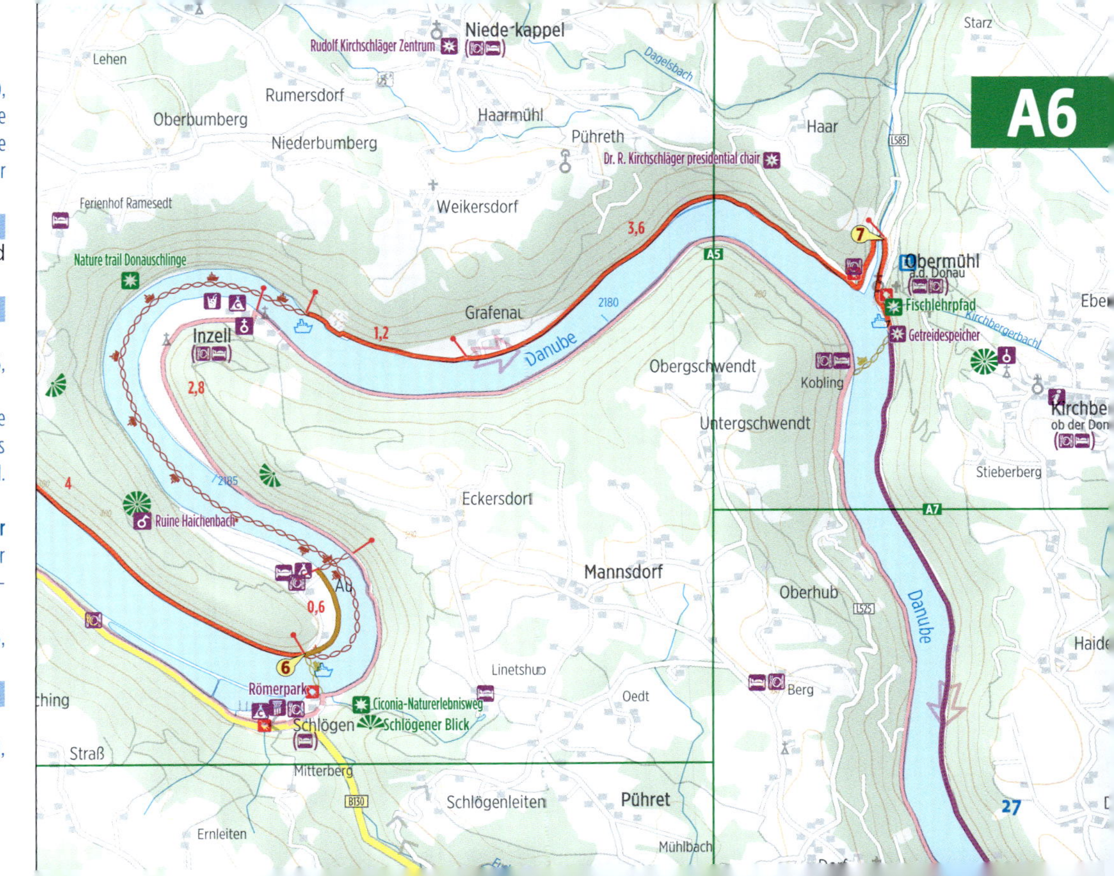

*The danube between Grafenau and Obermühl*

- **Donaufähre Obermühl-Kobling (Ferry)**, Obermühl 13, ☎ 0664/8298728, ☎ 0664/73493393, ☉ April/Oct. 9am-5pm, May/Sept. 8am-6pm, June-Aug. 8am-7pm. The ferry is operated by the Jausenstation Donauterrasse am Limes and Pension Idylle in Kobling and can be called by bell. @ xgi521en
- **Getreidespeicher (Old grain silo)**, Obermühl 1. On the eastern edge of town, this grain silo was built with a conspicuous 16 m high roof in the year 1618, and served as a customs post. This significant renaissance-period structure was almost lost when the river rose following construction of the hydro-electric plant downstream.
- **Fischlehrpfad (fish nature trail)**, Obermühl 13, ☎ 7216. On a 2 km long nature trail you will learn interesting facts about the fish living in the Danube. @ rlj415en

### Obermühl to Feldkirchen     23.5 km

**7** Turn right after the bridge and follow the road through the village past the historic grain silo and the ferry landing — after 7 km you round the inside of another tight bend in the river — continue along the narrow, paved road beside the river — you pass the houses of **Exlau** and **Point** before passing under the bridge where the Große Mühl joins the Danube — ride up onto the bridge and cross to the stream.


The route is interrupted in Untermühl by the steep, rocky slope below Neuhaus Castle, which is only passable along the "Felsensteig", a narrow track along where bicycles are not allowed to pass. You can either take the ferry 800 m down the river to bypass this section or across to Kaiserau on the right bank. Don't come late, there is no evening service.

## Untermühl (Sankt Martin im Mühlkreis)
prefix: 07232

- **Fähre Untermühl - Kaiserhof - Bremsberg (Ferry)**, ☎ 07273/62210, ☉ April-Sept 9am-6pm. Stations: Kaiserhof/Kaiserau, Untermühl and Bremsberg. The ferry can be called by radio. @ fab181en
- **Donaublick Kettenturm**, Felsensteig, ☎ 210518. In the early 2010s, the ruins of the former chain tower in the rugged cliff near Untermühl below the castle were revitalized and turned into a viewing platform. The 180 m long chain of the toll tower, which once served to block the Danube, was brought to France by Emperor Napoleon as a kind of souvenir and is now in the Army Museum of the City of Paris. @ ywh664en

Take the ferry past the Felsensteig — from the ferry landing continue downstream along the towpath — **8** pass a small harbour before reaching the **Kraftwerk Aschach** (Hydroelectric power station) — continue on the street

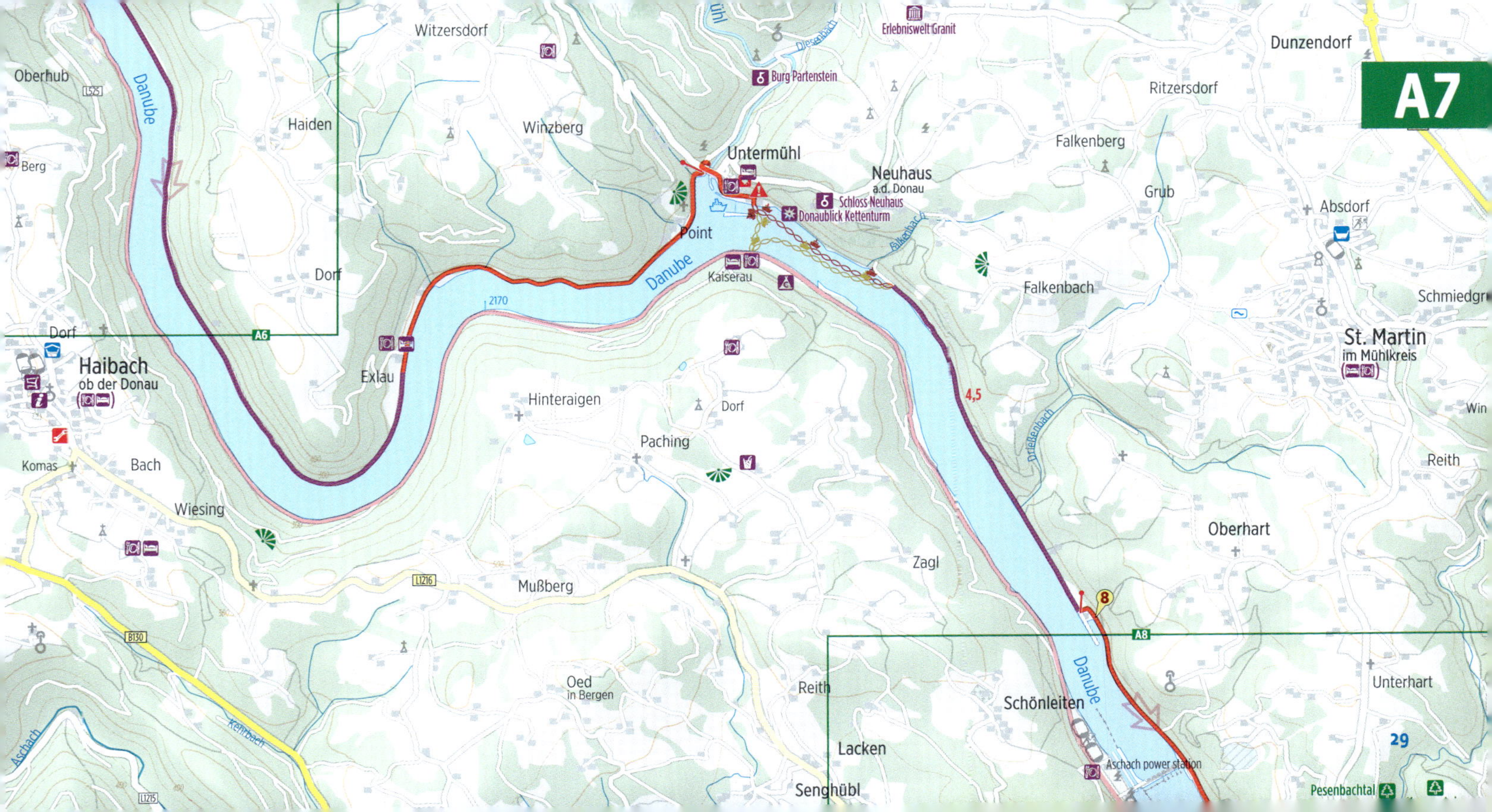
A7
A6
A8
Danube
Oberhub
Berg
Haiden
Witzersdorf
Winzberg
Untermühl
Burg Partenstein
Erlebniswelt Granit
Dunzendorf
Ritzersdorf
Falkenberg
Grub
Neuhaus
a.d. Donau
Schloss Neuhaus
Donaublick Kettenturm
Absdorf
Point
Dorf
Danube
Kaiserau
Falkenbach
Schmiedgr
St. Martin
im Mühlkreis
Dorf
Haibach
ob der Donau
Exlau
2170
Hinteraigen
Dorf
Win
Komas
Bach
Paching
4,5
Reith
Wiesing
Oberhart
L1216
Zagl
Mußberg
8
A8
Danube
Oed
in Bergen
Reith
Unterhart
Schönleiten
Lacken
29
Senghübl
Aschach power station
Pesenbachtal
L1215

*Swimming lakes Weidet*

along the river bank into **Oberlandshaag** ~ pass under the bridge and follow the left bend ~ turn right after the fire brigade ~ proceed about 300 m towards **Unterlandshaag** ~ **9** ride straight where the street makes a left turn.


Follow the street to the left to take the shorter alternative route to Feldkirchen.

Continue out of the village and follow the quiet country lane as it winds its way between fields and scattered farmsteads ~ in Feldkirchen, turn right at the first major intersection to the Danube.

## Feldkirchen an der Donau

prefix: 07233

**i** **Tourismusverein (Tourism association)**, Hauptstr. 1, ✆ 7190, @ ojl166en

**&** **Pfarrkirche Feldkirchen (Parish church)**, Marktpl. Special about this church are the freestanding early Gothic church tower as well as the rococo interior. @ cjy156en

### Feldkirchen to Ottensheim — 13.5 km


An alternative route from Feldkirchen to Ottensheim via the Walding zoo is shown on the map A9 in orange.

## Route via Walding — 16 km

### Walding

prefix: 07234

**&** **Tiergarten & Reiterhof (Zoo & Riding Stables)**, Mursberg 42, ✆ 82759 @ The area around the farm is home to 200 native and exotic animals that can be observed up close. @ ckj512en

The route leads from Feldkirchen back to the Danube ~ in **Weidet** follow the sharp bend to the right ~ **10** turn left at the small wooden chapel ~ you reach the Danube after the bridge across the drainage canal ~ the route follows this straight, well-paved path along the river.

After about 1.5 km you reach the Feldkirchen lakes, which can be reached by a narrow path that leads down from the embankment and to a narrow bridge across the drainage canal.

**Weidet** (Feldkirchen an der Donau)

prefix: 07233

- ✳ **Jetlake Wasserskilift (Jetlake cable waterski)**, Badeseestr. 6, ☎ 20520. Cable waterski and wakeboard, obstacle course, stand-up-passling and much more, ⓦ tms753en
- ✳ **Motorikpark Feldkirchen** 24 20 stations as a challenge for concentration and body coordination, for all ages. ⓦ mni728en
- 🛁 **Die vier Badeseen (The four bathing lakes)**, Badeseestr., ☎ 7190, ⓦ eoc535en

Continue down the path along the Danube.

About 3 km after the lakes there is the opportunity to visit Goldwörth, a place with a history of gold panning.

**Goldwörth** (Feldkirchen an der Donau)

- 🏛 **Brauchtumsmuseum (Museum of local traditions)**, Göldwörther Str. 44, ☎ 07233/7604, ☎ 0664/3259157 Ⓒ In the former Gasthaus Wiesinger, exhibits on everyday culture as well as information on festivals and customs in the region are on display. ⓦ euj544en

## Gold and pearls from the Danube

*The search for gold and pearls in the Danube may have been relatively small industries compared to main activities like fishing, shipping and energy production, but they made interesting contributions to the river's cultural history. The "pearl-fishers" especially favoured the Danube's small tributaries from north. The best pearl-creeks are streams with relatively low levels of lime. The clear-as-water to reddish-green pearls grow in the approximately 10 cm long river mussel (Margaritana margaritifera) when the mussel starts depositing mother-of-pearl on a sand-corn. The process takes some 15 to 20 years,*

and only one in 500 to 2000 mussels produce a single pearl.

The Passau diocese organized the systematic harvest of pearls in the region, and for many years "Passau pearls" enjoyed great popularity. The pearls were treasured not just in the immediate region – the Linz bishop's miter is decorated with river pearls from the Danube. Gold generated a similarly small but steady source of wealth. Despite the apparent futility of the activity, there is evidence of a number of gold prospectors, even from relatively recent times. In 1733, for instance, 93.3 grams of panned gold from Linz was sold at the Vienna Mint, and at Mauthausen prospectors, mostly gypsies, produced a small but steady supply of gold. Place names like Goldwörth, which has a history dating back to the 11th century, testify to the long history of gold mining and panning along the Danube.

The methods used by prospectors were relatively simple. River gravel was sifted through a wooden grating. The gravel stayed in the grating, sand was washed away, while traces of gold and other minerals were caught in a woolen cloth. Then a magnet was used to extract iron ore, and the remaining gold traces were thickened with mercury. The resulting mass was put in a leather pouch through which the mercury was filtered. At the end of this arduous process a tiny amount of gold remained in the pouch. Using these methods, a successful prospector produced about one hazelnut-sized lump of gold per year. It is estimated that the total amount of gold extracted from the Danube amounts to about 20 kilograms. This small amount sufficed, however, to strike ducats in Bavaria between 1756 and 1830, and to gold-plate the communion chalices at the Klosterneuburg and Göttweig abbeys.

Continue along the embankment to a small boat landing before the **Ottensheim power station 11**

> **TIP** If you like to continue on the south bank, here at the hydraulic power station you can cross the river.

Follow the paved path to the left towards Ottensheim ~ the path takes you along a rowing regatta course, making a small detour to cross the Pesenbach creek ~ the bicycle path ends at the regatta centre and you continue along the access road ~ after the left bend turn right across the bridge over the Große Rodl creek.

> **TIP** At this point, turning left, you can reach the village of Hagenau with the Model Railway.

A9
Semleiten
Oberndorf
Bergheim
Jörgensbühl
Unterlandshaag
Rosenleiten
Freudenstein
Käferbach
Tiergarten Walding
2,5
B131
Feldkirchen
a.d. Donau
Filialkirche
Pesenbach
2,5
3,6
4
Pfarrkirche
Zehetner
Vogging
B131
Schwarzgrub
A8
Mühldorf
Ach
Pösting
1,8
Rodl
Hofham
Schloss Mühldorf
7
Lindham
Höflein
Audorf
Große Rodl
2
Au
B131
Weidet
Haid
Ottensheim
10
Purwörth
l2155
Brauchtumsmuseum
Motorikpark
Goldwörth
Hagenau
4,5
4
A10
Dampfbahnerclub
Jetlake
1,6
Danube
9
Pesenbach
1,5
Danube
point
l2153
Hydro-electric power plant Ottensheim-Wilhering
Fischlehrpfad
Wörth
Unterschaden
11
Fall
erg palace
Eferding
Aschach
Aschacharm
3
Oberschaden
Innbach
Innbach
33

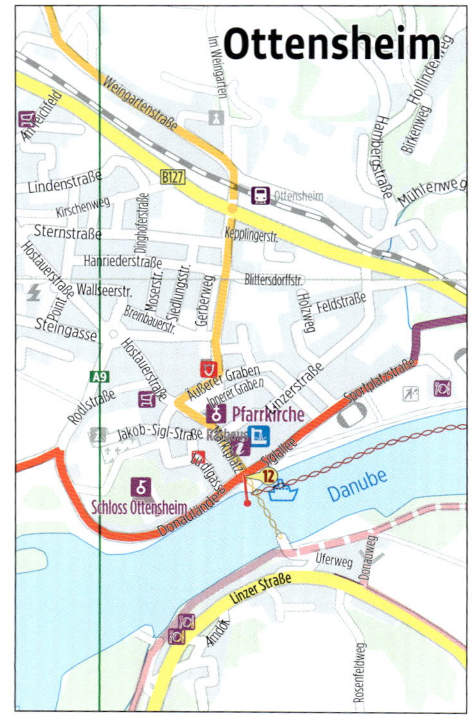





✳ **Dampfbahnerclub Linz - Modellbahnanlage (Model Railway)**, Hagenau 4, ✆ 0732/736657, ✆ 0699/13552545. Here you can admire the largest garden railway in Austria, on a scale of 1:8 on an area of approx. 4000 m². @ vjc787en

Continue towards Ottensheim — turn right at the next opportunity and follow the street **Donaulände** as far as the ferry landing. The historic centre of Ottensheim lies on the left.

## Ottensheim

prefix: 07234

🛈 **Tourist-Information (Tourist Information)**, Marktpl. 7, ✆ 8225530, ✆ 0699/10437643, @ akx863en

⛴ **Donaubus Ottensheim-Linz (May/June/Sept 9am-6.20pm, July/Aug Mon-Thu 9am-6.20pm, Fri-Sun 9am-7.20pm)**, Siglallee, ✆ 0699/11206173. Longitudinal ferry to Linz. You will find the landing stage of the Danube Bus on the north side 100 m below the ferry Ottensheim-Wilhering. In Linz, the Danube Bus lands on the north side immediately before the Nibelungen Bridge. @ fuk525en

⛴ **Fähre (Ottensheim-Wilhering Ferry)**, ✆ 0664/9254916, ⏱ Mon-Sat 6.15-19.20, Sun/Fri 8-19.20, @ mkp734en

⛪ **Pfarrkirche (Parish church St. Ägidius)**, Marktpl. 8. Built 1462-1520. The Nepomuk Chapel was added in the late 19th c. The oldest part of the church is the crypt with bones recovered from the old cemetery, and the mummified remains of a noblewoman. @ vpf253en

⛪ **Schloss Ottensheim (Ottensheim palace)**, Jakob-Sigl-Str. 17. The keep and the north and east wings are all that remain of the medieval castle that originally served as a Babenberger frontier outpost. Closed to the public. @ hth116en

✳ **Historischer Marktkern (Historic market)**, Marktpl., ✆ 8225530. Despite repeated market fires, a number of interesting houses have survived, including the "Kindlhaus" which plays a key role in one of the legends about the foundation of Ottensheim.

*The village owes its origin to its favorable location on the Danube and Rodl waterways. Ottensheim was once one of the most important trading hubs on the Danube. The name of the place could come from the knight Otini, who had a castle built on a hill directly on the Danube. A further derivation of the place name could come from the child house legend. According to this legend, Ottensheim owes its name to the birth of Emperor Otto IV in 1208. Historical facts refute this story, but this has never damaged the popularity of the house where Emperor Otto was allegedly born.*

### Ottensheim to Linz    10.6 km

**ALTERNATIVE** The cycle route between Ottensheim and Linz runs on a cycle path directly next to the main road. Alternatively, you can also take

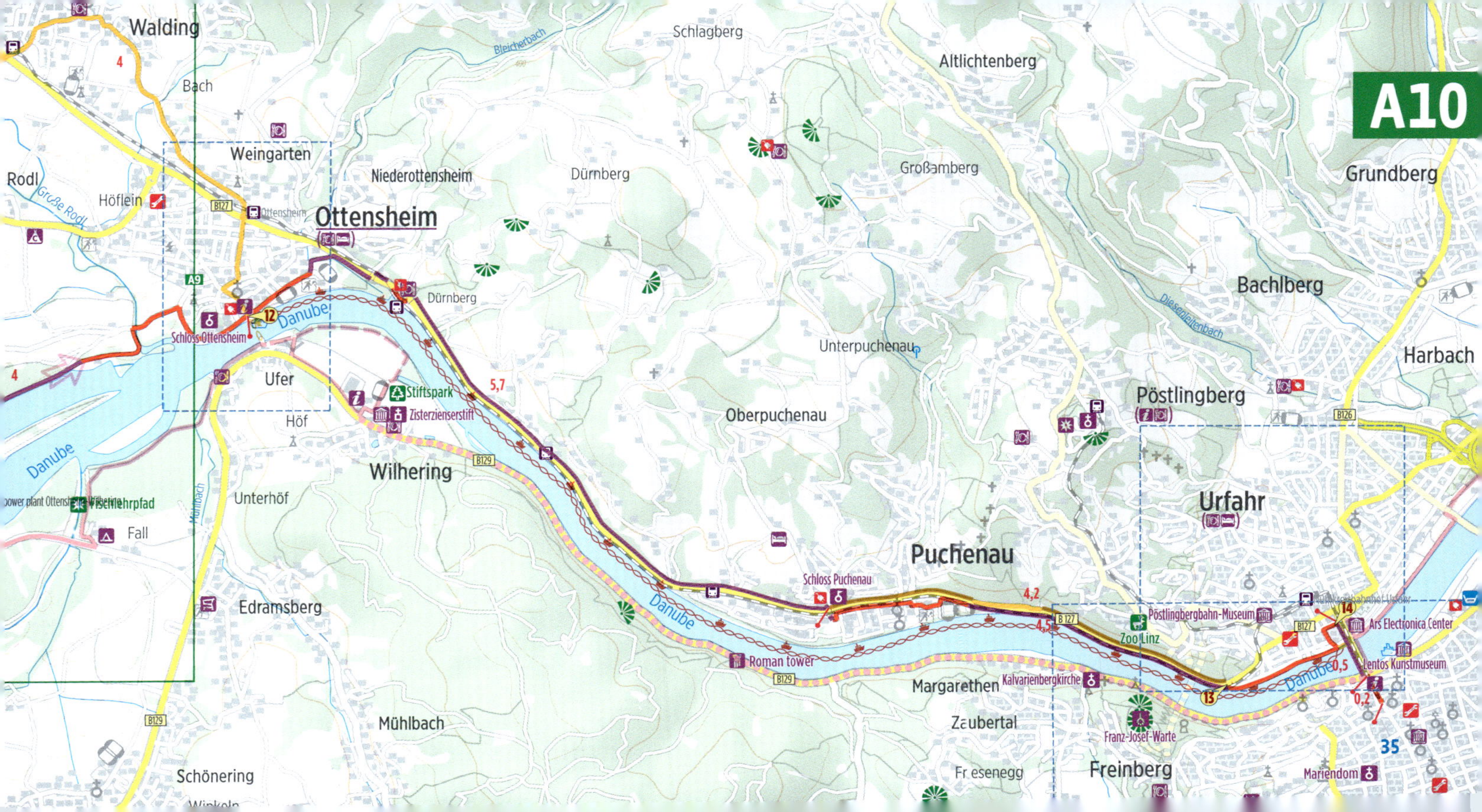

A10
Walding
Bach
Weingarten
Rodl
Große Rodl
Höflein
B127
Ottensheim
Niederottensheim
Dürnberg
Schlagberg
Altlichtenberg
Großamberg
Grundberg
A9
12
Danube
Schloss Ottensheim
Dürnberg
Ufer
Höf
4
Danube
Stiftspark
Zisterzienserstift
Wilhering
B129
Unterpuchenau
Oberpuchenau
Bachlberg
Dieselleitenbach
Pöstlingberg
B126
Harbach
power plant Ottensheim
Lehrpfad
Mühlbach
Unterhöf
Fall
5,7
Urfahr
Puchenau
Schloss Puchenau
Danube
Edramsberg
4,2
B127
Pöstlingbergbahn-Museum
14
Zoo Linz
B127
Ars Electronica Center
4,5
Roman tower
B129
Margarethen
Kalvarienbergkirche
13
Danube
0,5
Lentos Kunstmuseum
0,2
Mühlbach
Zaubertal
Franz-Josef-Warte
Freinberg
35
B129
Schönering
Fresenegg
Mariendom
Winkeln
4
Danube

the Donaubus longitudinal ferry. Shortly after the Ottensheim-Wilhering wire rope bridge you will find the Ottensheim-Linz Danube Bus landing stage.

**12** Straight on past the ferry into **Siglallee** and then into **Sportplatzstraße** ~ past the sports fields and then left according to the signs ~ follow the path over the Bleicherbach (creek) ~ left through the underpass and over the railway track ~ then turn right ~ on the asphalt road to the Dürnberg railway stop ~ shortly afterwards turn left under the road and follow

the cycle path in a right-hand bend ~ follow the cycle path alongside the road to Puchenau.

## Puchenau

**Schloss Puchenau (Puchenau castle)**, Karl-Leitl-Str. 1, ✆ 0650/4535543. Built in 1674 by Count Ernst Christof Schallenberg, the castle is located on a slope a little above the municipality of Puchenau and is used for flats as well as commercial space. @ ney317en

**TIP** From Puchenau to Linz, the cycle path now runs between the Danube and the railway tracks. In case of high water, however, it is necessary to switch to the roadside cycle path

to the left of the federal road. This alternative route is shown in orange on the map.

Follow the cycle path marking **R1** to the left ~ this leads in a right turn under the road ~ over the supermarket car park ~ right into **Gartenstadtstraße** ~ before the junction with the main road follow the marking to the right between the car parks ~ turn left, **Wilheringer Straße** ~ along the sports fields ~ continue between the Danube and the railway tracks ~ **13** on the outskirts of Linz the cycle path then merges into **Obere Donaustraße**.

 The **Danube bike trail** proceeds straight along the river. However, we recommend a stop in Linz.

To visit Linz, turn left before the bridge and follow the **Flussgasse** right into the **Fiedlerstraße.**

## Urfahr (Linz)

prefix: 0732

🏛 **Ars Electronica Center**, Ars-Electronica Str. 1, ✆ 72720 ⊕ "Museum of the Future". Fascinating architecture and changing LED façade lighting. ⓦ koc153en

🏛 **Pöstlingbergbahn-Museum**, Landgutstr. 19, ✆ 34007406 ↻ Museum about the Pöstlingbergtram. With driving simulator. ⓦ yqj358en

♿ **Pöstlingberg-Wallfahrtsbasilika (Pilgrimage church Pöstlingberg)**, Am Pöstlingberg 1, ✆ 7312280. The origin of the pilgrimage was the miraculous healing of Count Gundomer von Starhemberg. The easily-recognized church, a Linz landmark, was built 1738-47. ⓦ vtt311en

✳ **Grottenbahn am Pöstlingberg (Grotto train at Pöstlingberg)**, Am Pöstlingberg 16, ✆ 34007506 ⑦ The fairytale world for young and old, stories of dwarves, giants and enchanted princes. ⓦ uft654en

🦒 **Zoo Linz**, Windflachweg 1, ✆ 737180 ⑦ Halfway up the Pöstlingberg, with a fabulous view over the city of Linz, about 600 exotic and native animals are housed on an area of almost 4 ha. ⓦ ubx465en

🏊 **Familienoase Biesenfeld (Outdoor swimming area)**, Dornacher Str. 37, ✆ 3400-6670, ⓦ otc666en

Turn right onto the bicycle path onto the bridge – continue straight off the bridge to reach the **Linzer Hauptplatz** (main square) with the column of the Holy Trinity – you are now in the historic centre of Linz.

**Linz** see page 54

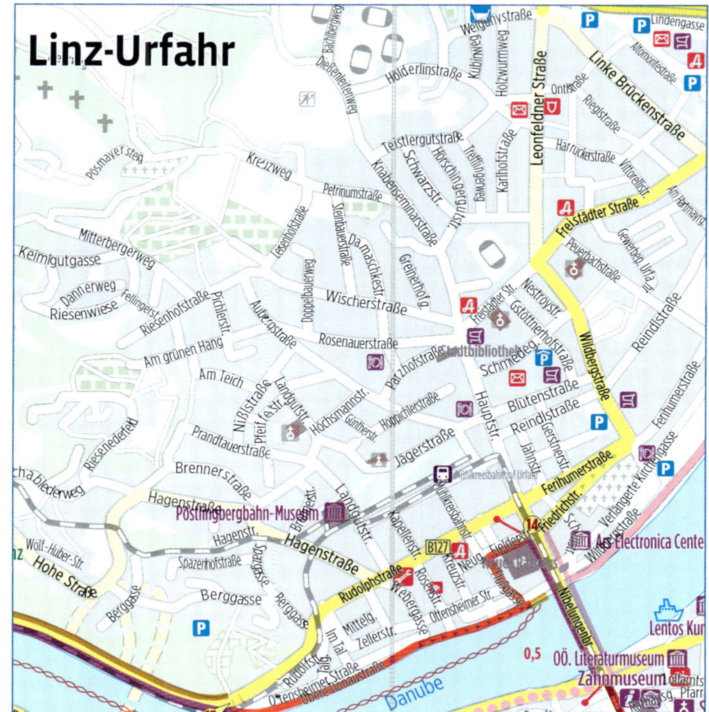

# Passau to Linz along the south bank

**95.9 km**

m/km: ↗ 2.3 (221m) ↘ 2.7 (258m) cycle path: 68 % unpaved: 1 % busy road: 9 %

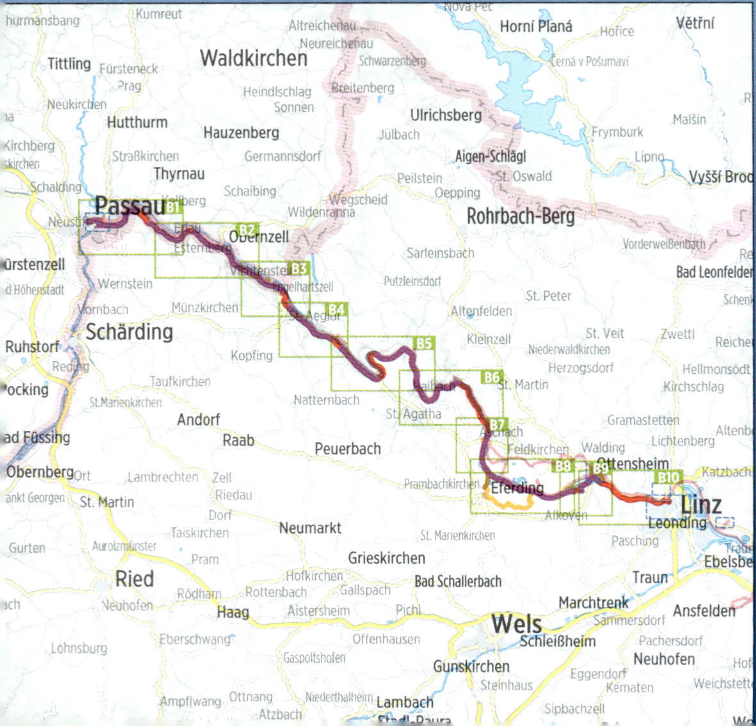


The bicycle route along the right, or southern, bank of the Danube begins in Passau, the city at the confluence of the rivers Inn, Danube and Ilz. After a short distance the route enters Austria and skirts the edge of the Sauwald, through Engelhartszell to Schlögen, where the river winds through an extreme S-curve, the Schlögener Schlinge (loop). At Aschach the Danube then enters the fertile Eferdinger Basin, where it passes through vegetable gardens and imposing old farms. End of this part of the Danube cycle tour is Linz, a city with numerous attractions.

On the right bank, the route runs on cycle paths and quiet side roads. Only the last 8 kilometers before Linz you cycle in heavier traffic on the main road. However, it is possible to switch to the left bank here. Climbs are rare.

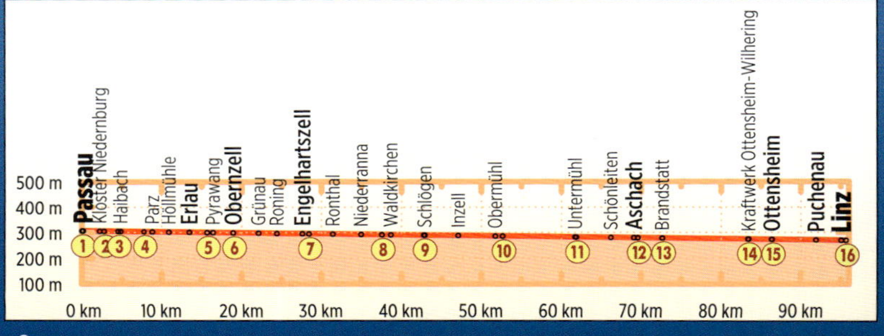

B1
Reut
Ries
Sandberg
Sieglgut
Erdbrüstbächl
Sieglberg
Stromlänge
Grubweg
Hals
Kuchlhof
turmsölden
berg
Anger
Passau
Untersölden
Lindau
Löwmühle
Aichet
Hörleuter Bach
Salzbach
Fattendorf
Schmiedemuseum
Kellberg
Wolfersdorf
Buchsee
Wingersdorf
Kapfham
Leithen
Schörgendorf
Pulvermühle
Kernmühle
B388
2222
B130
Achleiten
Danube
König-Max-Höhe
Veste Oberhaus
Ilzstadt
Obersölden
Parz
Hinding
Faberhof
Fritz-Schaffer-Promenade
St. Stephan
MMK
Danube
B388
Kräutergrabenbach
Dreiflüsseeck
Bahnhofstr.
Passau Hbf.
Danube
B85
regensburger Str.
Donau-Radweg
Donau-Radweg
t. Nikola
Universitätskirche St. Nikola
Inn
Römermuseum
Inn
Haibach
Freinberg
Höllmühle
B130
Edlhof
Erlau
Inn Bike Trail
Wallfahrtskirche Mariahilf
Innstadt
Rosenau
Neundling
Mühlbach
Erlau
Lindenthal
Hamberg
Neusaming
Anzberg
B2
Ingling
Rad
Schwendt
Waging
Saming
Aigen
Haibach
Kößlbach
Unteresternberg
Bräunbach
Dietz
Kugelrad
Hanzing
Achleiten
Untergscheidt
Lehen
Hareth
Kritzing
Mitteresternberg
Hö
Pyret
Gattern
Obergscheid
L1157
39
Esternberg
0,6
3,6
3,8

**1** The tour begins at the **Passau Hauptbahnhof** (main train station) ～ follow the sign "Zum Donauradweg" to the left into **Magalettigasse** ～ in a right-hand bend to Donaulände, turn right there ～ at a car park change to the riverbank path ～ always along the riverbank towards the city centre of Passau ～ straight ahead to **Römerplatz** and the **Luitpoldbrücke**.

> **TIP** For the north bank variant, cross the Danube via the Luitpold Bridge.

At **Römerplatz** turn right into **Lukas-Kern-Straße** ～ at the State Library turn right into **Jesuitengasse** ～ take the next left into **Michaeligasse** and immediately right again into **Schustergasse** ～ at **Residenzplatz** turn left ～ **2** turn right into **Innbrückgasse** and follow the street downhill ～ cross the river on **Marienbrücke** ～ at **Kirchplatz** turn left into Löwengrube ～ cross the river on the **Marienbrücke** ～ on the **Kirchplatz** left into the street **Löwengrube**.

**Innstadt** (Passau) ⓓ
prefix: 0851

🏛 **Römermuseum Kastell Boiotro (Roman Museum Boiotro)**, Ledererg. 43-45, ☏ 34769 ⓦ Exhibits include the excavated foundations of the Roman fort and archaeological discoveries from Passau and surrounding areas. @ jgu282en

♿ **Wallfahrtskirche Mariahilf (Pilgrimage church Maria Hilf.)**, Mariahilfberg 3, ☏ 2356. Important place of pilgrimage since 1622, first as a chapel, the church being constructed 1624-1627. Kaiser Leopold escaped the Turkish siege of Vienna here, prayer staircase with 321 steps. @ oio746en

Immediately turn left from Löwengrube down a widely-spaced stairs with a ramp down to the Inn ～ along the tracks on a partly unpaved and narrow path ～ just before the main road, turn left over the tracks and keep right, **Rosenauer Weg** ～ at the end of this lane a gravelled cycle path continues along the edge of an allotment settlement ～ **3** after the gardens the path becomes quite narrow ～ behind an old warehouse to a side road ～ after passing under the main road on the accompanying cycle path towards Achleiten ～ the cycle path changes to the left side of the road into Austria ～ **4** after about 1 km cross the main road and take the paved lane to the

B2
Haar
Matzenberg
Erlau
Edlhof
Wörth
5
Pfarrkirche
2
Burg Krämpelstein
Pyrawang
Winterhof
Scherleinsöd
Hamet
Diendorf
Obernzell
Unteresternberg
3,8
Hanzing
Dietzendorf
Unterbamberg
Oberbamberg
Danube
Keramikmuseum
Marktkirche
Schlossgarten
Schloss
Willersdorf
Niederndorf
Mitteresternberg
Hötzmannsdorf
Unterschacher
Deutschland
Österreich
3,6
6
Oberschacher
Hütt
Esternberg
Rechab
Schörgeneck
Kasten
St
Silbering
Reisdorf
Seebach
St. Jakob
Vollmannsdorf
Kohlbachmühle
Jetzendorf
Grünau
Endsfelden
Oberkiesling
Riedlbach
Pfamhof
Ruhmansedt
Oberachleiten
Unterachleiten
Gersdorf
Retzwinkel
Burg Vichtenstein
Unterkiesling
5
Moos
Lanzendorf
Enzendorf
Urschendorf
Vichtenstein
41
Aug
Roning
Wetzendorf

right along the woods – again on a roadside cycle path first on the right, then to the left of the main road.



## Esternberg

prefix: 07714

- **Gemeindeamt (Municipal office)**, Hauptstr. 33, ☎ 6655, @ qax536en
- **Solarfreibad (Public outdoor pool)**, Riedlbacher Str. 24, ☎ 6070, @ nof868en

Cross the road and continue through the settlement of Wörth and further on **5** along the right side of the road.

### Pyrawang (Esternberg)

- **Filialkirche (Filial church)**. The small church boasts frescoes from the 14th century, which were discovered in 1982. @ ghl873en

Continue on the bicycle path along the main road – **6** after 3 km you reach the landing of the ferry to Obernzell.



You soon reach Kasten.

### Kasten (Vichtenstein)

- **Filialkirche St. Jakob (Branch church)**. Small baroque church with a crucifixion relief from 1548, @ twx866en

*The fortified castles along the Danube and in other parts of upper Austria mostly date back to the 11th to 13th centuries. They were built and occupied by the nobility as the Bavarian Ostmark, the precursor to Austria, was reestablished following the defeat of the Magyar invaders at Unstrut in 933 and on the Lechfeld near Augsburg in 955.*

Continue on the bicycle path between the river and road to the hamlet of **Roning** – from here the bicycle path follows the river bank until it ends after the campground and outdoor pool by Engelhartszell.

*Signs along the way provide information about the Roman Limes in upper Austria.*

After the campsite, cross the main road and turn left onto the cycle path – on a parallel road to the B 130 along the village of Engelhartszell.



At the fire brigade, change to the main road – after a few hundred metres, turn right, **Stiftstraße**.

## Engelhartszell

prefix: 07717

- **Marktgemeinde (Tourist information)**, Marktpl. 61, ☎ 80550, @ ndq427en
- **Radfähre (Bicycle ferry)**, Nibelungenstr. 174, ☎ 0664/9937026, ☉ Apr/Oct 10:30 a.m.–5 p.m., May/Sept. 9:30 a.m.–5:30 p.m., June 9 a.m.–6 p.m., July/Aug. 9 a.m.–6:30 p.m. @ mff635en
- **Donauschifffahrt Wurm & Noé (shipping line service)**, Schiffsanlegestelle Engelhartszell, ☎ 0049/851/929292, ☎ 0732/783607, @ oaq457en
- **Hufschmiedemuseum (Farrier museum)**, Nibelungenstr. 11, ☎ 8059 ⑦ The 400-year-old farrier's smithy hails from a time when ships were pulled up the Danube by horses and was in use until 1951. Advance notice requested. @ dgh836en
- **Natura 2000 Infozentrum**, Marktpl. 61 ⑦ Interesting facts about the European Protected Area "Upper Danube and Aschach Valley" as well as the exhibition "Danube Stories" with ship's cabin, Danube rolling rope ferry etc. Admission free. @ anu418en
- **Schütz Art Museum**, Nibelungenstr. 36, ☎ 20320 ⊜ The modern museum building with the highest ecological standards houses exhibits by the most important representatives of classical modernism. There are regularly changing exhibitions. @ ulj543en

**Pfarrkirche Mariä Himmelfahrt (Parish church Mariä Himmelfahrt)**, Kirchenpl. 1, 7265. Nave and choir loft of the formerly Gothic market church were built between 1459-1503. kff671en

**Stiftskirche (Abbey church)**, Stiftstr. 6, 8010. Monastery church was consecrated in 1764 and represents a highpoint in 18th c. rococo stucco decoration. There are also impressive frescoes in the nave. bmf158en

**Stift Engelszell (Engelszell Monastery)**, Stiftstr. 6, 8010 7d The only Trappist monastery in Austria, founded in 1293 and with a stylistically pure rococo church (1754), is known for its liqueur, beer and cheese production. lxm878en

**Donaukraftwerk Schleuse Jochenstein (Hydro-electric power station Jochenstein)**, Am Kraftwerk 1, 912890. With the construction of the power plant in 1952-56, six bottlenecks for international shipping were removed over a length of 30 km. Via the lock you reach the "Haus am Strom" in Jochenstein, which brings the important topics of nature, energy and water closer to visitors in an experience exhibition. osk551en

**Kaiserliches Mauthaus (Imperial toll station)**, Energiepl. 51, 805516 7d Old high-water marks and a wall-painting about the history of the old town grace this 15th c building. Houses the Kulturkeller der Energie AG with changing exhibitions of renowned artists. dec873en

**Wassererlebnis Mini-Donau**, Stiftstr. 7, 805516 7d Six sections from the source to the mouth of the Danube provide insight into river dynamics, landscape and life on the water in the

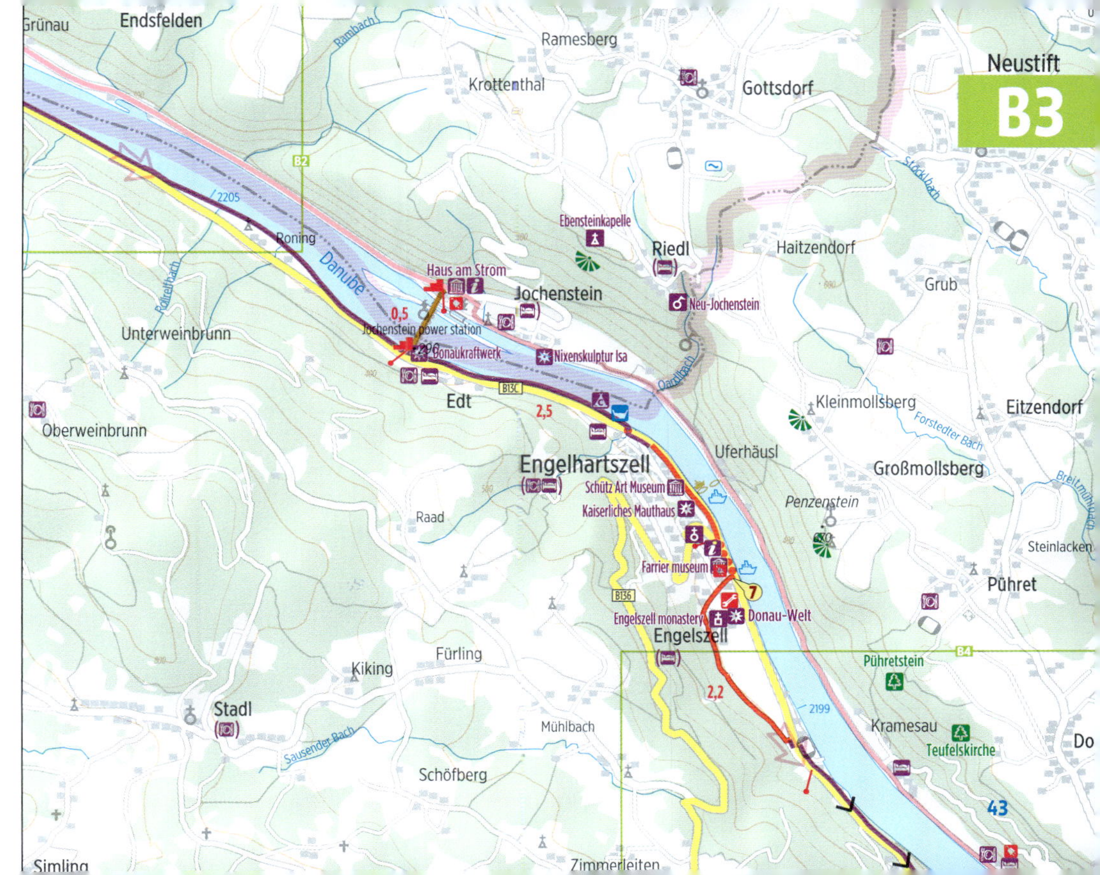

"Water Experience Mini-Danube". There is also a large aquarium and a sensory garden to marvel at and experience. @ tlt587en

✉ **Freibad (Public outdoor pool)**, Nibelungenstr. 113, ✆ 0664/8708787, @ tux467en

*The history of the Engelhartszell market, an important border and customs post since medieval times, is closely tied to the development of the Engelszell monastery. Founded as a Cistercian monastery in 1293 by the bishops of Passau, the monastery for many years served as a refuge for travellers and the summer residence of Passau's rulers. In the course of reforms instituted by Kaiser Josef II, the monastery was closed in 1786, after which its ownership changed repeatedly.*

*Religious life returned to the monastery in 1925, when it was occupied by German Trappists who had been driven out of Alsace. The strict rules by which members of this reformist Cistercian order live – silence, vegetarian food, early waking hours – give the monastery an aura of otherworldly asceticism. That the Trappists' are not completely alienated from the world is shown by their famous production of Liqueur and, since 2012, also a Trappist beer.*

**7** Turn right to the Engelszell monastery pass the monastery at the main road turn right onto the roadside cycle path shortly afterwards the cycle path changes to the left side of the road pass Oberranna.

### Oberranna (Engelhartszell)

🏛 **Römerburgus Oberranna (Roman fort)**, Oberranna 5, 📞 07717/805516 The remains are part of the Roman Limes. @ omh364en

After the Danube bridge, the cycle path leaves the main road turn left at the crossroads turn left again at the right of way into the town centre.

### Wesenufer (Waldkirchen am Wesen)

prefix: 07718

✳ **Skulpturenpark (Sculpture Park)**, Kager 2, 📞 0676/5383656. Life-sized mythological sculptures made of scrap metal on the banks of the Danube. @ ipm233en

🔰 **Naturschutzgebiet Kleines Kößelbachtal (conservation area)**, 📞 725511. "Valley of the Little Kösslbach", hillside, canyon forests and block heaps form this steep natural jewel. @ pli377en

Soon after the church, keep left at the fork **8** back on the B 130 continue on the roadside cycle path to Schlögen to the famous Schlö-

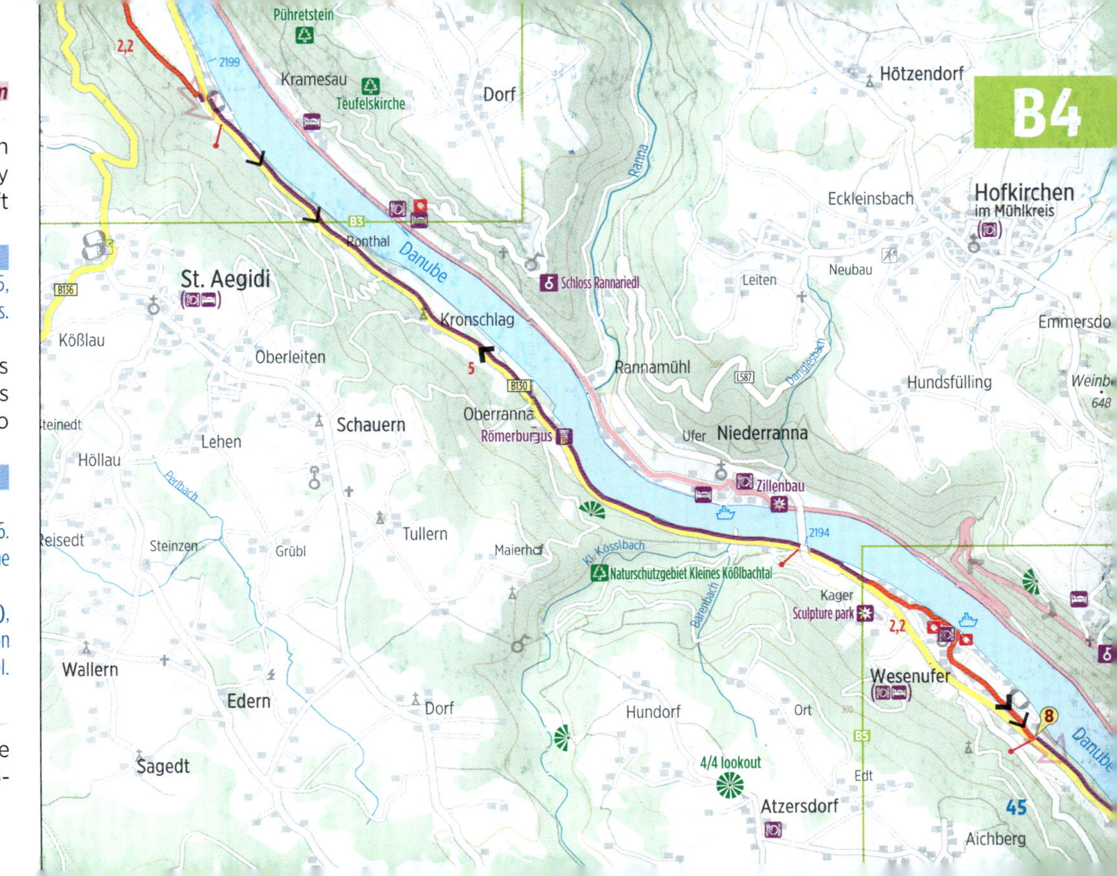

The Schlögen Loop

gener Schlinge ~ continue past the marina and camping, **9** then keep left onto the path into Schlögen.

### Schlögen (Haibach ob der Donau)
prefix: 07279

- **Radfähre Schlögen-Au (Bicycle ferry Schlögen-Au)**, ✆ 8212, ⟳ Apr./Oct. 10am-5pm, May/Sept. 9am-5pm, June-Aug. 9am-6pm, @ cbk653en
- **Donauschifffahrt Wurm & Noé (shipping line service)**, Schiffsanlegestelle Schlögen, ✆ 0049/851/929292, ✆ 0732/783607, @ lpq265en

- **Römerpark Schlögen (Roman park)**, Schlögen 2, ✆ 8235, ✆ 0677/61621401 ⟳ Numerous wall remains and over 4000 finds were uncovered during excavations. The fort's west gate has survived, and is the only existing Roman gate along the Danube in Austria. @ ghi473en
- **Aussichtspunkt Schlögener Blick (Lookout point Schlögener view)**, Steiner Felsen, @ pkh788en
- **Ciconia-Naturerlebnisweg (Ciconia nature trail)**, ✆ 8235. The hiking trail leads from Schlögen via Linetshub to Inzell passing several impressive lookout points around the Schlögener Schlinge. Further information is available from the Haibach tourist office. @ cni587en

## The Schlögen Loop

*Between Passau and Aschach the Danube takes a meandering course through the Bohemian highlands. In doing so, the river did not follow the geological border between the Bohemian plateau and the Alpine foothills, but instead forged its own path through the softer soils of the tertiary basin. The result was the scenic and winding valley downstream from Passau. At Schlögen, however, the river encountered a granite ridge that turned the river back, forming the Schlögen loop. Geologists still speculate about how this was possible.*

*The inaccessibility of the wooded slopes has helped create an environment in which many species of flora and fauna can be found. The spring and fall are seasons in which the Danube valley presents itself in especially vibrant colors, giving the valley a touch of wilderness. This impression is countered by the many inviting meadows and inns along the riverbank, which testify to the valley's centuries-long use.*

### Schlögen to Aschach      26.7 km
Follow the course of the path to Inzell, the Danube cycle route continues here only on the south bank.
*On the way you can see the ruins of Haichenbach on the other bank.*

### Inzell (Haibach ob der Donau)
- **St. Nikolaus Kirche (St. Nikolaus Church)**. The renovated little church is said to have been built in 1155 by an imperial count, who was rescued here from the floods. @ wpd636en

In the village the route returns to the river follow the path to Kobling.

### Kobling (Haibach ob der Donau)
- **Donaufähre Kobling-Obermühl (April/Oct. 9am-5pm, May/Sept. 8am-6pm, June-Aug. 8am-1pm)**, ✆ 0664/73493393. The ferry is operated by the Jausenstation Donauterrasse am Limes

B5
47
nufer
Marsbach
Schloss Marsbach
Lehen
Rumersdorf
Oberbumberg
Niederbumberg
Rudolf Kirchschläger Zentrum
Niederkappel
Haarmühl
Pühreth
Haar
Unteredt
Dr. R. Kirchschläger presidential chair
Steinerber
L585
Danube
Freizell
Zillenvermietung
B4
Dorf
Ferienhof Ramesedt
Nature trail Donauschlinge
Weikersdorf
Grafenau
Danube
2,80
Obermühl
a.d. Donau
Fischlehrpfad
Kirchbergerbachl
Getreidespeicher
Seibersdo
Ebersdorf
Aichberg
Buchen
Inzell
2,8
Danube
5
Obergschwendt
Kobling
Kirchberg
ob der Donau
Waldkirchen
am Wesen
Ruine Wesen
5,5
B130
Graben
Untergschwendt
Stieberberg
10
Wolkersdor
Ruine Haichenbach
Eckersdorf
Witzersdo
kmairing
Au
1,4
Mannsdorf
Oberhub
B6
L525
Danube
Erledt
Paschinger Hügl
Pasching
Römerpark
Ciconia-Naturerlebnisweg
Schlögen
Schlögener Blick
Linetshub
Berg
Oed
Haiden
Straß
9
Mitterberg
Pühret
Ve tsberg
B130
Schlögenleiten
Ernleiten
Mühlbach
Waldbach
Dorf
A tenberg
Fuchsbach
6

Aschach

and Pension Idylle in Kobling and can be called by bell. @ iql857en

Continue along the road ~ **10** turn left and continue down the well-paved towpath along the Danube, Haibach lies above on the right.

### Haibach ob der Donau
prefix: 07279

*i* Gemeindeamt (Municipal office), Kirchenpl. 4, ✆ 8235, @ ltv222en

⬆ Hallenbad (Swimming hall), Römerstr. 16, ✆ 821514, @ eul352en

The next place you come to, Kaiserau, is about 10 km downstream.

### Kaiserau (Aschach an der Donau)
prefix: 07273

⛴ Fähre Kaiserhof - Untermühl - Bremsberg (April-Sept. 9-18 h), Kaiserau 1, ✆ 6221-0, ✆ 0664/5313327. Stations: Kaiserhof/Kaiserau, Untermühl and Bremsberg. The ferry can be called by radio. @ ulf241en

**11** Pass the inn and its large campground ~ leave Kaiserau on the narrow street that serves residents along the river ~ when the Aschach dam comes in sight stay right at the fork ~ continue to Aschach ~ after the Fisherman Museum turn left onto the cycle path.

### Aschach an der Donau
prefix: 07273

*i* Tourismusverein (Tourism association Aschach an der Donau), Kurzwernhartpl. 5, ✆ 6355, ✆ 0664/4082200, @ pgt741en

🏛 Schopper- und Fischermuseum ("Schopper" and Fisherman Museum), Schopperpl. 2, opposite the info point, ✆ 0664/4797704 ⊜ The museum presents on two floors the extinct craft of the Schopperei, as well as the history of the commercial and leisure fishing in Upper Austria. The "Schoppen" in Zillenbau was the stuffing of the joints between the wall boards of the Zillen with moss. @ lwb161en

⛪ Pfarrkirche (Parish church), Kirchenpl. 1. The Gothic structure was built in 1490, and was expanded in the 19th c. according to

Oberhub
L525
Danube
Burg Partenstein
Ritzersdorf
Haiden
Winzberg
Untermühl
Neuhaus
a.d. Donau
Falkenberg
Grub
B6
Berg
Absdorf
Schloss Neuhaus
Donaublick Kettenturm
Falkenbach
Dorf
Point
11
Danube
Falkenbach
6
Kaiserau
2170
St. Marti
im Mühlkre
3,8
Dorf
Haibach
ob der Donau
B5
Exlau
Hinteraigen
Dorf
Ibach
Grub
Komas
Bach
Paching
Driefenbach
Reitl
Wiesing
L1216
Mußberg
Zagl
Oberhart
B130
Oed
in Bergen
Reith
Schönleiten
Unter
Kehrbach
Lacken
Aschach
Aschach power station
B7
6,5
L1215
Senghübl
Pesenbachtal
49
Stauf Ruin
Donaukraftwerk
Vornholz
Gfehret
Hart
ob Haizing
L1216
Sommerberg

*Eferdinger Becken*

plans drafted by Clemens Holzmeister. The altar includes the highly prized "Cross of the Danube," which washed ashore in Aschach in 1693. @ nve351en

🛡 **Schloss Aschach (Aschach castle)**, Harrachstr. 1, ✆ 7181, ✆ 0699/18181004, ✆ 0699/18181001. The complex was built around 1606 on the occasion of the marriage of Charles of Jörger and was one of the most important profane Renaissance buildings in Upper Austria. Under the architect Lukas von Hildebrandt a major reconstruction took place in 1709. Today privately owned, it offers opportunities for castle tours, accommodation or relaxation in the green area including a café. @ kak255en

✳ **Donaukraftwerk (Danube power plant)**, Schopperpl. 16. In the reservoir of the former largest run-of-river power plant in Europe, biotopes have been created which are home to rare animal and plant species. @ tre285en

✳ **Historischer Ortskern (Historic town centre)**. Most of the old houses with their charming courtyards and arbors are built in the Gothic or Renaissance styles. Many of the facades bear stucco work from the 18th and 19th centuries. @ qdv137en

✳ **Zehner-Trauner**, Schopperpl. 2, ✆ 640312. Open-air part of the Schopper and Fishing museum. The wooden river boat was built by 3 old "Schopper" according to original plans for the 1994 state exhibition in Engelhartszell. @ sqo736en

*The old customs station at Aschach was drawn into the great peasants' revolt of 1626, when* rebels captured and plundered the city repeatedly. Shipping and ship building dominated the local economy until the early 20th century. Today Aschach is home to a handful of what may be the last living "Schopper," the name given to the craftsmen who build the 20 meter, up to 15 ton flat-bottomed barges that once plied the Danube.

A number of handsome old houses along the Danube recall the town's heyday as a centre of shipping on the river.

## Hartkirchen

prefix: 07273

🛡 **Pfarrkirche (Parish church)**, ✆ 6374. Local records establish that the church existed as early as 898, making it the oldest church in the region. Around 1750 it was redecorated in the baroque style and furnished with imposing frescos, late-baroque illusionary paintings and rich decorations. @ sxk628en

## Aschach to Linz     26 km

To reach the left bank turn right just before the Danube bridge in Aschach. After 400 m turn left onto the bridge's ramp.
On the right bank continue along the river bank
**12** you pass under the Danube road bridge
you continue downstream on the bicycle

path directly along the river
after 3 km you reach Brandstatt
— at Brandstatt in a right turn over
a Danube tributary **13** turn left
at the end of the harbour back to
the Danube.


**13** From here you can take a
detour to Pupping.

## Pupping

prefix: 07272

- **Tourismusverein (Tourist Office)**, Pupping 13,
  ✆ 2331, @ gnm841en
- **Shalomkloster (Shalom Monastery)**, Pupping 4, ✆ 5896. As early as 1477, the Counts
  of Schauenberg brought the Franciscans to
  Pupping for pastoral care, where the pilgrimage church of St. Wolfgang already stood.
  Since 1998, the monastery has been run along
  the lines of the "San Masseo" house near
  Assisi and also offers a small monastery shop.
  @ jdy121en
- **Klostergarten (monastery garden)**, Pupping 4, ✆ 2331. The area, divided into 12 parts,
  presents the variety of local vegetables and
  herbs. @ ogh474en

## Brandstatt (Pupping)


The alternative route via Eferding begins just outside of
Brandstatt. This route is partially signposted and passes through
pleasant farmland on the way to
this historic town. The route is
shown in orange on the map.

### Eferding

prefix: 07272

- **Stadtmarketing und Tourismus (Tourism
  association Eferding)**, Stadtpl. 31, ✆ 5555-1711,
  @ ucw761en
- **Fürstlich Starhemberg'sches Familienmuseum und Stadtmuseum Eferding (Princely
  Starhemberg Family Museum and Eferding
  City Museum)**, Kirchenpl. 1, ✆ 5555-160,
  ✆ 2394 ☺ You will gain insight into the
  family history of the old noble family and the
  development of Austria's third oldest city.
  @ bpj334en
- **Stadtpfarrkirche Eferdinger Dom (Eferdinger
  cathedral)**, Kirchenpl. 2, ✆ 2241. Built in late
  gothic style, neogothic high altar from 1890.
  Stair to choir in the form of a double spiral
  staircase. @ nai533en

**Schloss Starhemberg (Castle)**, Kirchenpl. 1, ℓ 2301 ◔ Mentioned in 1255 as the castle of the Passau bishops. In 1785, the south and west wings were rebuilt in the classicist style under Prince Georg Adam von Starhemberg. Medieval cellar, knights' hall, ancestors' hall, ruling rooms. @ iql667en

**Stadtplatz (Town square)**. With Trinity Column and town houses. Most of the houses have classical facades. A special feature is the Lebzelterhaus Vogl (No. 27). Consisting of two Gothic houses, the façade was redesigned in the Baroque style and now houses a café-confectionery.

**Erlebnisbad (Adventure pool)**, Ludlg. 11, ℓ 0664/88241870, @ oib246en

*Eferding was given its town privileges already in 1222 and is therefore one of the oldest towns in Austria. The town is even mentioned in the Nibelungenlied (Song of the Niebelungs), where Kriemhild rested „Ze Everdingen".*

### Inn (Fraham)

**Wiesmühle**, Inn 20. The four-storey mill was built in 1828 with the stones of the demolished town gate of Eferding. Today the water power is used to generate electricity and the sawmill is operated. The mill is closed down. @ tpj145en

### Trattwörth (Fraham)

**Rosarium Gruber (Rose garden)**, Trattwörth 3, ℓ 0664/4647227 ⑦ Following the example of a baroque border garden, the complex was designed with over 1,000 roses. @ fxm517en

From Brandstatt continue along the riverbank as far as the power station at Ottensheim-Wilhering **14** — turn right onto the service road in front of the entrance to the transformer station.

**At the power station you can cross the Danube to the north bank all day.**

After the bridge over the Innbach take the sharp left turn before the campground — follow the asphalted cycle path past the fish nature trail.

**Fall** (Wilhering)
prefix: 07226

**Fischlehrpfad (Fish nature trail)**, Faller Str. 28, ℓ 225512. Along the Innbach, 40 display boards bring the native fish and aquatic animal species, including some that are already extinct, closer. @ smi645en

You cross the Mühlbach as you reach **Ufer** — turn left after the bridge and follow the path along the river to the ferry landing **15**.

**Ufer** (Wilhering)

**Fähre (Ferry)**, Uferweg 1, ℓ 0664/9254916, ◔ Mon-Sat 6.15-19.20, Sun/Fri 8-19.20. @ xhb656en

**The official Danube cycle path changes here to the north bank. The route on the south side is not an official cycle path and is very busy. Nevertheless, we would like to mention it as a more direct and faster route.**

To reach Wilhering and the route to Linz along the south bank, ride up the road from the ferry landing — keep left onto the bicycle path along the main road and ride to Wilhering.

### Wilhering
prefix: 07226

**Stift Wilhering mit Klosterpforte, Café, Shop (Wilhering Abbey)**, Linzer Str. 4, ℓ 231112 ◒ The exhibition deals with the 875-year history of Wilhering Abbey with reference to the following themes: Order of the Cistercians, Collegiate Church of the Assumption, life in the monastery and artists in Wilhering Abbey. The rooms of the Meierhof contain works by the artists Fritz Fröhlich and P. Balduin Sulzer. Guided tours by appointment. @ rfq728en

**Stiftskirche Mariä Himmelfahrt (Mariä Himmelfahrt abbey church)**, Linzer Str. 4, ℓ 231114. The construction of the church in 1733-51 created one of the most outstanding sacred rooms of the Rococo period in Austria, the special significance of which is primarily based on the interior. @ luj341en

**Zisterzienserstift (Cistercian Abbey)**, Linzer Str. 4, ℓ 231112, ℓ 231114 ◒ Founded in 1146, the monastery shapes both the

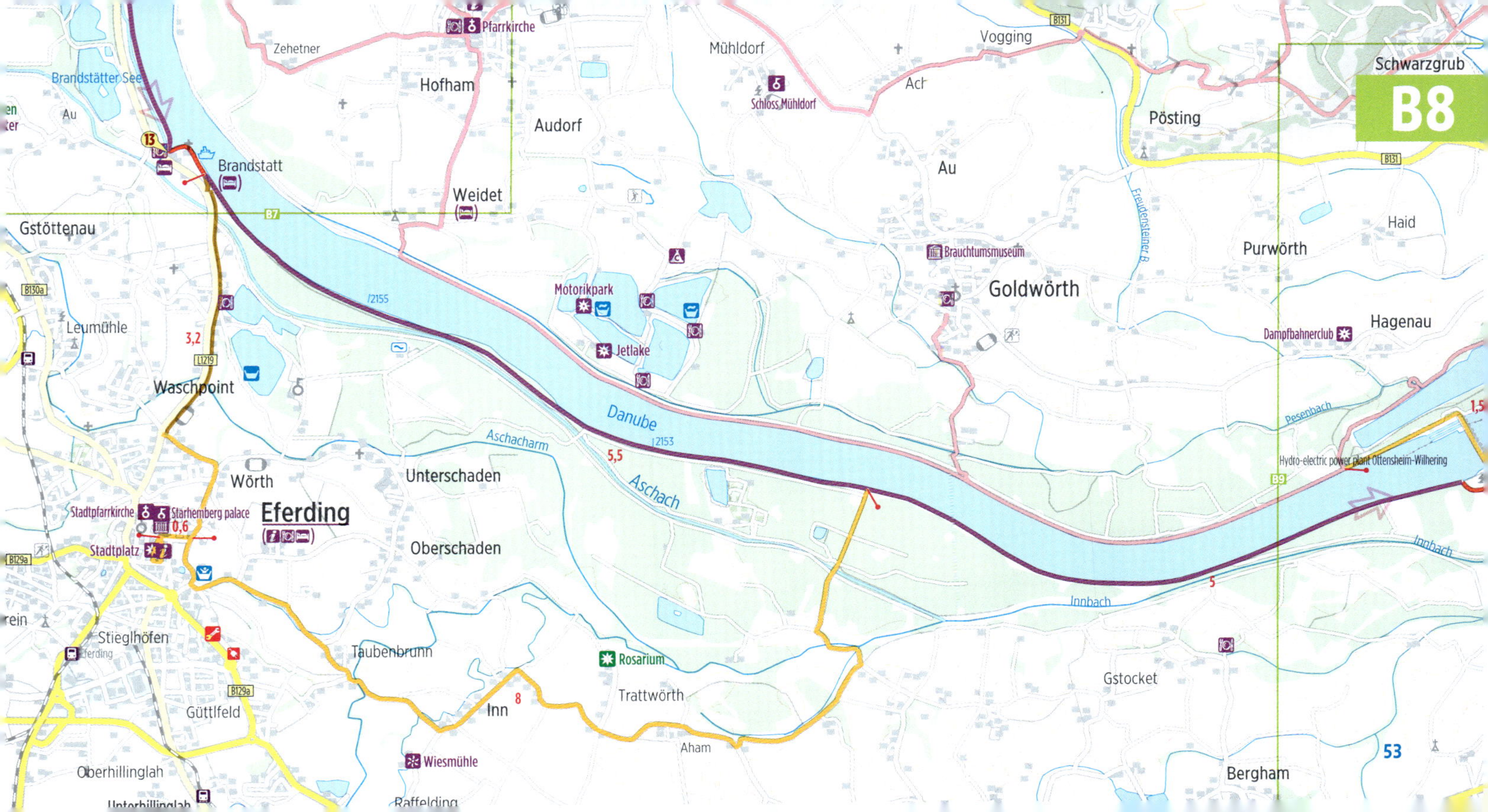

B131
Schwarzgrub
B8
Pösting
Vogging
Ach
Au
Mühldorf
Schloss Mühldorf
Haid
Purwörth
Brauchtumsmuseum
Goldwörth
Hagenau
Dampfbahnerclub
Zehetner
Hofham
Audorf
Weidet
Pfarrkirche
Brandstätter See
Au
13
Brandstatt
B7
Gstöttenau
B130a
Leumühle
I2155
3,2
L1219
Waschpoint
Motorikpark
Jetlake
Danube
I2153
5,5
Freudensteiner B.
Pesenbach
1,5
B9
Hydro-electric power plant Ottensheim-Wilhering
5
Wörth
Unterschaden
Aschacharm
Aschach
Innbach
Stadtpfarrkirche  Starhemberg palace
0,6
Eferding
Oberschaden
Stadtplatz
B129a
rein
Stieglhöfen
Eferding
Taubenbrunn
Rosarium
Gstocket
Innbach
B129a
Güttlfeld
Inn  8
Trattwörth
53
Oberhillinglah
Wiesmühle
Aham
Bergham
Unterhillinglah
Raffelding

cultural and spiritual life of the region. After the fire of 1733, the church was rebuilt and decorated in the magnificent rococo style by Martino and Bartolomeo Altomonte and by Augsburg stucco artists. Guided tours by appointment. @ omu231en

🔵 **Stiftspark mit Baumlehrpfad (Abbey garden with tree trail)**, Linzer Str. 4, ☎ 231110. Modeled on an English garden and laid out in 1833. It includes a yew believed to be 800 years old, and a large orangery in classicist Biedermeier design. @ ngx186en

If you have decided to take the busy main road to Linz simply follow the road from Wilher-



ing along the Danube to Linz — you pass the Calvary Church of St. Margarethen.

## St. Margarethen (Linz)

prefix: 0732

🔵 **Kalvarienbergkirche St. Margarethen**, Zaubertalstr. 9a, ☎ 775137. The church, built in its present form in 1688, was a hermit's hermitage and hospice. The Way of the Cross, built in the 19th century with several life-size wooden figures, shows a view of Jerusalem. @ jiv477en

Keep right just before the **Nibelungen bridge** and ride up to the end of the bridge — **16** here you turn right to reach the historic centre on the **main square**.

## Linz

prefix: 0732

🔵 **Donauschifffahrt Wurm & Noé**, Untere Donaulände 1, ☎ 783607, ☎ 0851/929292. Regular boat trips between Passau and Krems, harbour tours. Bicycle transport € 2. @ xjj576en

🔵 **Francisco Carolinum (State gallery)**, Museumstr. 14, ☎ 772052200 ⊜ The House of Photo and Media Art is a place for modern, contemporary art and photography. It is also dedicated to teaching the history of art of the 20th century with reference to Upper Austria. @ xyj314en

🔵 **Lentos Kunstmuseum (Lentos art museum)**, Ernst-Koref-Promenade 1, ☎ 70703600 ⊜ An architectural jewel directly on the banks of the Danube, built to house the top-class works of art of the city of Linz. The museum's appearance is dominated by a glass facade illuminated at night. Thus this museum of modern art sets a visible accent not only during daytime. @ jab315en

🔵 **Nordico Stadtmuseum (Nordico - City museum)**, Simon-Wiesenthal-Pl. 1, ☎ 70701901 ⊜ It has a rich collection from the fields of art, archaeology, folk art, photography and is used for continuously changing exhibitions. @ dfa742en

🔵 **OK Linz (OK centre for contemporary art)**, OK Pl. 1, ☎ 772052500 ⊜ Exhibition and production house for contemporary art. Symposia, mediation work and live acts broaden the activities on offer. @ moc743en

🔵 **OÖ. Literaturmuseum (Literary museum)**, Adalbert-Stifter-Pl. 1, ☎ 7720/11294 ⊜ The home of Adalbert Stifter, the author of "Nachsommer" and "Witiko," for 20 years before his death in 1868. Today a museum on Stifter and upper Austrian literature. @ jog746en

🔵 **Schlossmuseum (Palace museum)**, Schlossberg 1, ☎ 772052300 ⊜ The Schlossmuseum Linz provides a comprehensive insight into the natural, cultural and artistic history of Upper Austria from prehistory and early history to the 21st century on more than 10,000 m² of exhibition space. Around the permanent exhibition of the Upper Austrian Provincial Museum, special exhibitions highlight current international and regional, as well as cultural, natural and contemporary history topics. @ gyg487en

🏛 **voestalpine Stahlwelt (voestalpine steel world)**, voestalpine-Str. 4, ☎ 050304/158900 ⏲ Experience steel as material on five levels in the house and mix different types of steel yourself. @ lha571en

🏛 **Zahnmuseum (Tooth museum)**, Hauptpl. 1 🚏 Modern and architecturally designed exhibition rooms house ordination facilities from the past 120 years. @ nsh271en

🏛 **Zeitgeschichte Museum (Museum of Contemporary History)**, voestalpine-Str. 1, ☎ 050304/158900 🚏 During the construction and operation of the Reichswerke Hermann Göring in Linz, thousands of foreign men and women, young people and children were forced into forced labour. The Contemporary History MUSEUM is dedicated to their fate. @ tls358en

⛪ **Mariendom (St. Mary's Cathedral)**, Herrenstr. 26, ☎ 946100. Largest Austrian church building, capacity for 20,000 people, built between 1862 and 1924. Remarkable are the painting windows with depictions of Upper Austrian history. @ jbg656en

⛪ **Martinskirche (St. Martin's church)**, Römerstr. 21, ☎ 777454, ☎ 946100. Regarded as the oldest church in Austria surviving in its original form (known since 799). The foundations of a Carolingian king's residence were discovered above a Roman foundation. @ mis731en

⛪ **Minoritenkirche (Minorite church)**, Promenade 24, ☎ 943472. This charming rococo building was built in the 2nd half of the 18th c. in a neighbouring building of the Minorite monastery founded in 1236. @ eif258en

⛪ **Stadtpfarrkirche (Linz parish church)**, Pfarrpl. 4, ☎ 776120. Originally a Roman basilica. The 1648 baroque new building includes a wall-mounted gravestone for the heart and entrails of Kaiser Friedrich III. @ ycp742en

⛪ **Linzer Schloss (Linz Palace)**, Schlossberg 1, ☎ 772052300 🚏 The Roman Lentia Castle used to be located on the site of today's castle. In its eventful history, the castle was also in Bavarian hands for a number of years, served as the state capital and military hospital, was a prisoner house and barracks. Today it houses the Upper Austrian Provincial Museum. @ obw532en

⛪ ✳ **Franz-Josef-Warte (Franz-Josef observation point)**, Römerstr. 96 ⏱ At the highest point of Linz's Freinberg, after climbing the

*Landstraße Linz*

numerous steps of the observation point (1888), you are rewarded with a magnificent view over Linz, the Danube, Urfahr and the Pöstlingberg. @ jce844en

**Dreifaltigkeitssäule (Trinity column)**, Hauptpl. The 20 m high baroque column was created out of gratitude for the rescue from war danger, plague and conflagration around 1700, today a landmark of Linz. @ ohl836en

**Musiktheater**, Am Volksgarten 1, ☎ 7611400. Opened in 2013 as the most modern opera house in Europe. The building was designed by London architect Terry Pawson. @ rlk813en

**Brucknerhaus**, Untere Donaulände 7, ☎ 76120, ☎ 775230. Modern concert and congress hall and centre of the Linz Bruckner Festival with acoustics that are internationally regarded as exemplary. @ ubh471en

**Erlebniswelt am Pöstlingberg (Pöstlingberg mountain railway)**, Hauptpl., ☎ 34007000 ⑦ The steepest adhesion mountain railway in the world impresses with its unusual and idyllic route. From the main square it goes directly up to the Pöstlingberg - to the highest viewpoint above Linz. @ yra872en

**Landhaus**, Landhauspl. 1, ☎ 772011161. As a Renaissance building from the 16th century, the Upper Austrian official building offers some sights such as the remarkable arcade courtyard with the planet fountain. @ pri213en

**Mozarthaus (Mozart house)**, Altstadt 17, ☎ 70702009. In this Renaissance building from the 2nd half of the 16th c. Wolfgang Amadeus Mozart was a guest of Count Thun and composed the "Linzer Sinfonie" and the "Linzer Sonate". @ sts181en

**Botanischer Garten (Botanical Garden)**, Roseggerstr. 20, ☎ 7070, ☎ 70701870 ⑦ Attractive park on 4.25 ha with over 10,000

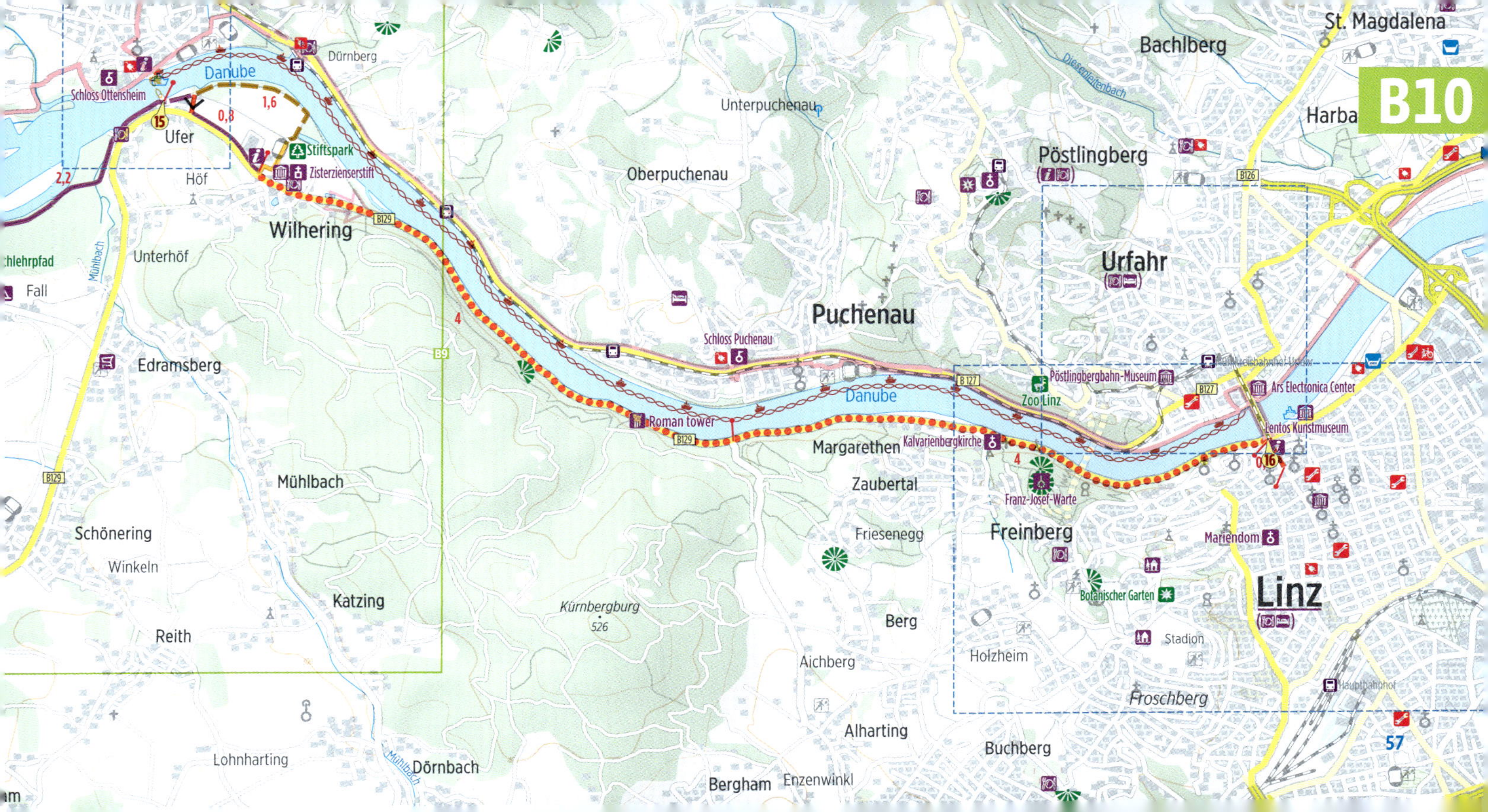

B10
St. Magdalena
Bachlberg
Harba
Diesenleitenbach
B126
Pöstlingberg
Unterpuchenau
Oberpuchenau
Urfahr
Danube
Dürnberg
Schloss Ottensheim
1,6
0,8
15
Ufer
Stiftspark
Höf
Zisterzienserstift
Puchenau
Wilhering
B129
Schloss Puchenau
Pöstlingbergbahn-Museum
B127
Zoo Linz
B 127
Ars Electronica Center
chlehrpfad
Mühlbach
Unterhöf
2,2
Fall
B9
Danube
Edramsberg
Lentos Kunstmuseum
4
Roman tower
B129
Margarethen
Kalvarienbergkirche
16
Zaubertal
4
Mühlbach
Franz-Josef-Warte
Schönering
Freinberg
Friesenegg
Mariendom
Winkel
Katzing
Botanischer Garten
Reith
Berg
Linz
Kürnbergburg
526
Stadion
Aichberg
Holzheim
Froschberg
Alharting
Hauptbahnhof
Lohnharting
Dörnbach
57
Bergham
Enzenwinkl
Buchberg

species, well-known cactus collection, rosarium, alpinum and tropical house. @ qpa446en

, Schörgenhubstr. 16, 34006680, @ ier363en

, Untere Donaulände 11, 34006630, @ vqk111en

, Ramsauerstr. 12, 34006660, @ bio326en

*Centuries ago, when salt and iron ore were the most important commodities, a large market was built at the site of the Roman settlement of Lentia. Kaiser Maximilian's "Brückenbrief" in 1497 launched the developments that made Linz and its annual fair known across Europe in the 16th and 17th centuries. The huge medieval square influenced the city's economic development until early industrialization. Today the city harbour has taken over this role. Europe's first large industrial factory was in Linz.*

*In more recent years the city has been gaining an international reputation as a city of culture that combines the qualities of an important centre of industry and trade with a lively and attractive contemporary arts scene. One example is the Ars Electronica, which since 1979 has been giving renowned artists the opportunity of giving artistic form to the newest technological advances. It takes place – together with the Bruckner festival – every year and reaches its highpoint with the Linz "Klangwolke," an outdoor music extravaganza.*

*Linz is also internationally known as a centre of computer art. In 2009, Linz was honored as a European Capital of Culture, further cementing the city's reputation as an industrial centre that has successfully transformed itself into a forward-looking and modern centre of culture.*

*Danube and Linz palace*

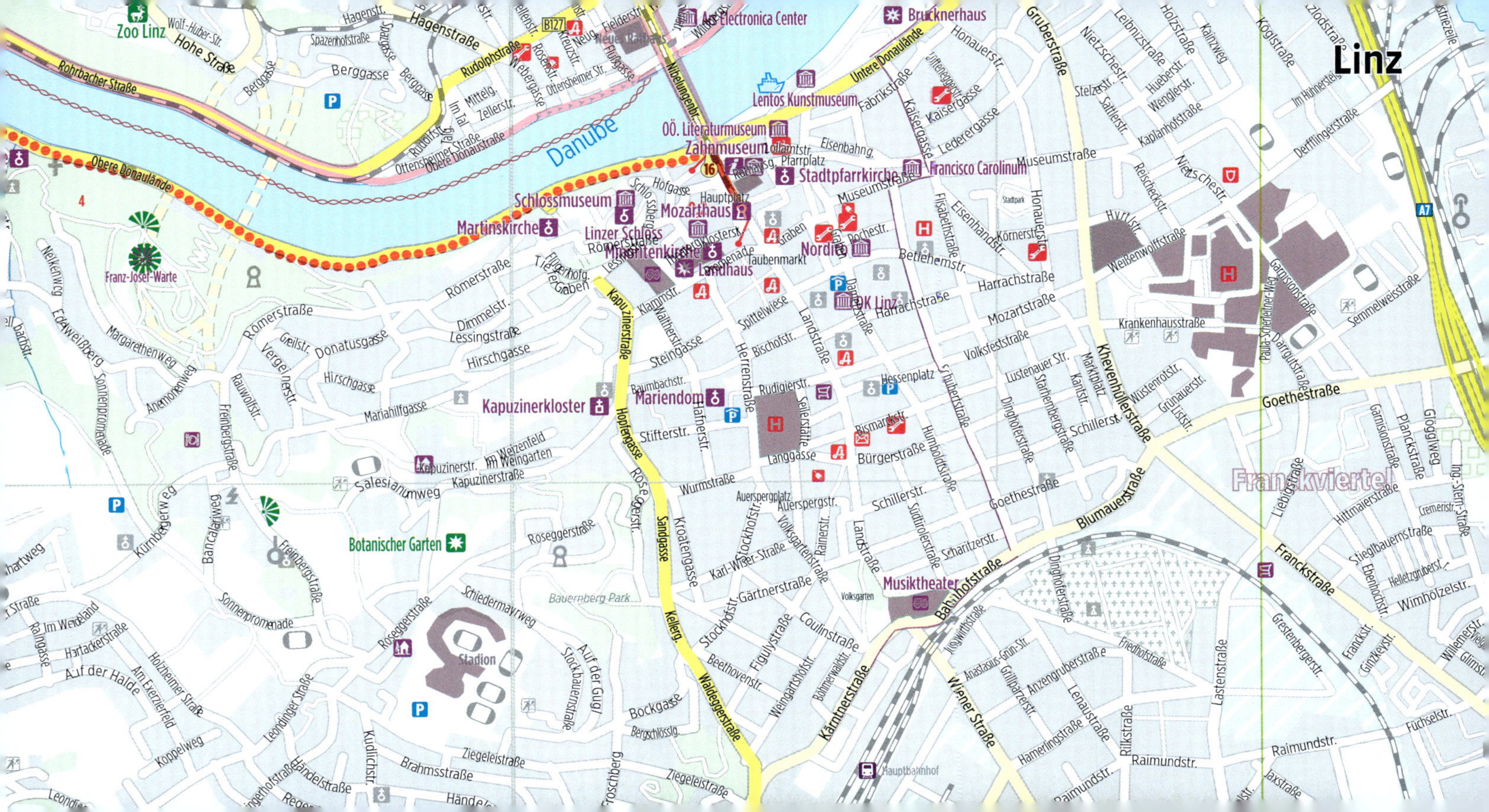

Linz
Zoo Linz
Wolf-Huber-Str.
Hohe Straße
Hagenstraße
Hagenstr.
Spazenhofstraße
Berggasse
Berggasse
Berggasse
Rohrbacher Straße
Rudolphstraße
B127
Neue Brücke
Nibelungenbrücke
Ars Electronica Center
Brucknerhaus
Gruberstraße
Leibnizstraße
Nietzschestr.
Holzstraße
Im Hühnersteig
zlodstraße
Köglstraße
Honauerstr.
Stelzerstr.
Sattlerstr.
Hueberstr.
Wenglerstr.
Kaplanhofstraße
Derfflingerstraße
Nietzschestr.
A7
Untere Donaulände
Fabrikstraße
Kaisergasse
Ledergasse
Museumstraße
Lentos Kunstmuseum
Danube
Obere Donaulände
Obere Donaulände
Ottensheimer Straße
Oö. Literaturmuseum
Zahnmuseum
Pfarrplatz
Stadtpfarrkirche
Francisco Carolinum
Museumstraße
Reischlstr.
Hyrtlstr.
Weißenwolffstraße
Garnisonstraße
Semmelweisstraße
Krankenhausstraße
Schlossmuseum
Mozarthaus
Hauptplatz
Stadtpark
Honauerstr.
Körnerstr.
Elisabethstraße
Eisenhandstr.
Martinskirche
Linzer Schloss
Römerstraße
Minoritenkirche
Landhaus
Graben
Nordico
Betlehemstr.
Harrachstraße
Mozartstraße
Volksfeststraße
Franz-Josef-Warte
Römerstraße
Römerstraße
Tiefer Graben
Hofgasse
Klammstr.
Promenade
Taubenmarkt
AK Linz
Dametzstraße
Harrachstraße
Nelkenweg
Dimmelstr.
Lessingstraße
Donatusgasse
Hirschgasse
Hirschgasse
Walther str.
Steingasse
Herrenstraße
Bischofstr.
Landstraße
Spittelwiese
Hessenplatz
Lustenauer Str.
Starhembergstraße
Marktplatz
Kantstr.
Grünauerstr.
Wüstenrotstr.
Kapuzinerstraße
Baumbachstr.
Rudigierstr.
Seilerstätte
Bismarckstr.
Humboldtstraße
Dinghoferstraße
Schillerstraße
Mariahilfgasse
Kapuzinerkloster
Mariendom
Pfarrstr.
Flafner str.
Bürgerstraße
Franckviertel
Kapuzinerstr.
Im Weingarten
Stifterstr.
Langgasse
Wurmstraße
Auerspergplatz
Auerspergstr.
Schillerstr.
Südtirolerstr.
Goethestraße
Hopfengasse
Rainerstr.
Scharitzerstr.
Blumauerstraße
Liebigstraße
Hittmaierstraße
Cremeristr.
Salesianumweg
Roseggerstraße
Sandgasse
Kroatengasse
Karl-Wiser-Straße
Volksgartenstraße
Landstraße
Dinghoferstraße
Stieglbauernstraße
Ebelsbergerstr.
Helletzgruberstr.
Botanischer Garten
Roseggerstraße
Kellerg.
Waldeggstraße
Stockhofstr.
Gärtnerstraße
Coulinstraße
Volksgarten
Musiktheater
Bahnhofstraße
Franckstraße
Wimhölzelstraße
Freinbergstraße
Bancalari
Schiedermayrweg
Bauernberg Park
Stockholstr.
Figulystraße
Bismarckstr.
Anastasius-Grün-Str.
Grillparzerstr.
Friedhofstraße
Lastenstraße
Sonnenpromenade
Roseggerstraße
Beethovenstr.
Weingartshofstr.
Böhmerwaldstr.
Wienerstraße
Kilswirthstraße
Dinghoferstraße
Lenaustraße
Grestenbergerstr.
Stadion
Auf der Gugl
Stockbauernstraße
Bockgasse
Bergschlössl
Kärntnerstraße
Wiener Straße
Hamerlingstraße
Rilkestraße
Franckstr.
Ginzkeystr.
Fuchsstr.
Leondinger Straße
Am Exerzierfeld
Holzheimer Straße
Kudlichstr.
Ziegeleistraße
Brahmsstraße
Froschberg
Ziegeleistraße
Hauptbahnhof
Anzengruberstraße
Raimundstr.
Raimundstr.
Koppelweg
Am Exerzierfeld
Händelstraße
Regerstr.
Bergschlössl
Händelstr.
Raimundstr.
Jaxstraße
Leonding

# Linz to Emmersdorf along the north bank

**106.9 km**

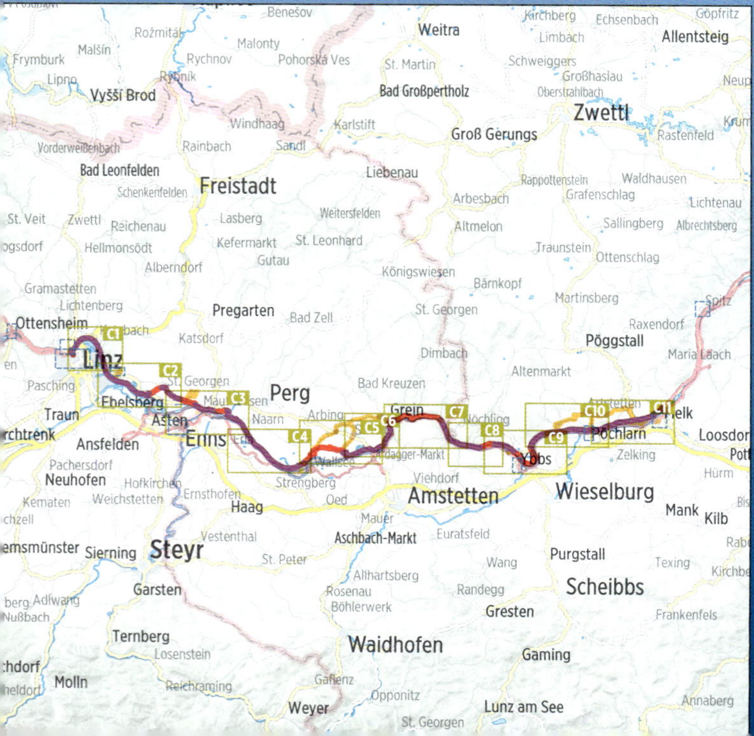


m/km: ↗ 0.7 (80m) ↘ 1.3 (141m) cycle path: 69 % unpaved: 0 % busy road: 10 %

Downstream from Linz, the Danube bicycle trail returns to the green and fertile Austrian countryside, bringing the bicycle tourist through pretty towns like Steyregg and Grein, past cultural attractions like the open-air museum in Mitterkirchen, and historical sites, including the Mauthausen concentration camp, a somber remnant of Germany's and Austria's Nazi past. The bicycle route passes the fascinating Strudengau, the much-feared narrows where the Danube churns and races, to the gentle Nibelungengau that the river passes to reach Melk.

A route is only available on the northern, or left, bank of the river from Linz to Abwinden. The route follows bicycle paths and quiet country lanes to Emmersdorf, with the exception of the stretch along the road by Struden. The only climbs are to be found on the excursion to the concentration camp memorial at Mauthausen.

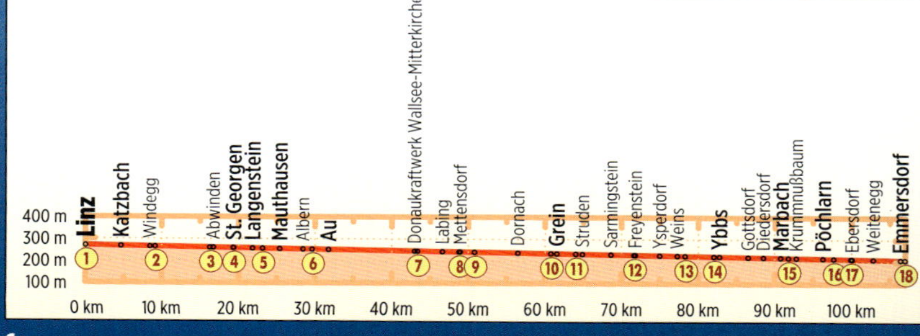

### Linz to Abwinden      15.9 km

Those riding from the north bank simply continue on the bicycle path along the river after passing below the bridge.

Coming from the **1** main square **Hauptplatz**, cross the Danube over the **Nibelungen Bridge** directly in front of the Ars Electronica Center, turn right onto the cyclist and pedestrian ramp zigzag at walking speed down to the left bank of the Danube past the Danube beach and keep left shortly before the bridge take the right-hand bend under the bridge shortly after, pass under the maze of bridges of the motorway bridge always along the embankment and past Lake Pleschingen.

> **TIP**
> After 2 km ride up to the crown of the dike, beyond which lies the Pleschinger See (lake) with its beaches, campground and various recreational facilities.

### Plesching (Steyregg)
prefix: 0732

- Pleschinger See (Pleschinger lake), Seeweg, ☎ 3400-6000, @ ltw644en

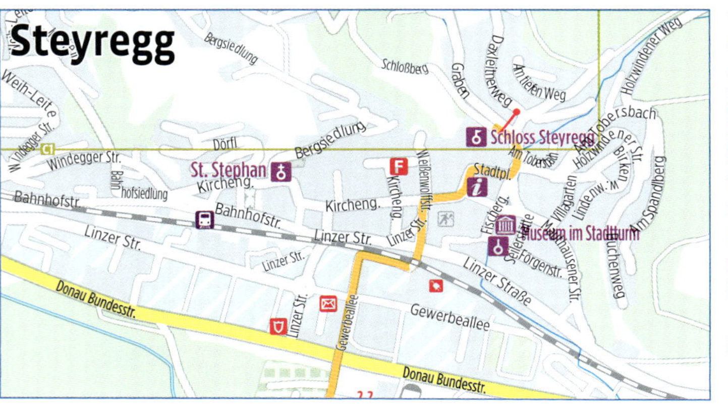


Continue on the former towpath along the Danube **2** you pass below a road bridge and a railway bridge.  After 1.5 km you reach a turn-off. From here a well-marked, paved path leads into the centre of Steyregg, which is dominated by the imposing castle.

## Steyregg

prefix: 0732

**Stadtgemeinde (Municipal office)**, Weißenwolffstr. 3, ☎ 640155, @ tqu315en

**St. Stephan (St. Stephan Parish church)**, Kircheng. 32, ☎ 640008. This 14th c. church includes early frescos that were rediscovered in 1951. @ iwr735en

**Schloss Steyregg (Steyregg palace)**, Schlossberg 1, ☎ 640054. Today's buildings date mostly from the 16th and 17th c. Formerly a medieval castle stood here, built on even older foundations. Includes extraordinary frescoes in the castle's chapel (14th c.). @ arw312en

**Museum im Stadtturm (Museum in the city tower)**, Stadtturmg. 11, ☎ 640677 ⊘ ⓒ The museum in the tower, dating from the 15th century, shows finds from the Steyregg Stone Age settlement up to the early Middle Ages and deals with the geology of the region. @ srt777en

C2
Schörgend
Windegg
Götzelsdorf
Weingraben Zottmann
Denneberg
Steyregg
Lehen
Hasenberg
Knierübl
Schloss Steyregg
Pürach
St. Stephan
Museum im Stadtturm
Gröbetsweg
Pulgarn
Klosteranlage Pulgarn
Kutzenbergsiedlung
Danube
1,5
2,2
B3
Luftenberg
a.d. Donau
Kruckenberg
Fetzysworld
Statzing
Große Gusen
Aßgitzer Straße
L569
2125
5,7
Heimathaus
St. Georgen
a.d. Gusen
Traun
Weikerlsee
Stollenanlage B8 Bergkristall
Bahnhofsiedlung
Bahnhofstr.
4
Frankenberg
3,2
Abwinden
Steining
Solar-City
B3
C3
Große Gusen
Gusen
Aubach
KZ-Gedenkstätte
Traundorf
3
Danube
3,8
Cowboy-Museum-Fatsy
B3
Langenstein
fer
B1
2,20
L569
Ausee
Berglitzl
Hydro-electric power plant Abwinden-Asten
2115
Ebelsberg
Pichling
63
Burgruine Spielberg

▣ **Badesee (Swimming lake)**, Im Freizeitpark 1, ☎ 640155 83, @ bym334en

### Pulgarn (Steyregg)

▣ **Klosteranlage Pulgarn (Pulgarn abbey)**, Pulgarn 1, ☎ 0732/640017. Established in 1303 as a hospital for the sick and needy. Today part of the St. Florian canonical abbey. The one-time chapel space includes impressive frescos from the time of the abbey's founding. The late-Gothic abbey church (1512) is distinguished by its excellent acoustics and interior spaces. @ qig626en

✱ **Fetzysworld**, Salmsee, ☎ 0660/9060960. Wakeboard and Wakesurf school, @ ths253en

Continue along the river ~ 2 km after the turn-off to Steyregg, the cycle path leads around a marina ~ continue along the river towards the Abwinden-Asten hydroelectric power station.

**3** The Danube cycle path turns left on the north bank and leaves the river for a while. If you want to change to the south bank, go straight ahead here and cross the Danube. **3** Keep left at the fork and immediately left again at the crossroads ~ over a branch of water ~ after the bridge immediately right into the cycle path and ride through the underpass ~ at the crossroads right to Abwinden.

### Abwinden (Luftenberg an der Donau)

## Abwinden to Mauthausen     10.4 km

Continue straight on the road through Abwinden ~ you pass the St. Georgen a. d. Gusen train station.

From here you can board a train for an excursion into the Mühlviertel and the impressive historic town of Freistadt.

Turn right onto the bicycle path about 400 m after the station ~ over a small bridge ~ left at **Wimminger Straße** **4** turn right at the T-intersection with the main street, the centre of St. Georgen a. d. Gusen lies to the left.

### Sankt Georgen an der Gusen
prefix: 07237

ℹ **Gemeindeamt (Municipal office)**, Marktpl. 12, ☎ 2255, @ kgx588en

🏛 **Heimathaus (Town museum)**, Färberg. 4, ☎ 3496 ↻ ↺ The collection includes prehistoric and early finds, technical exhibits from the light play period, a historical blacksmith's shop and a model of the gigantic "Rock Crystal" gallery. @ ooy736en

▣ **Stollenanlage B8 Bergkristall (Tunnel system)**, ☎ 07238/226951. From March 1, 1944, prisoners had to dig tunnels into the sandstone hill in this gallery complex in which Messerschmitt aircraft fuselages were built. On some days of the year the gallery is open for guided tours. @ vxo248en

✱ **Naturdenkmal Weingraben (Natural monument)**, Im Weingraben, ☎ 22550 ㉔ In an abandoned quarry, about 30 minutes' walk from the town centre, a biotope was created in which already extinct animal and plant species settled elsewhere. @ omj784en

▣ **Aquarella (Outdoor swimming area)**, In der Au 19, ☎ 2278, @ uey782en

The route now leads through Gusen.

### Gusen (Langenstein)

▣ **Berglitzl**, am Seyerberg. This important prehistoric cult site is located south of the village of Gusen. @ xoc222en

✱ **KZ-Gedenkstätte Gusen (Gusen concentration camp memorial – visitor's centre)**, Georgestr. 6, ☎ 07238/226922 ⊜ The visitor centre was opened in 2004 and documents the history of the concentration camp with plans and photos. Between 1939 and 1945 at least 71,000 people were imprisoned in the camp, of whom minimum 38,500 died. @ urv538en

*Tourists with an interest in archaeology might take note of the 12-meter hillock about one kilometer south of Gusen. This "Berglitzl" is a memorial to the region's prehistoric settlers – a granite formation that was able to defy the river's wearing powers and protect a camp used by hunters at the end of the last Ice Age (about 12,000 BC). It is the oldest proven human settlement in upper Austria.*

C3
Gusen
KZ-Gedenkstätte
Langenstein
Berglitzl
L569
Burgruine Spielberg
Marbach
Todesstiege
Mauthausen Memorial
3,8
3,8
0,8
Wienergraben
5
B3
3,4
Brunngraben
Heimatmuseum
Schloss Pragstein
St. Nikolaus
Vormarkt
Mauthausen
Heinrichsbrunn
Reiferdorf
Enghagen am Tabor
Danube
0,8
2110
2,8
Albern
6
Obersebern
Brand
Waging
Oberzirking
Hart
Aisthofen
Furth
Neuhart
Hinterholz
B123
B3
Oberwagram
Niedersebern
Haid
Enghagen
Enns
B123
2115
Lorch
Kristeinbach
Calcaria
Wiener Straße
Westbahnstr.
Basilika St. Laurenz
Lagerhausstraße
Stadtturm
Burg
Mooser Weg
Historisches Schützenhaus
Ennsdorf
B1
Windpassing
Pyburg
A'bing
Stein
Au
a.d. Donau
2
Oberwasserkanal
Arthof
Marksee
Raad
B123a
Aist-Mühlbach
Aulehrpfad
Fish ladder
3,5
C4
St. Pantaleon
65
2105

Continue parallel to the main road to Langenstein ~ after the right-hand bend, turn left and ride into Langenstein ~ continue on **Georgestraße** into the village.

## Langenstein
prefix: 07237

- *ℹ* **Gemeindeamt (Municipal office)**, Hauptstr. 71, *☎* 2370, *@* ogh227en
- *♂* **Burgruine Spilberg (Spilberg ruin)**, Spilberg 1, *☎* 0699/18999815. The circular castle complex, surrounded by a 16 m high rampart wall, has a 35 m high Romanesque tower with battlements. Once an important moated castle. Nowadays it is privately owned. *@* vyo244en

Go straight through Langenstein ~ a long left-hand bend follows, then a right-hand bend.


At **5**, the excursion to the memorial site of the former concentration camp Mauthausen branches off to the left. The main route curves to the right.

## Mauthausen memorial      5.4 km

**5** Turn left and follow the road **Wienergraben** along the valley of the Rieder Bach (creek) for about 800 m.


There are two routes to the former concentration camp from here. The first is shorter and follows **Erinnerungsstraße** which turns off to the right here. After a 14 percent incline and 1 km one reaches the site. The second route is less strenuous but somewhat longer. For the second option, continue along the **Wienergraben** ~ you pass two quarries in which concentration camp inmates once worked ~ turn right on **Marbachstraße** at the crossroads by the inn ~ ride uphill through two switchbacks ~ turn right on **Kardenweg** by the Marbach Palace ~ ride between fields to the former camp.

Visiting hours for the memorial and the centre: 9-17:30. For further information see www.mauthausen-memorial.org.


If your bicycle is equipped with good brakes front and rear, take the short steep route to return to the valley floor and the main Danube bike route.

## The Mauthausen concentration camp

*The quiet and tidy landscape of the Mühlviertel section of the Danube river valley belies the horrors that occurred here during the Nazi dictatorship. Uncounted victims were "shot while escaping," plunged from the granite quarries' cliffs or died in the gas chambers and crematoriums in Mauthausen, Gusen and Melk. It is estimated that between 1938 and 1945 about 123,000 people were murdered at the Mauthausen concentration camp.*

Mauthausen Memorial

**5** Keep right and follow the Linzer Straße into Mauthausen — turn right on **J. Czerwenka Straße** — follow the street to the left after passing the outdoor pool — continue on the bicycle path along the main road into the historic centre of Mauthausen.

## Mauthausen
prefix: 07238

- **Mauthausen Tourismus (Tourist association Mauthausen)**, Vormarktstr. 3, ☎ 2243, ☎ 0676/3150151, @ abv821en
- **Donauradfähre Enns-Mauthausen (Danube bicycle ferry)**, Bundesstr. 3, ☎ 07223/82777, ☎ 0650/3915034, ☺ May, Sept. 9am-6pm, June-Aug. 9am-1pm. The bike ferry has room for 12 people incl. bike and takes you to your desired destination. In principle, the ferry runs in a triangle over the Danube and Enns at intervals of 5-10 minutes. @ wny577en
- **Apothekenmuseum (Pharmacy Museum)**, Schlossg. 1, Pragstein castle, ☎ 29363, ☎ 0681/10851815 ☺ Austria's only special museum for the history of pharmacies and medicine from antiquity to the 20th century. @ tov675en
- **Heimatmuseum (Museum of local history)**, Schlossg. 1, Pragstein castle, ☎ 5033 ☺ Contemporary and differentiated examination of the term "home" as well as the historical development of the old Danube market. @ haq457en
- **Pfarrkirche St. Nikolaus (St. Nikolaus parish church)**, Pfarrpl. 1, ☎ 2303. This late-gothic church features a handsome altar painting by Martin Johann Schmidt "the Kremser" 1796/97. @ ynp723en
- **Karner (Barbara chapel)**, Pfarrpl. 1. This former ossuary on the south side of the parish church shows in its circular Romanesque structure traces of figurative and ornamental wall paintings from the late 13th c. @ tef287en
- **Schloss Pragstein (Pragstein palace)**, Schlossg. 1, ☎ 29363, ☎ 22550. Worth seeing former moated castle on a rocky island in the Danube. In the castle a pharmacy museum, a local history museum can be visited. @ obh448en
- **Führungen (Guided tours)**, Schlossg. 1, ☎ 29363, ☎ 0664/2207721 ☺ Sightseeing and night watchman tours through the historic Donaumarkt Mauthausen. @ kaw324en
- **Mauthausen Memorial/KZ-Gedenkstätte (Mauthausen concentration camp memorial)**, Erinnerungsstr. 1, ☎ 22690 ☺ The memorial site brings the horrific history of the Mauthausen concentration camp closer. It leads through the numerous preserved buildings and facilities as well as the quarry. @ kbq587en
- **Ortsbild (Town centre)**. Especially noteworthy are the stately houses along the Danube, with their playful facades, most of which are done in 17th c. baroque style.
- **Freibad (Outdoor swimming area)**, Josef-Czerwenka-Str. 1, ☎ 3361, @ dcx888en

*The earliest known historic mention of the Mauthausen market dates to the year 1208.*

*Mauthausen*

*Local legend has it that Frederick Barbarossa wrecked the town after townspeople demanded a toll when he and his army of crusaders passed through Mauthausen. Not all travellers contested the toll as vigorously, a fact shown by the late Gothic church and other splendid structures that were financed by income from tolls.*

### Mauthausen to Mitterkirchen    18.9 km
Cross the road and continue on the riverfront bicycle path out of Mauthausen.

 On the Mauthausen Danube bridge between Heinrichsbrunn and Pyburg you can cross over to the other bank and onto the cycle route south of the Danube. You hereby cross the border between Upper and Lower Austria. ⚠ However, you have to climb a steep staircase with a bike rail onto the bridge.

You ride under the road bridge ～ after 500 m the bicycle path ends and you turn right onto the side street ～ follow the street through the village of Albern.

## Albern

After the hamlet on the priority road, turn right and towards **Obersebern** ～ turn right onto the bicycle path ～ **6** cross the Aist River on a bicycle bridge and then turn right towards Grein ～ ride on the top of the dike along the Aist and then beside the Danube ～ by Au you pass a camping ground, info point and Marina ～ continue on the cycle path along the dam.

### Au a. d. Donau (Naarn im Machlande)

✳ **Fischtreppe (Fish ladder).** It is considered Europe's largest fish ladder, which helps fish and other aquatic animals to overcome a barrage. @ pem313en

✳ **Aulehrpfad (Floodplain nature trail).** A hiking path posted with information about the plants and animals found in the river plain. @ wni174en

Continue on the path beside the river, which you follow for about 12 km to the **Wallsee-Mitterkirchen hydroelectric power station** ～ continue on the road past the sluices and barrage ～ you reach the **7** Radstation Mitterkirchen, a rest area for cyclists with information boards and water ～ turn left onto the road **Werksstraße** at the intersection.

 Turning right takes you to the barrage, which you can cross to the other bank of the Danube.

You cross a bridge before riding past the scattered houses of **Hütting** ～ the lightly-travelled road leads to Mitterkirchen.

## Mitterkirchen im Machland

prefix: 07269

ℹ **Radinfo (Bycicle tourist information)**, Hütting 30, ✆ 30373, ✆ 0664/7361454, ◷ April-June, Sept. 11am-5pm July, Aug. 10am-6pm, @ yfs476en

ℹ **Marktgemeindeamt (Municipal office)**, Mitterkirchen 50, ✆ 82550, ✆ 0664/3841745, @ lcj375en

🛁 **Badesee (bathing lake)**, Weisching 16, ✆ 0681/849955 00, @ fkt464en

### Mitterkirchen to Grein     16.2 km

Turn right after the playing fields ～ turn left after crossing the bridge over the Naarn River ～ at the T-intersection turn right into **Labing**.

 From here you can follow the signposted excursion route via Klam and turn left off the main road at this point in Labing. This tour requires some sporting ambition and a little road safety and meets the Danube again in Grein. The route is shown in orange on the map.

 All those who want to visit the Celtic village of Mitterkirchen are recommended to follow the excursion route in the direction of Klam as far as Lehen and to return to the main route from the museum via the main road.

## Via Clam Castle to Grein     13,7 km

### Lehen (Mitterkirchen im Machland)

🏛 **Keltendorf Mitterkirchen (Celtic village)**, Lehen 12, ✆ 07269/6611 ⑦ᵈ The remains of a large barrows field from the Hallstatt period (around 700 BC) were discovered here in 1980. Excavations lasted 10 years, and exposed sensational discoveries that drew international attention to the site. Today a reconstructed Celtic village provides insights into the lifestyle of the Danube's ancient residents. The open-air museum with a Hallstatt village

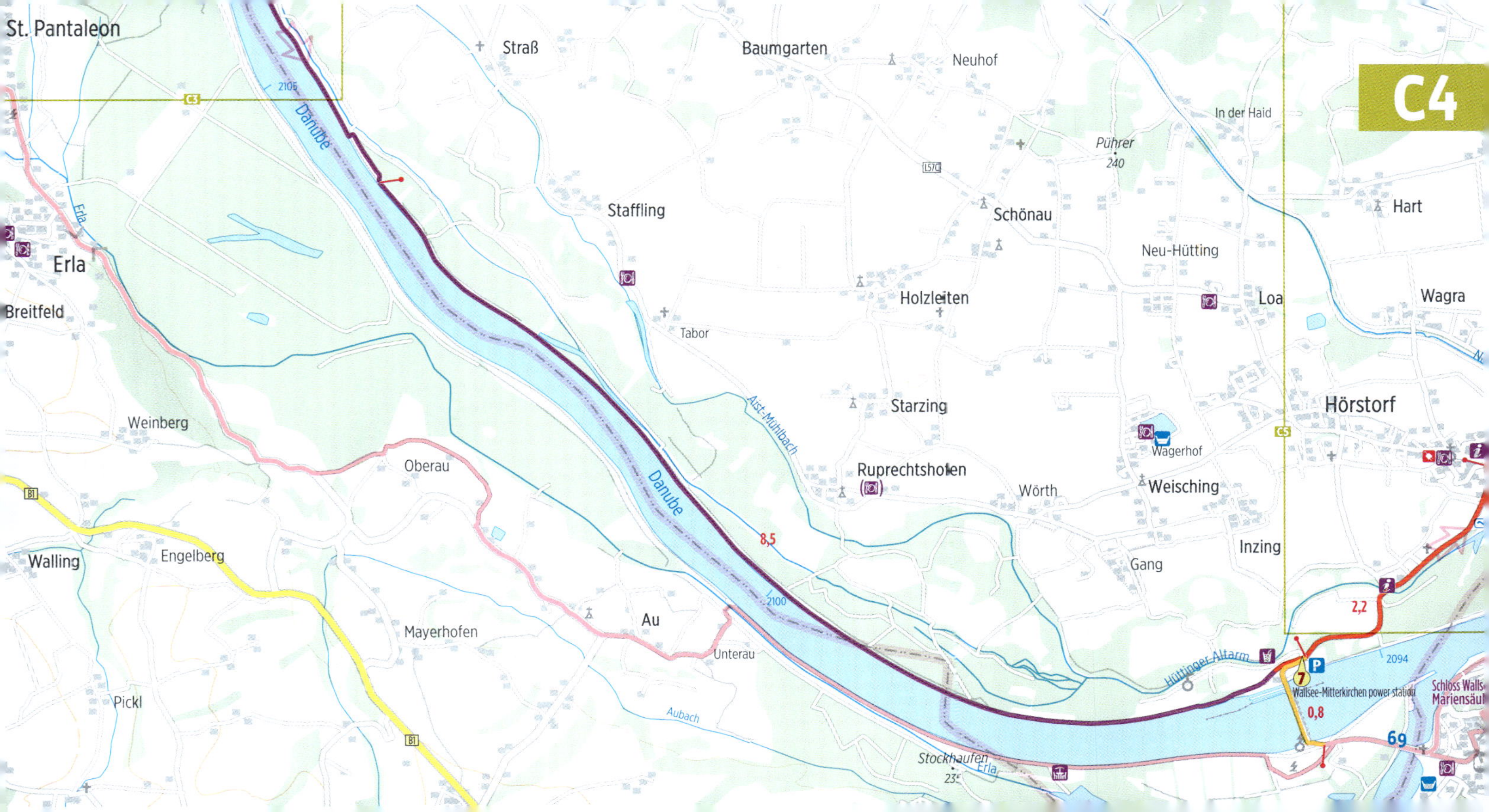

C4
St. Pantaleon
Straß
Baumgarten
Neuhof
In der Haid
Pührer 240
Hart
Schönau
L57C
Staffling
Neu-Hütting
Loa
Wagra
Erla
Holzleiten
Breitfeld
Tabor
Hörstorf
Weinberg
Starzing
Wagerhof
Oberau
Ruprechtshofen
Weisching
B1
Wörth
Inzing
Walling
Engelberg
Gang
8,5
Danube
Aist-Mühlbach
Mayerhofen
Au
2100
Unterau
Hüttinger Altarm
2094
Schloss Walls
Mariensäul
Pickl
Wallsee-Mitterkirchen power station
7
0,8
2,2
B1
Stockhaufen
Erla
23
69
Danube
2105
2,2

*Clam Castle*

complex with 20 buildings offers workshops and attractions for the whole family. @ buf345en

## Baumgartenberg

prefix: 07269

🛈 **Marktgemeindeamt (Municipial office)**, Baumgartenberg 85, ☎ 2550, @ lvi888en

⛪ **Stiftskirche (Abbey church)**, Baumgartenberg. The Romanesque basilica (1142), built in 100 years of construction, became a jewel of Baroque architecture in the 17th century. @ dji258en

## Klam

prefix: 07269

🛈 **Marktgemeindeamt (Municipal office)**, Klam 43, ☎ 7255, @ ymf686en

⛪🏛 **Burg Clam (Clam castle)**, Sperken 1, ☎ 7217 ⊜ One of the best preserved castles in Austria which not only boasts great architectural beauty, but also an interesting museum. Concerts with famous international artists take place in the amazing historical surounding. @ mqk674en

✳ **Klamschlucht (Klam gorge)**. 2 km hiking trail along the Klam creek, with boardwalks, bridges and waterfall. @ crn257en

## Saxen

🏛 **Strindberg-Museum**, Saxen 7, ☎ 07269/6828, ☎ 0664/4568919 ☾ The museum is dedicated to the stays of the great Swedish playwright August Strindberg in Saxen and Klam between 1893 and 1896. @ jpq247en

🌲 **Naturinformationszentrum (NIZ) (Nature Information Centre)**, Saxen 8, ☎ 0650/5464051 ⊜ Visitors learn interesting facts about the Machland and its importance for the animal and plant world. @ auy416en

Continue on the main road ⁓ in the left curve of the road turn right into the side road ⁓ continue towards Mettensdorf ⁓ **8** turn left as you reach the village ⁓ after the small stream turn right.

## Mettensdorf                                                     L

A narrow road leads out of the village ⁓ you pass the farms of **Pitzing** ⁓ keep right as you reach Eizendorf.

## Eizendorf

**9** Turn right again at the crucifix in the direction of the Danube ⁓ you ride through forest and cross a branch of the Naarn river before reaching a lake ⁓ turn left and ride away from the lake ⁓ follow the path to the right between fields down to the Danube ⁓ turn left and proceed along the river to Dornach. *The flat Machland ends at Dornach, where the Danube enters the picturesque Strudengau.*

## Dornach

⛪ **Schloss Dornach (Castle)**, Dornach 4. In 1890, Maria Theresa Princess of Thurn and Taxis had a manor house converted into

C5
Frühstorf
Puchberg im Machland
Kolbing
Deiming
Amesbach
Sperken
Klam
Burg Clam
Achatzberg
Schneckenreitsberg
Burgstall 355
Klamschlucht
Au
Kirchbichl
Steindl
Obergassolding
Saxen
Untergassolding
B3
Kirchstetten
Stiftskirche
Baumgartenberg
Strindberg-Museum
Naturinformationszentrum
...fkirchen
Hart
Kühofen
Froschau
Wetzelsdorf
Patzenhof
Hofstetten
Lehen
2,2
Gasoldinger B
Mettensdorfer Mühlbach
Wagra
Mitterkirchen celtic village
0,5
2,6
1
Mettensdorf
Eizendorf
Dornach
Schloss Dornach
Labing
Schwemmnaarn
8
3,5
Pitzing
9
...örstorf
Naarn
0,8
C4
Mitterkirchen im Machland
4,7
2085
1,2
Donauwellenpark
Ardagger-Markt
Hüttinger back water
Danube
Danube
2090
71
B119
2,2
4
2,4
B3
C6

Along the Danube near Grein

a palace. The neo-baroque building is privately owned and can only be visited from the outside.

Cross the bridge and before the railway line turn right onto the Treppelweg.



**Straight across you reach the village and a small bathing lake.**

The cycle path follows the course of the railway and passes Dornach — behind the pond, follow the cycle path to the right and over a footbridge.

*The valley is becoming markedly narrower here as the Danube heads into a difficult stretch of water long feared by ship captains.*

After 4.2 km the route reaches the bridge near Grein.

⚠ **The route between Grein and Ybbs/Persenbeug mostly follows the busy national road or bicycle lanes next to the road. For this reason we recommend the south bank for this stretch, especially for groups travelling with children. Take the bridge upriver from Grein or the ferry from Grein to Wiesen.**

To stay on the north bank route, continue on the bicycle path along the river into Grein **10** you pass to the left of the marina — cross a small bridge and ride past the camping ground — keep right and follow the path along the Danube.

## Grein a. d. Donau

prefix: 07268

- **Tourismusbüro (Tourist association)**, Stadtpl. 5, ☎ 7055, @ may152en
- **Donaufähre Umi Uma (Cycle and passenger ferry)**, Kreuznerstr. 45, ☎ 0664/47666871, ⏱ May, Sept. 9am-6pm, June-Aug. 8am-6pm, @ xlo358en
- **Oberösterreichisches Schifffahrtsmuseum (Shipping museum)**, Greinburg 1, ☎ 700718, ☎ 0664/9861981 ⊜ The museum has a collection of detailed models that give insights into the history of transportation on the Danube and its tributaries. @ kkc586en
- **Stadtpfarrkirche Hl. Ägidius (St. Ägidius parish church)**, Kirchenpl. A late-Gothic, heavily-rebuilt church with baroque altar that includes a painting by Bartolomeo Altomonte (1749). @ qkx182en
- **Schloss Greinburg (Greinburg palace)**, Greinburg 1, ☎ 700718, ☎ 0664/9861981 ⊜ The oldest residential palace in Austria was built between 1500 and 1700 and contains unique interior spaces and wall decorations: the imposing knights' chamber, palace chapel with its Christmas altar, fascinating net-vaulted ceilings, the Sala Terrena with its river-pebble mosaic, and the attractive arcaded courtyard. @ sss548en
- **Historisches Stadttheater und Stadtmuseum (Old city theatre and City Museum)**, Stadtpl. 7, ☎ 7055 ⊜ In Austria's oldest bourgeois theatre (1791), curiosities such as barricade seats, costumes, old props and exhibits reflecting the history of the city are shown. @ pqc374en
- **Altes Rathaus (Old town hall)**, Rathausg. 1, ☎ 2550. Unchanged since its construction in 1563 by the Italian architect M. Canaval. The adjacent grain silo was transformed into the famous Bürgertheater in 1791. @ rrr635en
- **Galerie in Granit (Gallery in granite)**, Kalvarienberg ㉔ Inspired by pre-Christian cultures, Miguel Horn created news sculpted in granite, so-called petroglyphs. @ qoq873en

- ✷ **Ortsensemble (Historic town centre).** Most of the houses in the centre of town date to the 16th and 17th c., though many have baroque facades. The town's bourgeois flair is especially evident in the 19th c. inns and taverns.

- ✳ **Stillensteinklamm (Stillenstein gorge)**, Gießenbach, 2 km to the east, ☎ 7055. The 200 m deep stream valley, marked by impressive stone formations, offers a great nature experience coming from the Mühlviertler Mittellandterrasse. @ roy588en

- ✉ **Freibad (public outdoor pool)**, Herdmannweg 1, ☎ 555, @ bpk744en

*The "Pearl of the Strudengau" – as local poets dubbed the city – at the entrance to the perilous Struden served as a base for river pilots and as a place to transfer and trade freight. The resulting prosperity helped give local citizens a taste for art, and in 1791 city fathers built a small theatre in the Rathaus. This theatre has achieved international fame for its many curious features, including a toilet separated from the audience only by a curtain, well-preserved locking seats for the most important citizens as well as a cell from which inmates could watch performances through narrow viewing slits. It is the oldest theatre in Austria to survive in its original form.*

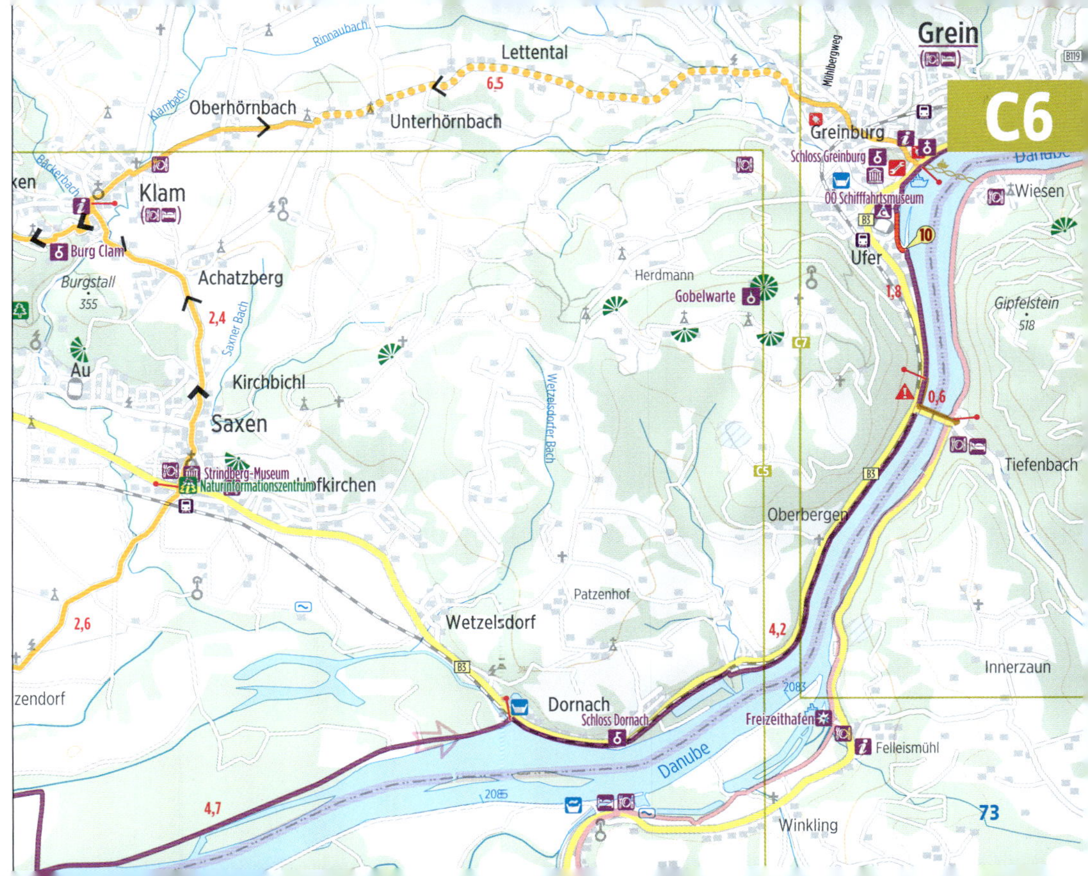

## Grein to Persenbeug         20.4 km


From Grein the bicycle route follows the busy main road. Although there is a bicycle lane available most of the way, this is really narrow and not quite safe.

At **11** you cross a bridge as you pass an old railway viaduct.


At **11** a smaller road branches off to the hiking trail to the nearby Stillensteinklamm. Public toilets.

Proceed down the **B 3** to Struden and Werfenstein castle.

### Struden (Sankt Nikola an der Donau)

prefix: 07268

🏰 **Burg Werfenstein (Werfenstein castle)**, Struden 5, ☎ 8025. Werfenstein is an example of the numerous castles and towers built over narrows in the river to enforce toll collection on the Danube. Historically documented as early as 1242, the complex was abandoned around 1500. @ ldh481en

Proceed to St. Nikola.

### Sankt Nikola an der Donau

ℹ️ **Gemeindeamt (Municipal office)**, St. Nikola 16, ☎ 07268/8155, @ qyf412en

⛪ **Schifferkirche (Boatmen's church)**, St. Nikola 15. Originally a Romanesque church which underwent Gothic and baroque (17th c.) renovations. The 4 Gothic reliefs of the side altar on the left (ca. 1500) are especially noteworthy. @ qkb767en

🏊 **Freibad (public outdoor pool)**, Marktpl. 1, ☎ 0664/73131629, @ exn561en

Ride past St. Nikola and continue down the B 3 — continue past Sarmingstein.

### Sarmingstein (Sankt Nikola an der Donau)

🏰 **Mautturm Sarmingstein (toll tower)**, Donau Bundesstr. 28 (24) The historic toll tower was part of a fortification and, with its toll house and sloping walls, formed a sovereign customs post. In 1968, the ruins of the tower were provided with a viewing platform and offer an impressive view over the village and the course of the Danube. @ bsd472en

**12** After almost 3 km turn right as you enter Hirschenau — follow the towpath along the river — you now ride into Lower Austria (Niederösterreich) — by **Ysperdorf** you cross the Ysper creek.


From here it is possible to start a side-trip up the beautiful Ysper valley, which is also one entrance to the wild and romantic Waldviertel area of Austria.

After 1 km turn left, taking the street away from the river — cross the tracks and go slightly uphill into Weins.


⚠️ The Donau Bundesstraße is closed for cyclists from here on (except for racing cyclists)!

### Weins

**13** At the end of the village the route continues on a bicycle path along the road — past the **Ybbs-Persenbeug hydroelectric power station** — proceed toward the centre — keep left of the palace, then turn right off the main road — the route follows **Schlossstraße** and

*Strudengau*

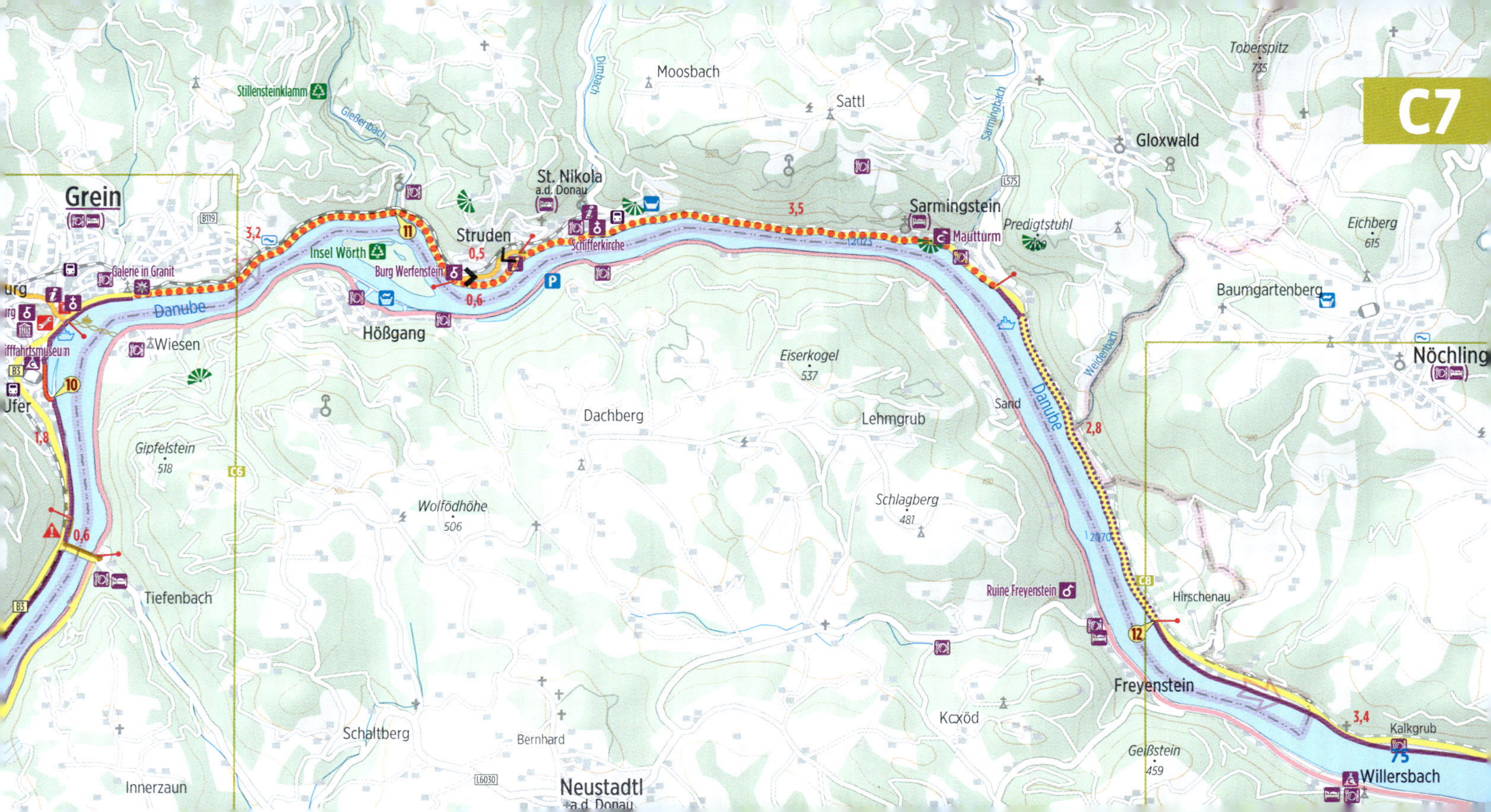

C7
Toberspitz
735
Moosbach
Sattl
Gloxwald
Dimbach
Sarmingbach
Stillensteinklamm
Gießenbach
St. Nikola
a.d. Donau
Eichberg
615
Grein
Sarmingstein
Predigtstuhl
B119
3,5
Struden
Mautturm
3,2
11
Insel Wörth
0,5
L575
Schifferkirche
Galerie in Granit
Burg Werfenstein
Baumgartenberg
urg
0,6
Danube
Nöchling
rg
Hößgang
B3
Wiesen
Eiserkogel
537
Sand
10
Ufer
Weidenbach
Danube
1,8
Dachberg
Lehmgrub
2,8
Gipfelstein
518
C6
Schlagberg
481
Wolfödhöhe
506
Ruine Freyenstein
Hirschenau
0,6
C8
12
Tiefenbach
Freyenstein
B3
Kɔxöd
3,4
Kalkgrub
Schaltberg
Bernhard
75
Geißstein
459
Willersbach
Innerzaun
L6030
Neustadtl
a.d. Donau

Ybbs-Persenbeug power station

**Hauptstraße** through the historic centre of Persenbeug.

## Persenbeug
prefix: 07412

**ℹ** **Marktgemeindeamt (Municipal office)**, Rathauspl. 1, ✆ 52206, @ ibg556en

**🏛** **Heimatmuseum (Local museum)**, Rathauspl., ✆ 52206 ⊜ On display are exhibits on the history of the community and the castle Persenbeug, birthplace of the last Austrian emperor - Karl I.) @ hnd825en

**⬡** **Schloss Persenbeug (Persenbeug palace)**, Schlosstr. 1, ✆ 5253196, ✆ 0664/6144119. The complex on the steep rock outcropping attained its current form after reconstruction by Eusebius v. Hoyos 1617-21. Owned by the Habsburgs since 1800. @ qvb348en

**✱** **Ortskern (Town centre)**. Among the numerous original Biedermeier houses you can find the Kleine and Große Schiffsmeisterhaus (small and large shipmasters' houses).

**✱** **Marktlinde (Market limetree)**, Rathauspl. The huge limetree next to the Floriani chapel is said to have been planted in 1300.

*Under the shipmaster Matthias Feldmüller (1801-50), Persenbeug was the most important shipbuilding town on the lower Austrian Danube. The town's "schopper" built about 20 ships a year. At the time the Danube carried about 850 ships and 25 rafts from Feldmüller wharf downstream each year. About 350 ships were dragged back upstream by horses using the towpath.*

### Persenbeug to Marbach     10.2 km
At Gasthof Böhm turn right into **Rollfährestraße** ⌐ straight on through the village **14** at the four-way intersection turn right ⌐ turn left to the bank of the Danube ⌐ this path leads out of the village and across the flat "peninsula", the Hagsdorfer Scheibe ⌐ follow the left bend into the village.

### Hagsdorf (Persenbeug)
Turn right at the intersection with the small wayside shrine ⌐ follow the paved lane out of the village ⌐ after 1.5 km turn right at the crossroads in the fields ⌐ then left at the cluster of houses ⌐ the next town is Gottsdorf, with a distinctive onion-roof church steeple.

## Gottsdorf (Persenbeug)

- **Badeteich (bathing pond)**, Hagsdorfer Str., ☎ 0680/2235695, @ wjd725en

Ride straight into the street along the shoreline, which becomes the **Donaustraße** – turn right just before the fire station (Feuerwehr) and follow the path past the playing fields – you come to ride between the main road and the river past **Metzling** – continue to **Granz**, where you pass the campground and the marina.
*A sign here notes that you are entering the Nibelungengau.*

## Marbach an der Donau

prefix: 07413

- **Gemeindeamt (Municipal office)**, Marktstr. 28, ☎ 7045, @ mtr763en
- **Herrenhaus (Manor house)**, Marktstr. Built in 1575, the Habsburg manor house with its two round corner towers bears the coats of arms of the families Starhemberg-Schaumburg and Löwenstein-Wertheim.
- **Nibelungenbad (Outdoor swimming area)**, Badg. 1, ☎ 7730, @ qqd675en
- **Taxi-Sitz (Bicycle transport taxi)**, ☎ 0676/5256340, @ rix255en

 In Marbach it is possible to start an interesting excursion into the southern Waldviertel with stops at Maria Taferl and the castles at

Artstetten and Leiben. This tour follows quiet country roads that include several daunting climbs. Good physical condition or an e-bike are required here. It is also possible to reach Maria Taferl by bicycle-taxi, which can bring bicycle and baggage straight to the pilgrimage site. Return to the main route either through Klein-Pöchlarn or through Weitenegg, just before Melk. The excursion is shown in the maps in orange colour.

## To Maria Taferl                    18,6 km

### Maria Taferl
prefix: 07413

- **Marktgemeindeamt (Municipal office)**, Nr. 35, 7040, @ efv133en
- **Wallfahrtsbasilika (Pilgrimage basilica)**, Nr. 1, 278 The foundation stone of the pilgrimage church was laid in 1660, after miraculous healings and light apparitions. The appearance is characterised by the master builders Georg Gerstenbrand, Carlo Lurago and Jakob Prandtauer. In the 18th century, the basilica was decorated with frescoes designed by Antonio Beduzzi. @ qsi478en
- **Mechanisches Alpenpanorama (Mechanical „Alpenpanorama")**, Nr. 6, 340. The mechanical work of art from 1910 behind the innkeeper's parlour of the "Zum Goldenen Löwen" inn

depicts everyday life and leisure activities of people at the turn of the century. @ ahx732en

### Artstetten-Pöbring
prefix: 07413

- **Marktgemeindeamt (Municipal office)**, Schlossstr. 1, 8235, @ bvp151en
- **Schloss Artstetten (Artstetten palace)**, Schlosspl. 1, 8006 The castle, built in the middle of the 13th century, preserves in the museum the memory of the heirs to the throne Archduke Franz

Maria Taferl, Basilica

Ferdinand and his wife, Duchess Sophie von Hohenberg. A thousand peonies and rare varieties of fruit and berries with aristocratic names adorn the historic garden and park. @ dyf737en

- **Freibad (Outdoor swimming area)**, Schulstr. 4, 8235, @ jyu157en

### Leiben
prefix: 02752

- **Marktgemeindeamt (Municipal office)**, Hauptstr. 34, 70042, @ rrp175en
- **Europaschloss Leiben (European palace Leiben)**, Schlossstr. 4, 70043, Visits only possible during events. The Renaissance castle from 1113 houses the Agricultural Engineering Museum with themed exhibitions such as: Tractors, soil cultivation, scales and successful models of technology. @ eag663en

### Marbach to Emmersdorf                    16.2 km

**15** From Marbach, the Danube cycle path follows the towpath when the main road moves away from the river bank, continue either up along the embankment or to the right of it along the towpath the village of Klein-Pöchlarn lies to the left.

### Klein-Pöchlarn
prefix: 07413

- **Marktgemeindeamt (Municipal office)**, Artstettner Str. 7, 8300, @ fqt154en

C9
Herrenhaus
15
Kleinmitterberg
Großmitterberg
Eichberg
485
Loja
Tümlingbach
Loßbach
B3
2050
Annastift
Wallenbach
Krummnußbaum
Neustift
Viehtrift
Doberg
460
Rottenhof
Diedersdorf
Wallfahrtskapelle
Weins
Knogl
Fürholz
Doberg
Rosenbichl
Säusenstein
13
3,5
Forsthub
Metzling
B3
4,5
Holzern
Danube
B3
Hofamt Priel
Kalz
Rehberg
C10
Donaudorf
C8
Holzian
Persenbeug
Sittenberg
340
L91
B36
0,8
Schloss Persenbeug
B3
Danube
Stift Säusenstein
Theresienkapelle
H. Donatus
L6013
Besucherkraftwerk Ybbs-Persenbeug
1
Heimatmuseum
Gottsdorf
Aigen
Wolfri
Marktlinde
14
Scharlreith
2060
Danube
2055
Roßberg
Reitern
Wolfsgrub
305
Ratzenberg
Theinstetten
Reitering
B25
Fahrradmuseum
Treppelstraße
Stadtmuseum
5,7
Maierhofen
Windhof
Freizeitzentrum
Hagsdorf
Reist
Berging
Ybbs
a.d. Donau
Reister Bach
Mitterndorf
Griesheim
Ybbs
Untereichen
Kolm
Plaika
Martin
bsfelde
Göttsbach
B25
Unterhaus
Sarling
Obereichen
Pfaffenberg
Neusarling
B1
Thalling
79
A1

☖ **Pfarrkirche (Parish church)**, Kirchenstr. 10, ☎ 8298. The church first mentioned in a document in 1391 is dedicated to St. Otmar. @ dlv161en

✳ **Schwibbögen**, Hufschmiedg. Two arches from the 15th century with coat of arms and dentil frieze.

✳ **Spiegelskulptur (Mirror sculpture)**, Dammkrone. Designed by the local artist Herbert Golser. @ ajj282en

✳ **Bienenpark (Bee experiencing world)**, Ötscherblick 12, ☎ 81627, ☎ 0664/1502840 ✉ In a natural environment, life and work of bees are documented. @ lcb623en

*Klein-Pöchlarn lies in the heart of the idyllic Nibelungengau. Klein-Pöchlarn experienced a rapid economic upswing due to the numerous clay and loam deposits. The former village flourished thanks to the so-called "Schwarzhafnerei". The clay was also mixed with graphite from the surrounding area, which gave the dishes hardness and shine. Another source of income at that time was the sale of alumina, which was transported by ships down the Danube to Vienna, Budapest and Belgrade.*

**16** Pass under the Danube bridge to Pöchlarn ~ continue on the crest of the dam ~ **17** at **Ebersdorf**, turn left off the dam at the fork.


Il you would like to visit the Benedictine Abbey of Melk on the other bank, stay on the dam to cross over the Melk power station. You can park your bike in the centre of Melk either in the bike shed with lockers at the Wachau Info Center or in Abt-Dietmayr-Straße and make your way to the monastery on foot. Take the bicycle path next to the main road along an old arm of the Danube towards Weitenegg.


This old arm of the Danube is a great place to go for a swim. In Weitenegg there is a romantic old castle ruin to explore.

### Weitenegg (Leiben)
prefix: 02752

🛏 **Freizeitzentrum (Leisure park)**, Weitenegg 8, ☎ 70042. Bathing beach with pedal boat hire, aqua jump, surfing facilities and much more. @ iyk842en

The next signposted distant goal is Krems, 36 km away ~ proceed to Luberegg.

### St. Georgen (Emmersdorf a. d. Donau)

✳ **Teddybärenwerkstatt (Teddy Bear Workshop)**, St. Georgen 4, ☎ 02752/71726, ☎ 0664/2786452. You can witness the creation of a teddy bear. Phone registration only. @ soy723en

### Luberegg (Emmersdorf a. d. Donau)
prefix: 02752

☖ **Schloss Luberegg (Luberegg castle)**, Luberegg 20. Built in 1780, the small palace subsequently served as the favourite residence of Emperor Franz II. The late Baroque exterior is complemented inside by early Classicist canvas wallpaper. Private property. @ ikq333en

☖ **Feuerturm Luberegg (Lighthouse and signal towers)**. These two ancient round towers once served the orientation of the rafters. @ wks771en

🛏 **Badestrand (Bathing beach)**, ☎ 70010, @ agr272en

Continue directly along the Danube ~ at **Seegarten** briefly turn left and then immediately right again on the cycle path next to the Danube road.


The bicycle path passes along the edge of Emmersdorf, but a short detour into the town's centre and its richly decorated bourgeois houses is worthwhile. If you have seen the film "Der Hofrat Geiger" or "Mariandl", you may recognise some of the locations in Emmersdorf and the entire Wachau region.

### Emmersdorf a. d. Donau
prefix: 02752

ℹ **Infostelle (Tourist infopoint)**, Beim Kreisverkehr, close to roundabout, ☎ 70010, @ gxd877en

ℹ **Marktgemeindeamt (Municipal office)**, Nr. 22, ☎ 71469, @ sae631en

C10
Grub
Obersteinbach
Pargatstetten
Reitern
Thalheimberg
585
Eichberg
515
Artstetten
Trennegg
Hasling
Schloss Artstetten
0,6
Hilmanger
0,8
Unterbierbaum
6,5
Obererla
Untertha heim
5,5
Thalheimbach
Untererla
Oberthalheim
Rindfleischberg
390
Marbach
Am Tonberg
Hirschensprung
515
Steinbach
Marbach
2
Wallfahrtbasilika Maria Taferl
Saulackenberg
360
Klosterberg
355
Bienenpark
Auratsberg
3,2
Klein-Pöchlarn
Marbach
a.d. Donau
Friesenegg
Krummnußbaum
a.d. Donauuferbahn
B3
Pfarrkirche
Großer Mühlberg
508
Steinbach
Schwibbögen
Kracking
Granz
C9
Kalvarienberg
5
Danube
Spiegelskulptur
C11
Danube
1,2
0,6
16
Herrenhaus
15
Nibelungendenkmal
B3
Stadtweiher
Schlosspark
4,5
2050
Oskar-Kokoschka-Geburtshaus
Pöchlarn
Loja
Krummnußbaum
Am Rechen
Pöchlarn
Diedersdorf
Annastift
Wallenbach
Brunn
a.d. Erlauf
Wallfahrtskapelle
Neuda
Neu-Pöchlarn
osenbichl
Neustift
Hinterleiten
Erlauf
81
hub
Metzling
B3
Steinwand
Kellerhäuser
B1
A1

Emmersdorf

⛴ **Brandner Schiffahrt (Shipping Brandner)**, ☎ 07433/259021 ⓐ Daily scheduled trips through the Wachau between Melk and Krems, bicycle transport approx. 2 Euro. Possibility of boarding and alighting only for groups if required. ⓦ sxl518en

⛴ **DDSG Blue Danube (Shipping)**, Donaustr., ☎ 01/58880 ⓐ Regular service between Melk and Krems, bicycle transport approx. 2 Euro. Tickets on board. ⓦ jey518en

🏛 **Kramurigwölb (Vault with antique things)**, Nr. 31, ☎ 71764 ⓒ More than 2000 handcrafted devices and utensils, including bizarre exhibits such as ankle cuffs, wooden refrigerators and an old noodle press, give an insight into the 17th to 19th centuries. ⓦ ywn617en

✳ **Ortsensemble (Town centre)**. The charming, elongated street square is lined with characteristic houses from the 16th to early 19th centuries.

✳ **Wachaubahn (Wachau Railway)**, Bahnzeile, ☎ 02742/360990-1000, ⏱ Mid-March-May, Sat, Sun & Fri; June-Oct daily. Between vineyards, ancient walls and the mighty Danube river, you can travel by local train between Krems and Emmersdorf without stress or traffic jams and experience great views of the beauty of the world cultural heritage. Bicycles can be taken along free of charge. ⓦ qul637en

**ALTERNATIVE** The main route through the Wachau region follows the left bank of the Danube, passing through one beautiful and famous location after another. Tourists who prefer to visit the charming little wine making villages that line the right bank can cross the bridge and select the alternative route.

At the level of the information pavilion, cross the road on the cycle path before the roundabout and then cycle on the cycle path on the left side of the road over the bridge ⁓ on reaching the right bank of the Danube, the cycle path forks ⁓ here turn left and follow the cycle path steeply downhill to Pielamunder-Allee ⁓ turn left.

**TIP** At Wachauer Straße you can turn left into Melk, you will reach the centre after about 2.5 km. For a visit to Melk Abbey, you can park your bike in the centre of Melk either in the bike shed with lockers at the Wachau Info Center or in Abt-Dietmayr-Straße and make your way to the Abbey on foot.

**Melk** see page 106

To continue along the south shore, turn right.

C11
83
Langthaler
Reith
Schallemmersdorf
Hart
Moosbach
Payerstetten
Antenaubach
Emmersdorf
Haidhof
Trennegg
B216
Hofamt
18
Leiben
Rantenberg
Schloss Leiben
Wachaubahn
Losau
Hasling
Kramurigwölb
Hub
Weinzierl
Dachberg
385
1
Neuweinzierl
Weitenbach
2,6
Sankt Georgen
Danube
Unterbierbaum
3
6,5
Hain
Seegarten
Luberegg
B33
B3a
Mampasberg
Stadelau
Henzing
385
Teddybärenwerkstatt
2036
B1
Weitenegg
Schloss Luberegg
molemelk
Melk
Kaumberg
Feuerturm
2,4
Lehen
B3
Freizeitzentrum
Stift Melk
Ebersdorf
Urfahr
1
Stiftskirche
Rindfleischberg
3,6
1,2
Spielberg
390
B3
3,4
Danube
1,2
Melk
Klosterberg
3,2
355
2,4
river power station Melk
C10
0,8
Klein-Pöchlarn
17
Neuwinden
KZ-Gedenkstätte
B1
onberg
B1
Freiningau
kirche
Schwibbögen
Maierhöfen
Winden
A1
1,2
16
Danube
0,6
Bergern
Wachauring
Schrattenbruck
Pöverding
A1
B1
Pöchlarn
Ornding
ark
Großpriel
Melk
Weyerbach
Matzleinsdorf
Kollapriel

# Linz to Melk along the south bank

**117.3 km**

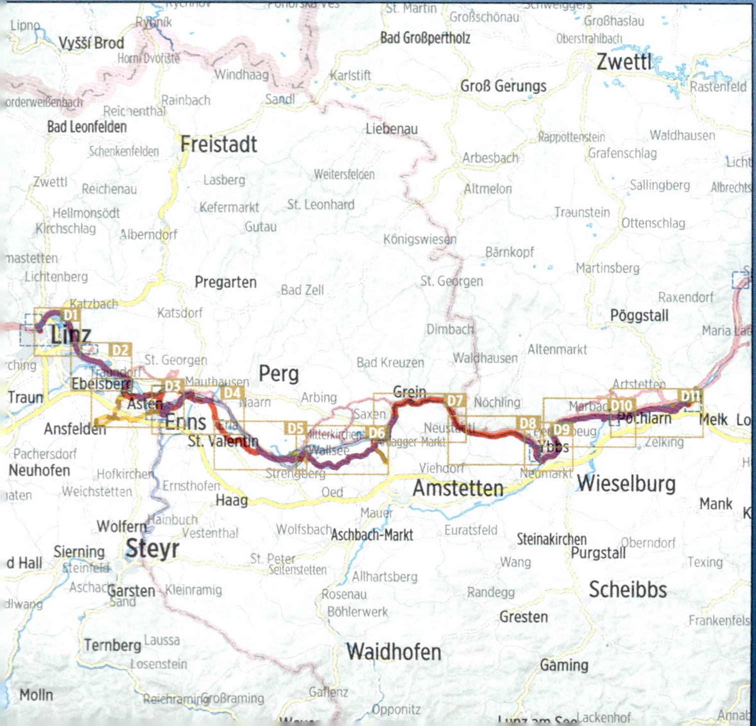


| m/km: ↗ 0.7 (81m) ↘ 1.2 (135m) | cycle path: 58 % | unpaved: 0 % | busy road: 0 % |
|---|---|---|---|

The Danube bicycle route on the southern side of the river leaves the capital of Upper Austria, Linz, and proceeds into the fertile Machland. Especially noteworthy here are the St. Florian monastery and, of course, Enns – Austria's oldest city. The route then passes through the enchanting "Most" region with its distinctive farms. The Danube becomes narrower and faster before reaching Grein and then rushes through the thrilling Strudengau. The crowning conclusion to this stage is the town of Melk and its world-famous Benedictine abbey.

Between Linz and Abwinden there is no Danube bicycle route on the right, or south, bank. In Abwinden you can cross to the right bank and proceed along quiet country lanes, farming roads and bicycle trails. This stage has no serious climbs and no stretches along busy roads.

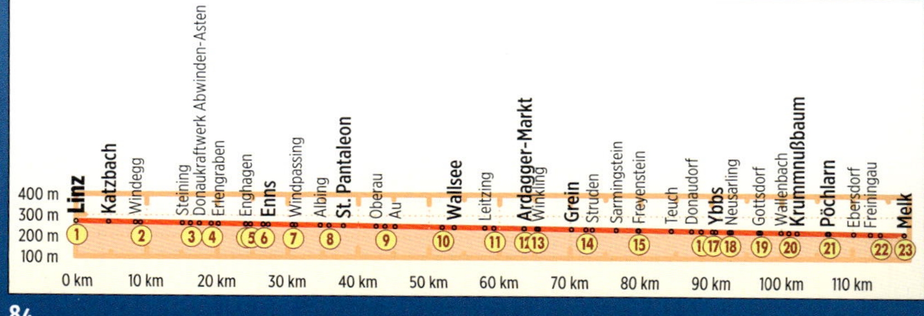

*Linz*

## Linz      see page 54

### Linz to Abwinden      15.9 km

The Danube bike trail runs on the north bank only from Linz to the Abwinden-Asten power station.

**TIP** The route description can be found in the previous section on page 59, maps C1 and C2. From waypoint **3** continue along the river bank and cross the river or the barrage of the hydroelectric power station.

**ATTENTION** Crossing at the power station is possible from April to October between 6am and 10pm.

### Abwinden to Enns      10.2 km

**Ausee** (Luftenberg an der Donau)
prefix: 07223

**Hohenlohe Ausee (Swimming lake),** Auseestr., ✆ 81802. Pedal boats, stand-up paddling, sandy beach, aqua park and much more. @ klb353en

**TIP** A little off to the west of the route is the village of Pichling.

### Pichling (Linz)
prefix: 0732

**Cowboy-Museum-Fatsy,** Traundorfer Str. 266, ✆ 791855, ✆ 0680/1404077 ↻ A time travel through "Little America" and the "Wild West" - Cowboys, Indians and pioneers. @ hej122en

**Pichlinger See (Pichlinger lake),** Raffelsstettnerstr., ✆ 305314, @ rjk712en

**Weikerlsee (Weikerl lake),** ✆ 34006000, @ vtk166en

Continue straight ahead on the paved road after crossing the river

**4** after 1.4 km turn left into the narrow lane.

 To take the excursion to St. Florian, continue straight ahead here and follow the green signs.

## Excursion to St. Florian     16 km

**In addition to the magnificent baroque abbey and other attractions, an excellent open-air agricultural museum awaits you.**

**4** Continue straight ahead ～ follow the right curve in the road ～ turn left across the railway bridge ～ after 500 m turn right into the side road and immediately left onto the bicycle path ～ turn right after riding through the underpass under the main road ～ follow the bicycle path into Asten.

### Asten
prefix: 07224

*i* **Gemeindeamt (Municipal office)**, Marktpl. 2, ☎ 663810, @ ejo475en

🏛 **Paneum (Chamber of Bread Wonders)**, Kornspitzstr. 1, ☎ 8821400 ⊜ The Paneum, the Chamber of Bread Wonders, focuses on one of the world's most important foodstuffs: the miracle of bread! @ weq328en

After the church ride straight ahead across the main street **Wiener Straße** ～ continue on **Ipfbachstraße** ～ left across the bridge ～ immediately turn right ～ you pass under the freeway as you ride out of Asten ～ continue straight ahead past the commercial buildings of Backaldrin and follow the field road to the open air museum **Sumerauerhof**.

### Samesleiten (St. Florian)

🏛 **Freilichtmuseum Sumerauerhof (Open air museum Sumerauerhof)**, Samesleiten 15, ☎ 0664/6007252391 ⊜ In one of the most beautiful square courtyards (13. century) there is a unique

collection of farm furniture, Gasselschlitten, carpenter's paintings and the farm. Works like: Baking, battles, must production, faithfully represented. @ jre445en

There you turn right ～ cross the main road and proceed to the T-intersection ～ turn left and follow the road into St. Florian ～ to reach the monastery take the first right after the **Marktplatz**.

### St. Florian
prefix: 07224

*i* **Marktgemeinde (Municipal office)**, Leopold-Kotzmann-Str. 1, ☎ 42550, @ pix823en

🏛 **Anton Bruckner in St. Florian**, Stiftstr. 1, ☎ 8902-0. In this newly conceived Bruckner Museum at St. Florian Abbey, the periods during which Anton Bruckner stayed at St. Florian Abbey are thematised on the basis of 9 stations. The published knowledge about Anton Bruckner, his work and his creative activity at the monastery is almost exclusively drawn from the monastery's rich archives in the form of original documents. Opening April 2024. @ tph214en

🏛 **Feuerwehrmuseum St. Florian (Firebrigade museum)**, Stiftstr. 2, ☎ 4219 ⊜ The museum presents the development of firefighting technologies as well as the social organization of fire departments. @ tha648en

🏛 **Stift-Kunstsammlungen (Abbbey Art collections)**, Stiftstr. 1, ☎ 89020 Ⓒ Various art collections can be seen at St. Florian

Abbey: Sculpture Collection, Glass Painting Collection, Gothic Gallery, Baroque Gallery, Graphics Collection and Contemporary Art. @ olt725en

**Stiftsbasilika Mariä Himmelfahrt (Abbey basilica)**, Stiftstr. 1. The baroque church with its perfect, festive effect is the main work of C. A. Carlone, the so-called Bruckner organ of Franz Xaver Krismann 1770-74 belongs to the most famous organs of its time. @ iqd378en

**Stift St. Florian (St. Florian Monastery)**, Stiftstr. 1, ℓ 890210. The baroque monastery of St. Florian is one of the largest and best-known monasteries in Austria. The monastery building was first documented in Carolingian times in the 9th century. A community of Augustinian canons has been documented since the 11th century. The magnificent Baroque buildings were built in the 17th and 18th centuries under the architects Carlo Antonio Carlone, Jakob Prandtauer and Johann Gotthard Hayberger. The impressive state rooms - Abbey Library, Imperial Marble Hall and Emperor's Room - are worth seeing, as are the crypt with Anton Bruckner's sarcophagus, the Abbey Basilica, the Abbey Collections and the "Bruckner Organ". @ hxn666en

**Hörerlebnis Brucknerorgel (Organ concerts)**, Stiftstr. 1, in the Abbey Basilica, ℓ 8902-0, ⊘ Mid May-Mid Oct, Mon, Wed-Fri, Sun at 14:30. Listening experience Bruckner organ event. @ uxm177en

**Literaturgarten (Literary garden)**, Stiftstr. 1, ℓ 8346. Clay tablets with sayings and quotations from writers accompany the visi-

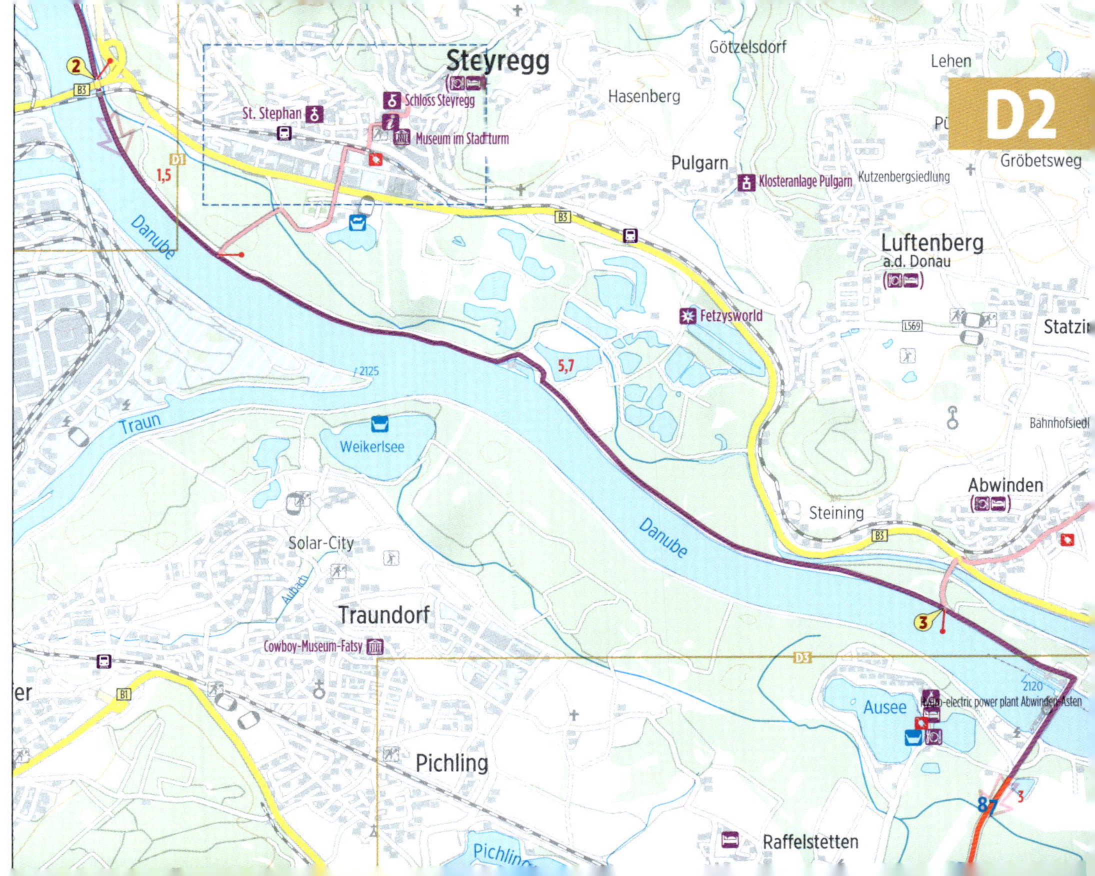

tors through the former kitchen garden of the Meierhof. @ qvo123en

📧 **Freibad (Outdoor swimming area)**, Badstr. 1, ☎ 8118, @ slg125en
*In the middle-ages the abbey emerged as the spiritual and economic centre of the region. Its schools for writing and painting were famous throughout Europe, and monastery organist Anton Bruckner (1845-55) brought even greater fame to St. Florian.*

## Hohenbrunn (St. Florian)

🏛 **Jagdmuseum Schloss Hohenbrunn (Hunting museum)**, Hohenbrunn 1, ☎ 07224/20083 ⓐ The art of hunting, and especially hunting traditions of Upper Austria, are presented in this baroque palace from 1722-32. @ kxh158en

From the monastery go right past Gasthof Goldener Löwe into **Fürstenberg street** downhill ~ at the crossroads go straight on, **Bachgasse** ~ follow the left-hand bend ~ at the priority road turn right onto the cycle lane ~ cross the roundabout to the Agricultural School ~ before there turn left into the paved lane between fields to Weilling ~ follow this road steadily to the Open Air Museum, there turn right ~ continue to **Samesleiten** ~ cross the main road there ~ the road takes you to a T-junction at the end of town, turn left

~ cross under the main road ~ turn right at the next opportunity ~ then pass under the motorway ~ you will soon reach the outskirts of Enns ~ now follow the cycle path that accompanies the main road ~ at the junction to the town centre, turn half left into **Stadlgasse**

~ continue to **Mauthausener Straße** ~ turn right there to the main square

## Enns see page 90

To take the main route to Enghagen, continue along the country lane from the turnoff at **4** ~ at the three-way junction turn left ~ in the right-hand bend straight on into the cycle path ~ at the crossroads turn left to the Danube ~ as far as Enghagen **5**.

### Enghagen (Enns)

🚢 **Donauradfähre Enns-Mauthausen-St. Pantaleon-Erla (Danube bicycle ferry)**, Ennshafen, ☎ 07223/82777, ☎ 0650/3915034, ⏲ Mai & Sept. 9-18 Uhr, Juni-Aug. 9-19 Uhr. The bike ferry has room for 12 persons incl. bike and takes you to the desired shore. In principle, the ferry travels in a triangle over the Danube and Enns at intervals of 5-10 minutes. @ ptw721en

**FORK** Here you can continue to the cycle ferry to Mauthausen to cross over to the other bank. On the route on the south bank, however, you cycle here to the historic town of Enns, which is well worth seeing.

## To the ferry

To get to the ferry, turn left towards the end of Enghagen to the Danube and follow the path to the ferry.

D3
Berglitzl
L569
B3
Hydro-electric power plant Abwinden-Asten
2120
2115
Burgruine Spielberg
2115
Heimatmuseum
Schloss
Raffelstetten
4
Enghagen am Tabor
Pichlinger See
Danube
D2
2,2
0,8 Kronau
2
Enghagen
5
Enns
Ipfdorf
Erlengraben
B1
1,8
Wiener Bundesstraße
B1
Kristeinbach
Lorch
Bruck
bei Tödling
Einsiedl
D4
Calcaria
Kircher Straße
A1
2,5
Fisching
Westbahnstr.
2,2
7
Windpassing
Enns
4,5
Asten
Basilika St. Laurenz
Mittelstraße
0,6
0,8
Norikum
Lagerhausstraße
6
Traunleiten
Kristein
0,4
Ennsdorf
Paneum
Stadtturm
B1
Burg
1
3,2
Historisches Schützenhaus
1,5
Augustiner-Chorherrenstift
Mooser Weg
Wiener Straße
0,8
Samesleiten
Entel
Stift-Kunstsammlung
Freilichtmuseum Sumerauerhof
Samesleitner Str.
3,2
Sankt Florian
Am Seisberg
Johann-Hoflehner-Str.
A1
L6247
Weilling
89
3,2
Oberndorf
Tillysburg
Rabenberg
A1

*Enns, Ennsegg palace*

Leave Enghagen on the route towards Enns ~ turn right at the priority road ~ cross under the motorway ~ follow **Mitterstraße** slightly uphill ~ follow Mitterstraße, which branches off to the left before the houses ~ at the large crossroads turn left into **Jägerstraße** through the settlement ~ in **Drosselstraße** turn right to **Mauthausner Straße** ~ continue to the right along the cycle path ~ cross under the railway bridge **6**

To get to the city centre, continue to follow Mauthausner Straße to the right.

## Enns
prefix: 07223

**Tourismus & Stadtmarketing Enns (Tourist information)**, Hauptpl. 19, *C* 82777, @ ydv788en

**Historisches Schützenhaus (House of Marksman)**, Schießstättenstr. 17, *C* 83681, *C* 0680/3077459 *C* Built in 1807, the civic shooting range features over 200 painted targets, the oldest dating from 1695. @ skt451en

**Museum Lauriacum**, Hauptpl. 19, *C* 85362 *7d* The II. Italian Roman Legion, national cult and city law, life in the civil city, agriculture, trade, burial culture and spatial art are shown. @ bph611en

**Basilika St. Laurenz**, Lauriacumstr. 4, *C* 822370 *7d* The Basilica of St. Lawrence was built in the 4th/5th century as an early Christian church on the remains of Roman walls. Since early Christian times, the most diverse architectural styles have been mixed in it. Around 1300, the church, which still exists today in this form, was built in the Gothic style. The archaeological excavations under the basilica and numerous finds from the Roman period tell of the emergence and spread of early Christianity in the province of Noricum. @ rxx327en

**Stadtpfarrkirche St. Marien (Town Parish Church)**, Kirchenpl. 6, *C* 82855. It is a picturesque Gothic building group, essentially built around 1270, consisting of the main church, Wallsee chapel, cloister and Franciscan monastery.

**Johanniter-Kapelle**, Mauthausner Str., *C* 82777. The chapel next to the Frauenturm (Woman's Tower) is impressive because of its murals dating from around 1320. Visit during guided sightseeing tour possible, @ tad226en

**Ehem. Landesfürstliche Burg (Former princely castle)**, Wienerstr. 9. Emperor Frederick III had the castle built in 1483 as the residence of the respective sovereigns and the bailiff. The inner courtyard with Gothic arcades is well worth seeing. @ nqb454en

**Schloss Ennsegg (Ennsegg palace)**, Schlossg. 4, *C* 82777, *C* Visits are possible as part of a city tour. The castle and its park invite you to marvel and relax. It was built in the years 1569/70 by the imperial council Dr. Gienger. Weddings take place in the castle. @ dde624en

**Calcaria - Römische Kalkbrennöfen (Roman lime kilns)**, Lorcher Str. 62, *C* 85362 *7d* Near the northern corner of the legionary camp lies the largest known Roman lime kiln complex of the Imperium Romanum. The best-preserved kiln can be visited in a protective building. @ wsy181en

**Stadtturm (City tower)**, Hauptpl. 1, *C* 82777 *7d* The 60 m high city tower was built in the 16th century under Emperor Maximilian II. Its four-storey ashlar structure combines Gothic and Renaissance styles and is particularly impressive due to its imposing architecture. For over 400 years, the city tower served as a church tower, fire alarm post, clock tower and city guard. Today it houses a modern hotel. The climb up the tower is rewarded with a wonderful panoramic view! @ jlu517en

**Hauptplatz (Main square)**. Many well-preserved houses are grouped around the city tower, the core is Gothic, but with Renaissance and Baroque facades, and all testify to a remarkable achievement in Austrian urban development.

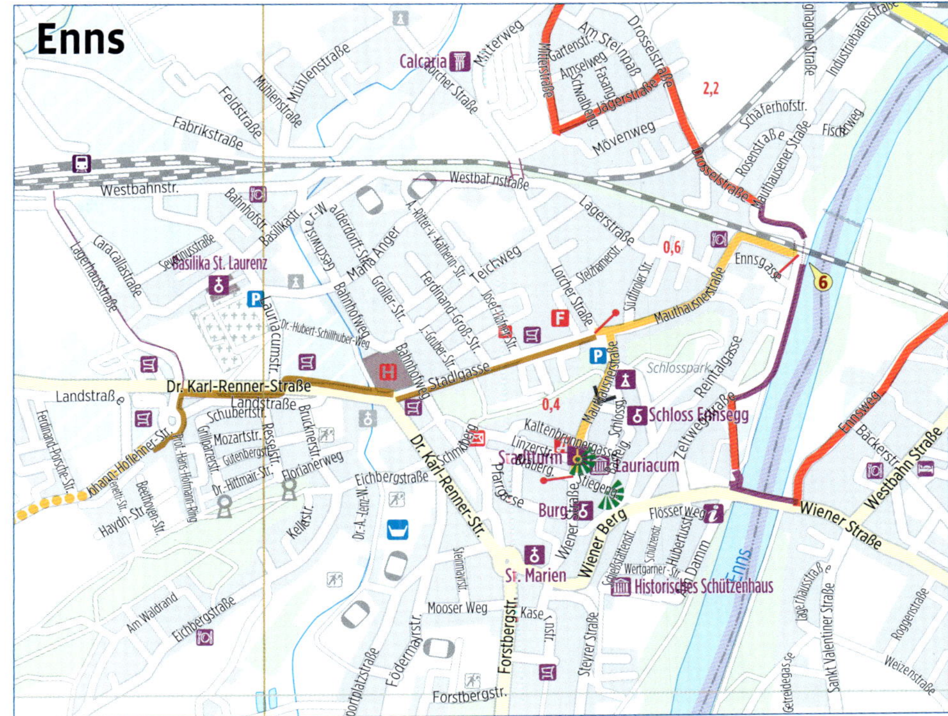

✳ **Stadtführungen (City tours)**, Hauptpl. 19, ☎ 82777 ⓦ Various city tours are offered, such as the 3 Towers Tour, Laurios Tour, Medieval City Tour, etc. @ kdn846en

🛏 **Freibad (Outdoor swimming pool)**, Födermayr-Str. 4, ☎ 82181232

The designation of Enns as the oldest city in Austria is based on two documents. The Roman civil town of Lauriacum received its town charter as early as 212, which can be documented by bronze tablet fragments with the relevant inscription. Exactly 1,000 years later the medieval town was granted this privilege again by Leopold VI. However, the town was already inhabited during the Stone Age and by the Celts.

The Romans built a large camp for the second Italian legion at the strategically important location at the mouth of the river Enns. Parts of the surrounding moat are still visible today, the Porta principalis dextra and the Porta decumana are still marked. To the west of the camp, the civil town of Lauriacum extended towards Kristein and the slopes of Eichberg, which has been developed since 1951. Under Charlemagne, the camp became Pfalz Lorch. The spiritual centre of the Roman city was a *predecessor of today's St. Laurenz Basilica. Excavations during the 60s have shown that this place of worship has been used continuously since the 2nd century. The Celtic-Roman temple was followed in the 4th century by an early Christian heated building. The present basilica dates back to the first quarter of the 14th century. It is a three-nave Gothic pillar basilica with a straight closed choir. The Roman and Romanesque walls uncovered during the restoration of the church have been made accessible in a crypt. The medieval city walls have also been preserved with various towers. In the town centre there are still Gothic houses with quiet inner courtyards, but many of which have been given Baroque show sides.*



### Enns to Wallsee                    27.1 km

**6** Straight ahead onto **Zeltwegstraße** — at the end of the cycle path turn left at the junction, **Ennslände** — turn left across the Enns — immediately afterwards turn left again onto **Ennsweg**. — ride straight along the edge of **Ennsdorf** and under the railway line — continue straight — keep left by the railway embankment — follow the path under the rail and road bridges and back along the road embankment — follow the left bend to an intersection — turn right — at the next side street turn left — **7** turn left at the T-intersection — turn right into the paved cycle path — at the underpass of the B 123 turn right towards Wallsee.



Turn left onto the road — cross the road and go under the railway — straight ahead along the small road — after the canal, turn left in the direction of Wallsee — the path first follows the course of the canal and then passes the settlement of Albing — at the confluence of the canal with the Danube, the route briefly touches the Danube bank and runs along the embankment.



forests, providing for a pleasant change of scenery before returning to the Danube after 10 km.

**8** Turn right by the playing field into the paved lane and ride away from the dike — turn left at the T-intersection and ride past the farms of Stein — proceed straight to St. Pantaleon.

### St. Pantaleon-Erla

prefix: 07435

ℹ **Gemeindeamt (Municipal office)**, Ringstr. 13, ☏ 7271, @ ylh475en

First straight ahead — at the fork in the road after the church, follow the signs for the Danube cycle path to the left — past Erla and over a small hill — over a little bridge — follow the signs to the left — take a large bend to the right — **9** at the priority road, turn left — past the farmsteads of **Au** — just before the Danube, over the second protective dyke and back up to the cycle path on the outer dyke crest.

*At the end of the straight stretch of the dam, you can already make out the silhouette of the mighty castle complex of Habsburg Castle and the market town of Wallsee-Sindelburg*

D4
93
Niedersebern
Haid
B3
Albern
Obersebern
Brandstatt
Au a.d. Donau
Hainbuchen
Heinrichsbrunn
Reiferdorf
Vormarkt
St. Nikolaus
Heimatmuseum
Schloss Pragstein
Enghagen am Tabor
Danube
4
2115
Enghagen
5
Lorch
Lorcher Straße
Mühlstraße
2,2
Enns
4,5
0,6
6
0,4
Stadtturm
Burg
Mooser Weg
Historisches Schützenhaus
Ennsdorf
Enns
B123
1,8
0,8
1,4
0,5
Pyburg
7
Windpassing
Albing
4,7
8
Stein
2110
Aist-Mühlbach
Aulehrpfad
Fish ladder
Naarn im Machlande
i
St. Pantaleon
i
Arthof
Marksee
Raad
B123a
Wagram
Oberwasserkanal
Erla
Stögen
Weingarten
D3
D5
1,2
Erla
Breitfeld
Danube
2108
2106
Rems
B1
Aichet
Kötting
A1
L6247
B1
Wimm
Oberwasserkanal
Enns

Market square Wallsee

Continue to the **Wallsee-Mitterkirchen hydroelectric power station** ~ turn right by the gate and ride around the fenced area past the transformer station.


At the power station it is possible to cross the Danube and continue on the north bank.

Straight ahead across the old arm of the Danube.


**10** At this point you have the choice of an alternative route through Wallsee to take in the beautiful historic market square.

## Alternative route over Wallsee    2 km

**10** Turn right in the left bend onto **Josefstraße** ~ follow the road through its curves ~ right on the street **Donauberg** ~ turn right opposite the palace to reach the market square (**Marktplatz**). *The market square in Wallsee, with its 17th century facades and monuments, is considered one of the most beautiful historic market squares along the Danube.*

Ride straight along **St. Severin-Straße** then left onto **Ardaggerstraße** ~ in the right bend you rejoin the main route.

### Wallsee-Sindelburg

prefix: 07433

ℹ **Gemeindeamt (Municipal office)**, Marktpl. 2, ☎ 22160, @ jjs676en

🏛 **Römermuseum (Roman museum)**, Donauberg 1, ☎ 2380, ☎ 2270 ◔ ◔ Learn more about how Roman soldiers lived and Roman domestic life. Exhibits also include some of the largest Roman bowls. @ iqe181en

⛪ **Pfarrkirche Sindelburg (Sindelburg parish church)**, Sindelburg 1. Gothic-baroque church includes two altar paintings by "Krem-ser Schmidt" and the grave of the imperial daughter Marie-Valerie. In immediate vicinity of the parish church you can enjoy a magnificent panorama of the Mühlviertel, the Danube valley and the Ötscher. @ cei747en

⛪ **Schloss Wallsee (Wallsee palace)**, Schloss Wallsee 1. Built by Heinrich VI von Wallsee between 1368 and 1388 on the site of a Roman settlement. Greatly expanded in the 17th c. and renovated in the late 19th c. The private residence can only be viewed from the outside. @ lmc318en

✳ **Barocke Mariensäule (Baroque Marian column)**. Build in 1710, a work by the Viennese sculptor Benedikt Stober, imperial memorial and Anna chapel. @ pxk588en

🏖 **Beach & Wassersportzentrum Wallsee (Water sports centre Wallsee)**, Altarmstr. 2, ☎ 0664/1049604, ☎ 0664/1049604. From water skiing and wakeboarding to beach volleyball and little-known sports equipment at Fun Corner. @ pns875en

## Wallsee to Ardagger    11.5 km

**10** For the main route follow the left-hand bend ~ in the right-hand bend left-straight ahead and along the edge of the forest ~ at the cross path right back to the main road ~ here left and leave Wallsee on the cycle path, which soon changes the side of the road ~ in Sommerau over a channel and then straight ahead ~ at the end of the

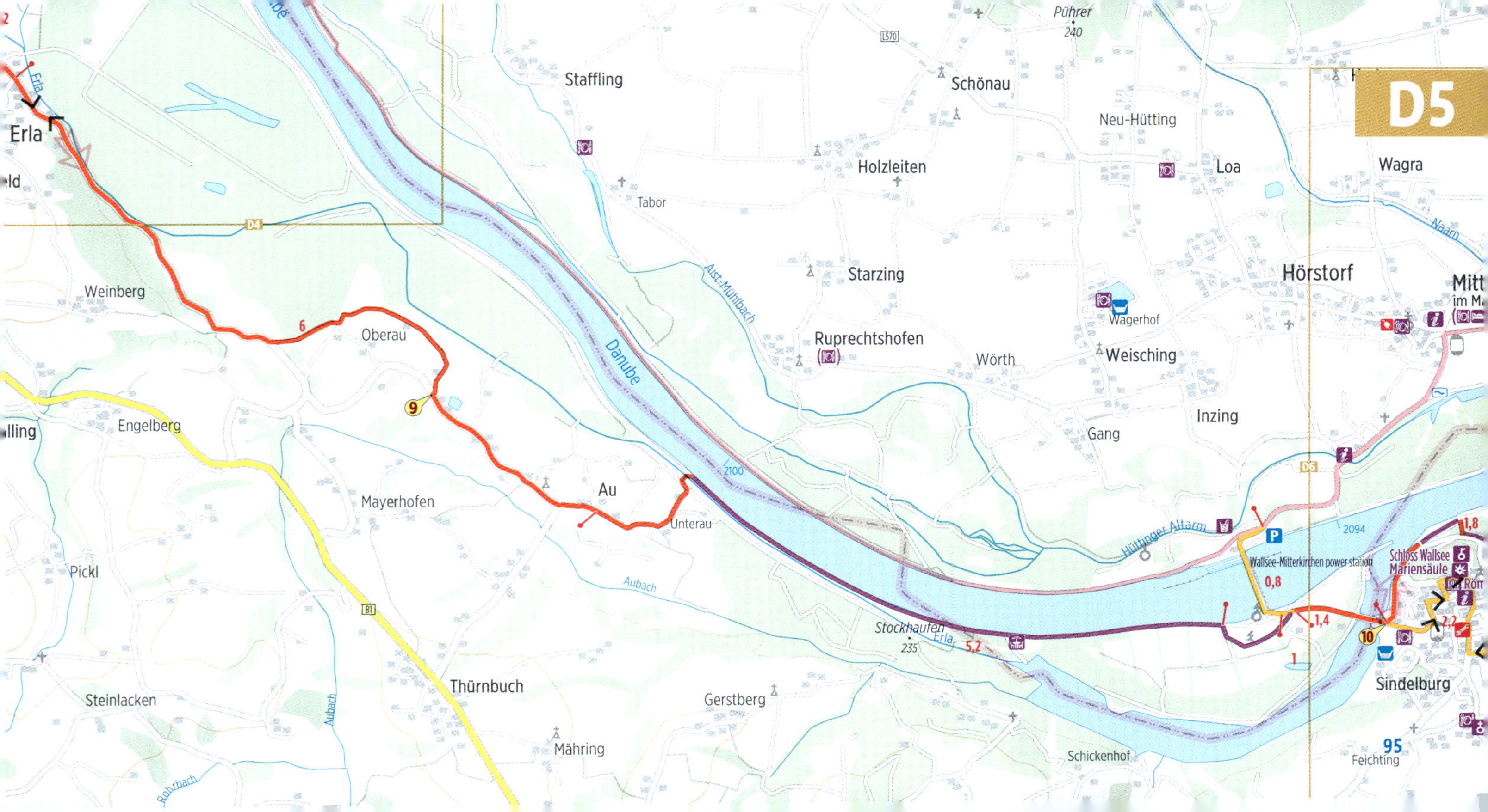

D5
95
Erla
Id
Weinberg
Engelberg
Illing
Pickl
Steinlacken
Mayerhofen
Oberau
Au
Unterau
Thürnbuch
Mähring
Gerstberg
6
9
Staffling
Tabor
Holzleiten
Starzing
Ruprechtshofen
Wörth
Schönau
Neu-Hütting
Loa
Wagra
Pührer
240
Hörstorf
Wagerhof
Weisching
Inzing
Gang
Mitt
im M
Danube
Aist-Mühlbach
Naarn
L570
D4
B1
Aubach
Aubach
Rohrbach
Stockhaufen
235
Erla
5,2
2100
2094
Hüttinger Altarm
D6
Wallsee-Mitterkirchen power station
0,8
1,4
1
10
Schloss Wallsee
Mariensäule
Rön
1,8
2,2
Sindelburg
Schickenhof
Feichting
95

village the road turns left ~ through the village of Leitzing.

### Leitzing (Ardagger)

✳ **Riesenmostbirne (Giant cider pear)**, Leitzing 1, ✆ 07479/6351. The wooden 6 m high and 4,5 m wide pear is called the "gate to the Mostviertel". Inside it illustrates the development of the Mostbirne in the course of the year. @ bcd714en

Keep left by the inn and continue on the path along the road ~ **11** after another 1.5 km turn left towards Grein and Ardagger-Markt ~ follow the bicycle path along the road once again ~ cross the bypass road and ride into Ardagger-Markt ~ **12** in the village area, the cycle path ends and you continue on the local road in a left-hand bend.

Before continuing into the Strudengau we recommend a short excursion to the abbey church in Ardagger Stift, with its unique Margarethe windows, and the MostBirnHaus, which is dedicated to the cider pears and cider so popular in the region. The route is shown on map D6 in orange.

### Ardagger Markt (Ardagger)
prefix: 07479

ℹ **Marktgemeindeamt Ardagger (Ardagger municipal office)**, Markt 55, ✆ 7312, @ kln518en

✳ **Donauwellenpark (Danube waves park)**, Markt 58, ✆ 7312. Amusement park designed in the form of a ship with beach volleyball court, giant swing, skater park and much more, surrounded by "Danube waves" formed from earth. @ kdb221en

▭ **Donaustrand (Danube beach)**, ✆ 7312 ㉔ open access

### Ardagger Stift (Ardagger)
prefix: 07479

⛪ **Stiftskirche (Abbey Church)**, Stift Ardagger 3, ✆ 7246 ㉔ The oldest part is the three-nave Romanesque crypt from 1049. The centerpiece of the church is the famous Margaret window in the east choir (1240), the oldest figurative stained glass in Austria and perhaps in the German-speaking world. @ tns243en

✳ **MostBirnHaus**, Stift 14, ✆ 6400 ☺ On a multimedia journey into the world of pears there is a lot for young and old to try out. Accompany the little fruit on its way to the delicious pear must. 700 m² indoor experience, 4,500 m² pleasure garden, adventure and play area, tastings and much more. @ bvp471en

## Ardagger to Hößgang      8,8 km

Towards the end of the village, take the left-hand bend straight ahead ~ up to the bypass road and cross it at the Schatzkastl inn ~ there, follow the Danube cycle path to the right ~ keep left at the fork ~ **13** at the next fork, turn left again.

### Freizeithafen Ardagger (Ardagger)

⚓ **Donauschifffahrt Ardagger (Danube shipping Ardagger)**, Freizeithafen, ✆ 07479/6464. Easter until 26 Oct., Sa, Su/holiday. Round trips in Strudengau. @ ysb887en

✳ **Freizeithafen Ardagger (Recreational harbour)**, Felleismühle 6, ✆ 0664/4137931. Lively life awaits you at the Ardagger leisure harbour. A barbecue hut, a children's playground, an information stand and the Danube shipping pier can be found here. @ uiq264en

Follow the bicycle path between the river bank and the main road until you reach the next bridge across the Danube ~ after passing under the bridge turn left and continue on this pleasant minor road ~ you pass the village of **Wiesen** and continue along the road to Hößgang, where you enter the section of the river known as the Strudengau.

*The route nears the dangerous narrows at Struden. The Hausstein rock near the island of Wörth caused notorious eddies that made the passage especially tricky to navigate. The village of Hößgang is named after the canal which was excavated long ago to enable ships to bypass the river's sharp bend at Struden.*

### 14 Hößgang (Neustadtl an der Donau)
prefix: 07471

D6
Hofstetten
Lehen
Wagra
Mitterkirchen celtic village
Mettensdorf
Pitzing
Eizendorf
Wetzelsdorf
Patzenhof
Dornach
Schloss Dornach
Freizeithafen
Labing
Naarn
Schwemmnaarn
Danube
Mitterkirchen
im Machland
2085
Winkling
Hüttinger back water
Donauwellenpark
Ardagger-Markt
Danube
2090
Bach
Schloss Wallsee
Mariensäule
Wallsee
Römermuseum
5,7
Kir
Sindelburg
Empfing
Pfaffenbach
Stiftskirche
Grenerarm
11
MostBirnHaus
Hummelberg
Moos
Stephanshart
Pfarrkirche
4
Sommerau
Landgerichtsbach
Leitzing
Riesenmostbirne
Albersberg
Ardagger Stift
Pfaffenberg
Schweinberg
Dorf
Zeitlbach
Zeitlbach
97

**ℹ Marktgemeindeamt (Municipal office)**, Marktstr. 16, ☎ 22400, @ eeo325en

**✳ Insel Wörth (Isle Wörth)**, ☎ 22400 ⟳ The only surviving real Danube island is a nature reserve and can be explored on guided tours. Entry point ferry: Grein or Wiesen, @ pwt154en

**▭ Naturbadeteich (Natural swimming pond)**, Hößgang 65 ㉔ Open access

*The Danube valley narrows further, the granite rocks now reach the shore. To the left you have a wonderful view of the legendary island of Wörth on the former Donaustrudel and Werfenstein Castle.*

### Hößgang to Ybbs                                    18.9 km

The route briefly veers away from the river as it passes around a swimming pond ∿ continue another 12 km downriver to Freyenstein.

**15 Freyenstein** (Neustadtl an der Donau)

**♂ Ruine Freyenstein (Freyenstein Ruin)** ㉔ The castle ruins, which were built around the year 1200 - supposedly on an old Celtic cult site - are enthroned on a wooded hill above the village.

*The ruins of a castle are perched above the village on a wooded bluff over the river. It is said to be haunted by a legendary river ghost, "Prince Nöck," who comes out only at full moon and is rarely seen.*

The route continues along the river past **Willersbach** ∿ the river gradually becomes wider and less turbulent as you leave the Strudengau ∿ after 7 km you reach a T-intersection by the **16 Ybbs-Persenbeug hydroelectric power station.**

**❚ TIP** At the bridgehead there is an information point for cyclists.

### Kraftwerk Ybbs-Persenbeug (Ybbs an der Donau)

**♿ Besucherkraftwerk Ybbs-Persenbeug (Visitor power plant)**, Donaustr. 2, ☎ 0650/3002236, ⟳ Guided tour: Apr.-Oct., Mon-Fri 2 p.m., Sat/Sun/Fri 1 p.m. and 3 p.m. The oldest Danube power station provides an insight into the fascinating world of hydroelectric power generation. @ bdk821en

At the southern end of the Ybbs-Persenbeug power station, take the cycle path ∿ after the bike information, turn left ∿ down to the bank ∿ along the **Donaulände** to Ybbs **17** into the **Peter Rosegger Promenade** via **Kaiser-Josef-Platz** through the atmospheric Old Town.

### Ybbs an der Donau
prefix: 07412

**ℹ Nibelungengau Info-Center (Info Center Nibelungengau)**, Stauwerkstr. 86, ☎ 55233, @ osj475en

**🏛 Fahrradmuseum (Bicycle museum)**, Herreng. 12, ☎ 20098 ⑦ᵈ The museum takes the visitor on a journey through time into the history of the bicycle. There are, among other things, wooden running wheels, pedal crank wheels as well as high wheels to visit and partly also to try out. @ lwi262en

**🏛 Stadtmuseum (Town museum)**, Herreng. 23, ☎ 0676/6173933 ⟳ Historical development, the Danube navigation and ship mastery as well as Roman finds are illustrated. @ rpa816en

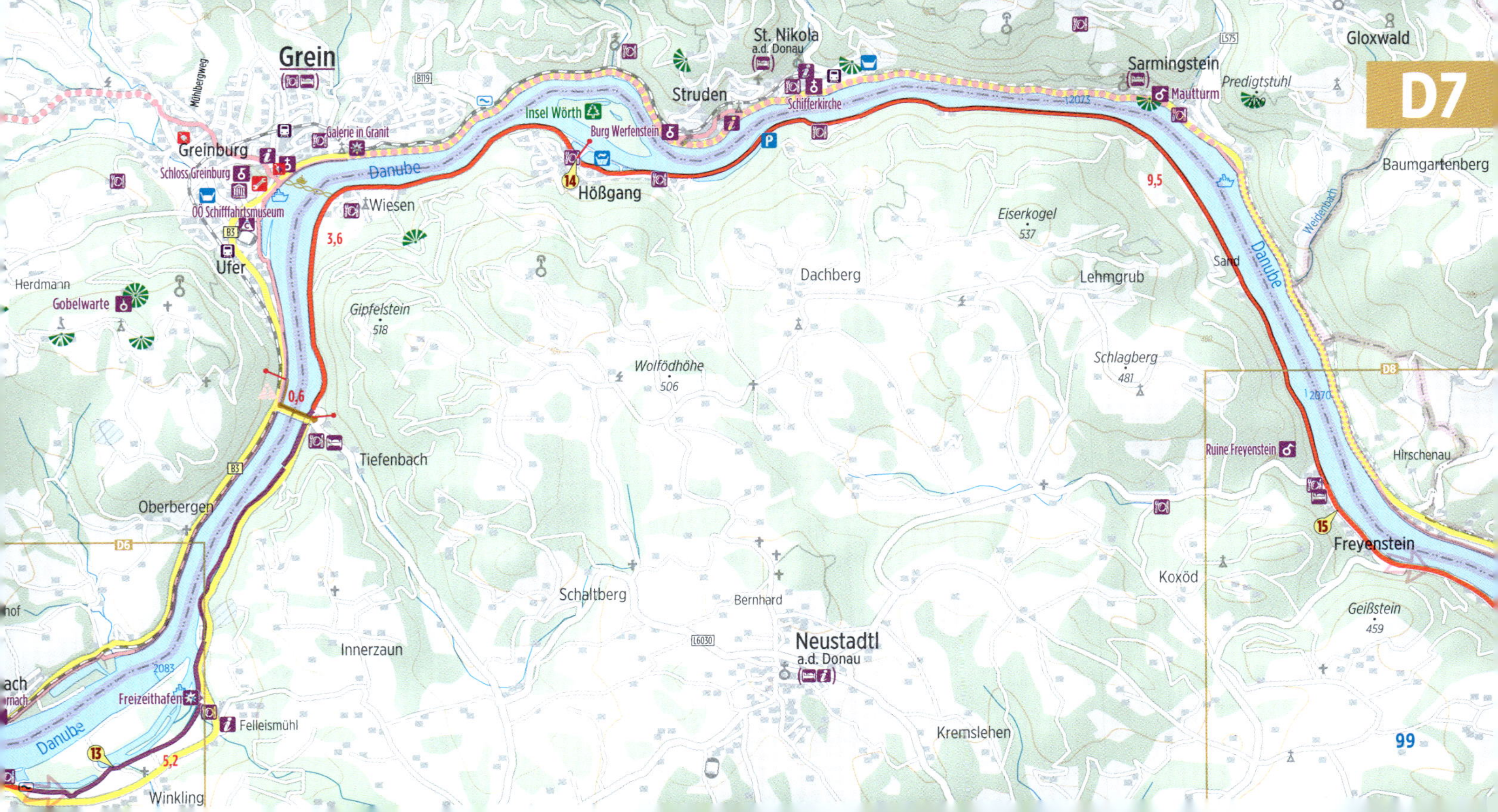

D7
Gloxwald
Sarmingstein
Predigtstuhl
Mautturm
L575
2073
Baumgartenberg
St. Nikola
a.d. Donau
Struden
Schifferkirche
Weidenbach
9,5
Grein
B119
Galerie in Granit
Insel Wörth
Burg Werfenstein
Danube
14
Hößgang
Eiserkogel
537
Sand
Danube
Greinburg
Schloss Greinburg
OO Schifffahrtsmuseum
Wiesen
3,6
Dachberg
Lehmgrub
B3
Ufer
Herdmann
Gobelwarte
Gipfelstein
518
Wolfödhöhe
506
Schlagberg
481
D8
2070
0,6
Tiefenbach
Ruine Freyenstein
Hirschenau
B3
Oberbergen
15
Freyenstein
D6
Schaltberg
Bernhard
Koxöd
Geißstein
459
2083
Neustadtl
a.d. Donau
99
Freizeithafen
Felleismühl
Danube
Kremslehen
13
5,2
Winkling

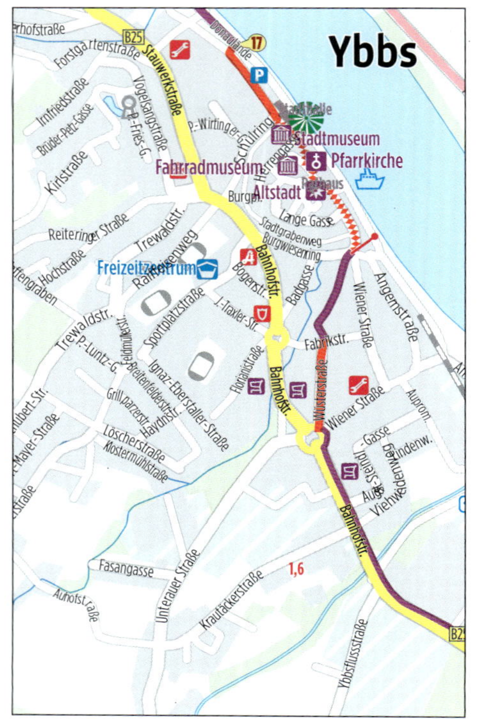




- **Pfarrkirche St. Lorenz (St. Lorenz parish church)**, Kirchenpl., ☎ 52654. Triple-naved church with net-vaulted ceilings built around 1500. The pulpit, organ and the beautifully gilded altar date from 1730. @ kiv748en
- **Altstadt (Historic centre)**, Hauptpl. Ybbs has been widely commended for the exemplary efforts to restore and preserve the old Renaissance houses and remaining parts of the city defenses.
- **Ybbsiade**. Annual two- to three-week cabaret and cultural festival in April. @ xlr472en
- **Flussbad 3er**. Natural river bath in the middle of the Natura 2000 area. @ ool568en
- **Freizeitzentrum & Hallenbad (Indoor swimming pool)**, Sportplatzstr. 6, ☎ 52525, @ osf174en

### Ybbs to Pöchlarn        15.4 km

Go further on into **Wiener Straße** ~ at the crossroad between **Wiener Straße** and Burgwiesenring follow the path in the middle ~ cross **Fabrikstraße** ~ continue straight to the roundabout ~ keep left onto the bicycle path along the **Bahnhofstraße** and ride out of Ybbs ~ turn left immediately after crossing the Ybbs River and follow the path along the Ybbs to the Danube ~ follow the path to the left after passing the houses of Unterhaus

and proceed between the river and the railway line ~ you pass the hamlet of **Aigen** and reach Säusenstein.

### 19 Säusenstein (Ybbs an der Donau)

- **Pfarrkirche Hl. Donatus (St. Donatus parish church)**, Kirchenberg. The late-baroque church high above the village includes interesting wall paintings and an altar painting by Paul Troger (1746).
- **Theresienkapelle (Theresien chapel)**, Säusensteiner Str. ☎ The last remnants of a former Cistercian monastery (14th c.), a rib-vaulted room is attached to a renovated baroque palace. @ ebp624en

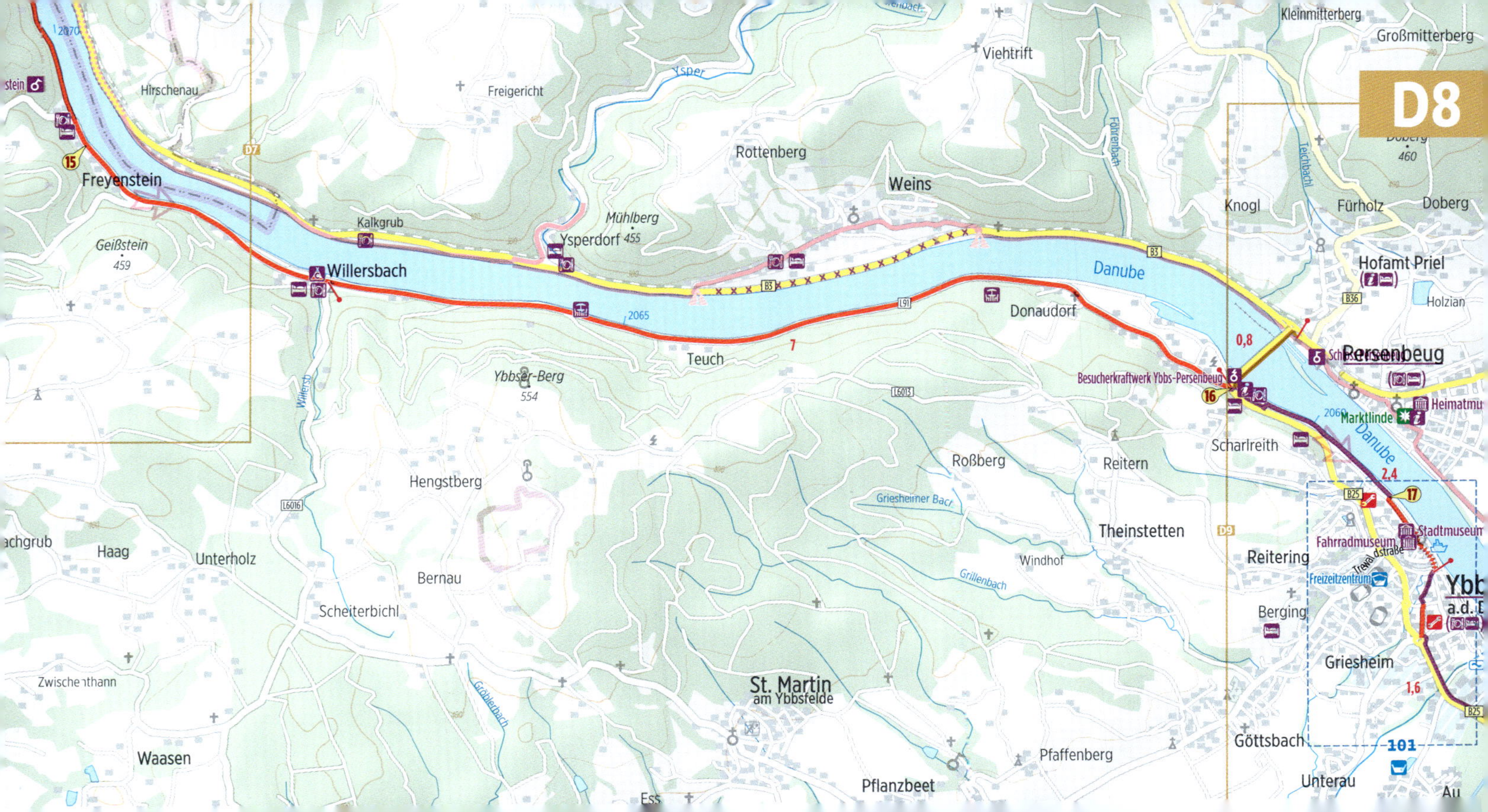

D8
Kleinmitterberg
Großmitterberg
Viehtrift
Doberg
460
Rottenberg
Weins
Knogl
Fürholz
Doberg
Hirschenau
stein
Freigericht
Ysper
Freyenstein
15
Kalkgrub
Mühlberg
Ysperdorf 455
Hofamt Priel
Holzian
Geißstein
459
Willersbach
Danube
B3
B3
Persenbeug
Schloss
Donaudorf
0,8
Teuch
2065
L91
Heimatmu
7
Besucherkraftwerk Ybbs-Persenbeug
Ybbser-Berg
554
L6013
16
Marktlinde
Scharlreith
2066
Danube
Roßberg
Reitern
2,4
Hengstberg
Griesheimer Bach
Theinstetten
17
B25
Willersd
D9
L6016
Fahrradmuseum
Stadtmuseum
Reitering
Treva dstraße
Freizeitzentrum
chgrub
Haag
Unterholz
Windhof
Ybb
Bernau
Grillenbach
a.d.
Scheiterbichl
Berging
Gröblerbach
St. Martin
Griesheim
am Ybbsfelde
1,6
Zwische thann
Waasen
Göttsbach
101
Pfaffenberg
B25
Pflanzbeet
Unterau
Ess
Au

**Stift Säusenstein (Säusenstein abbey),** Schlossstr. 14. Turkish wars, an abbot who disappeared with the monastery treasury and looting by dismissed soldiers threatened the existence of the monastery from its foundation in 1336 until it was dissolved at the end of the 18th century. Privately owned. @ wrg517en

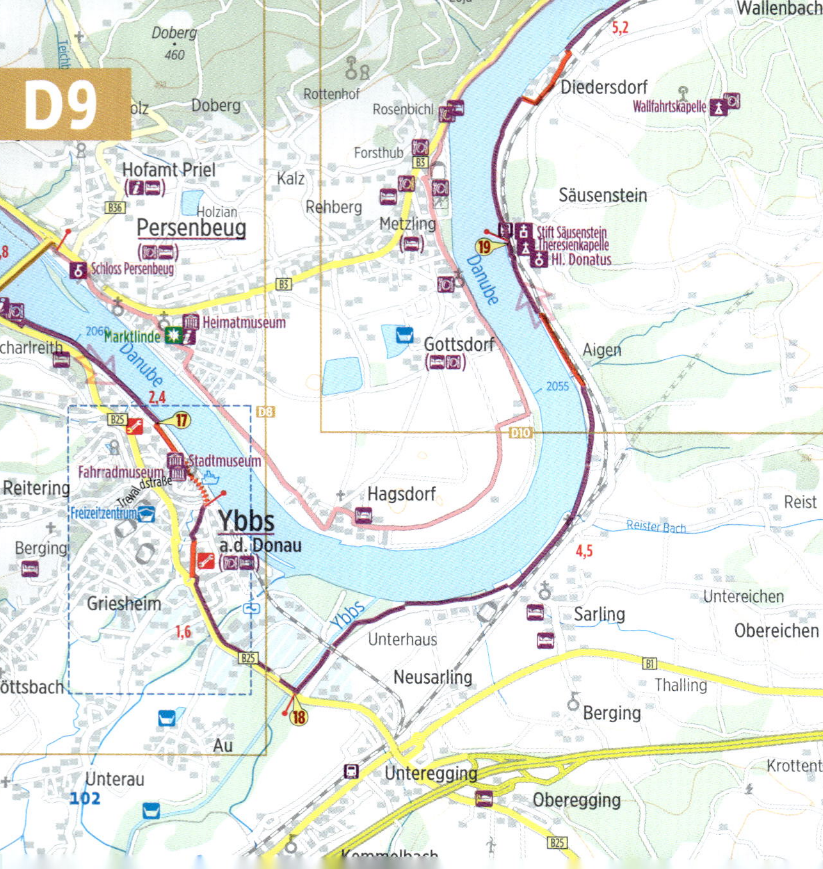

Continue along the riverfront to **Diedersdorf** along the railway line, then follow the street through the village before the railway underpass turn left and return to the path along the Danube.

## Wallenbach (Krummnußbaum)

**Wallfahrtskapelle (Pilgrimage chapel),** Wallenbach 6. As early as 1805, the spring was thought to have a healing effect. The new chapel was built in the 20th century according to the plans of the Viennese architect Erwin Plevan. @ npc331en

Near **Wallenbach** the route turns away from the river up to a road turn left onto the road and ride to the harbour **20** turn left onto the towpath after the Krummnussbaum harbour.

TIP Continue straight ahead if you wish to reach the centre of Krummnußbaum.

## Krummnußbaum

prefix: 02757

**Gemeindeamt (Municipal office),** Rathausstr. 8, ✆ 2403, @ yug781en

Continue down the river for 3 km to the confluence of the Erlauf and Danube ride up the Erlauf river and keep right onto the dike to reach the bridge cross the Erlauf and turn left to return to the path along the Danube proceed past Pöchlarn.

## 21 Pöchlarn

prefix: 02757

**Stadtgemeinde (Town office),** Kirchenpl. 1, ✆ 2310, @ pkp734en

**Oskar-Kokoschka-Geburtshaus (Oskar Kokoschka house),** Regensburgerstr. 29, ✆ 7656, ✆ 231014 The birthplace of the painter, who was born here in 1886, shows the life and works of the artist. Special exhibitions are held every year from May to October. @ cjy313en

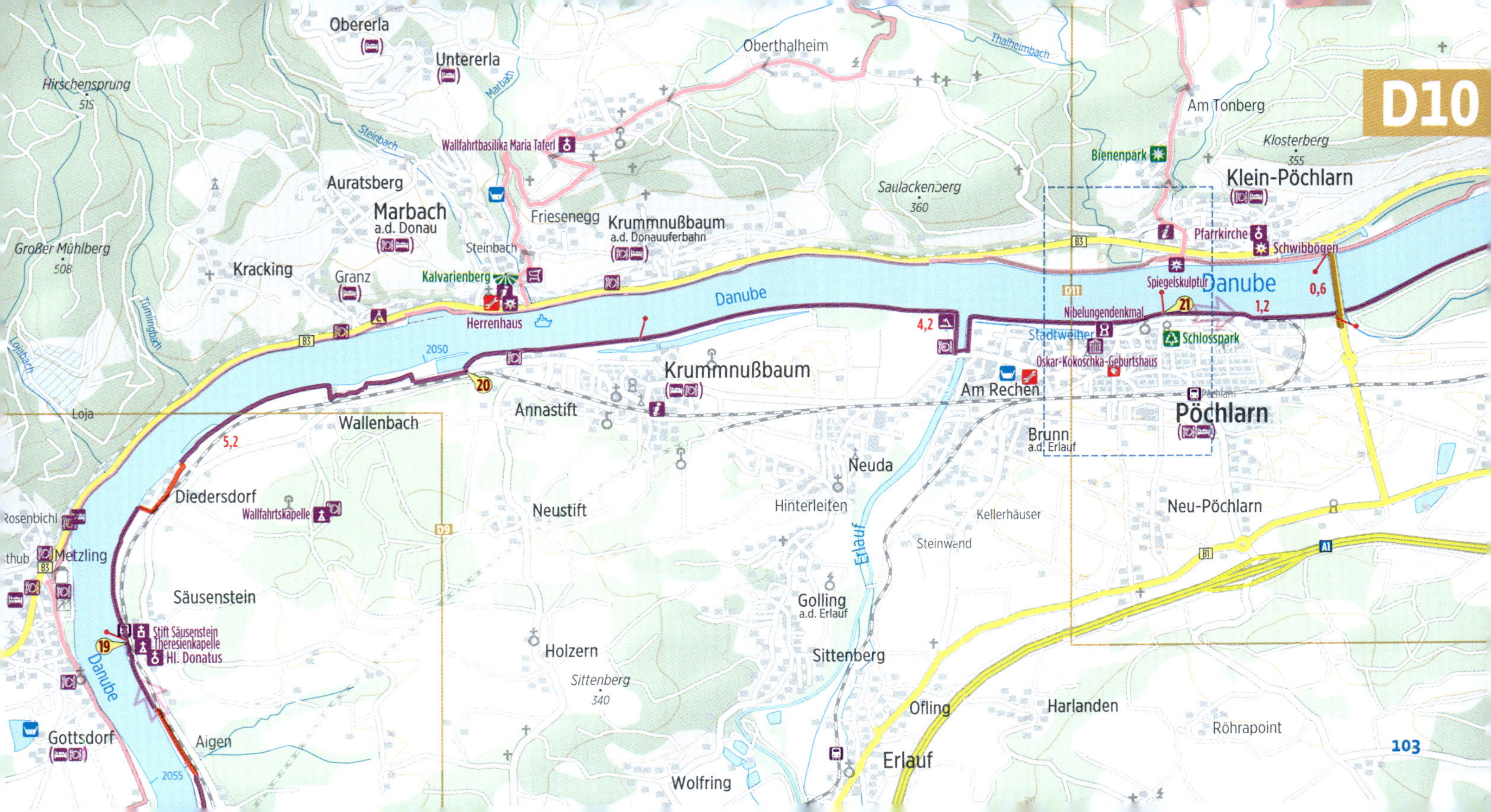

D10
103
Hirschensprung
515
Obererla
Untererla
Oberthalheim
Thalheimbach
Am Tonberg
Klosterberg
355
Bienenpark
Klein-Pöchlarn
Auratsberg
Wallfahrtsbasilika Maria Taferl
Saulackenberg
360
Marbach
a.d. Donau
Friesenegg
Krummnußbaum
a.d. Donauuferbahn
Pfarrkirche
Schwibbögen
Großer Mühlberg
508
Kracking
Steinbach
B3
Danube
Spiegelskulptur
0,6
Granz
Kalvarienberg
1,2
Herrenhaus
Danube
Nibelungendenkmal
21
Stadtweiher
4,2
Schlosspark
B3
2050
Krummnußbaum
Oskar-Kokoschka-Geburtshaus
Loja
20
Annastift
Am Rechen
Pöchlarn
Wallenbach
Pöchlarn
5,2
Brunn
a.d. Erlauf
Neuda
Neu-Pöchlarn
Diedersdorf
Wallfahrtskapelle
Hinterleiten
Kellerhäuser
Neustift
Steinwand
D9
Rosenbichl
B1
A1
Metzling
B3
Säusenstein
Golling
a.d. Erlauf
Stift Säusenstein
Theresienkapelle
19
Hl. Donatus
Holzern
Sittenberg
Danube
Sittenberg
340
Ofling
Harlanden
Röhrapoint
Gottsdorf
Aigen
Erlauf
2055
Wolfring

# Pöchlarn

Pöchlarn

🏛 **Stadtmuseum im Welserturm (City museum in the Welser tower)**, Regensbuger Str., ☎ 2310, ☎ 0664/4821090 ⟳ Permanent exhibition: "ARELAPE - Roman Pöchlarn" and finds from the Roman period. Annual special exhibitions. ⓦ aiq588en

🏛 **Tischlereimuseum (Carpentry museum)**, Sandtorg. 9, ☎ 2310, ☎ 0664/4821090 ⓒ Historic machines and hand made tools from carpentry workshops are on display in this unique museum in the city centre. ⓦ nab382en

♿ **Pfarrkirche Maria Himmelfahrt (Assumption parish church)**, Pfarrpl. 1, ☎ 2251, ☎ 0676/826633304. Built 1389-1429 and renovated in the baroque style in 1766. The church's exterior is marked by inlaid grave memorials and Roman stones. The interior features good paintings by Martin Johann Schmidt (Kremser-Schmidt). ⓦ olw471en

♟ **Nibelungendenkmal (Nibelungen memorial)**, Donaulände, ☎ 231030. Monument with 16 mosaic coats of arms from important locations from the Song of the Nibelungen, ranging from Worms to Esztergom and Verona. ⓦ pxb267en

✳ **Welser Turm (Welser Tower)**, Regensburger Str., ☎ 2310 ⓒ Built in 1484, the complex initially served as a fortification against Matthias Corvinus of Hungary, and later as a settlement for the Wels merchants (salt trade). ⓦ nrq643en

🌲 **Schlosspark (Palace park)**, Nibelungenstr. With centuries-old trees, pavilion and amusements.

🏊 **Stadtbad (Public baths)**, Rechenstr. 9, ☎ 0676/7316566, ⓦ akg811en

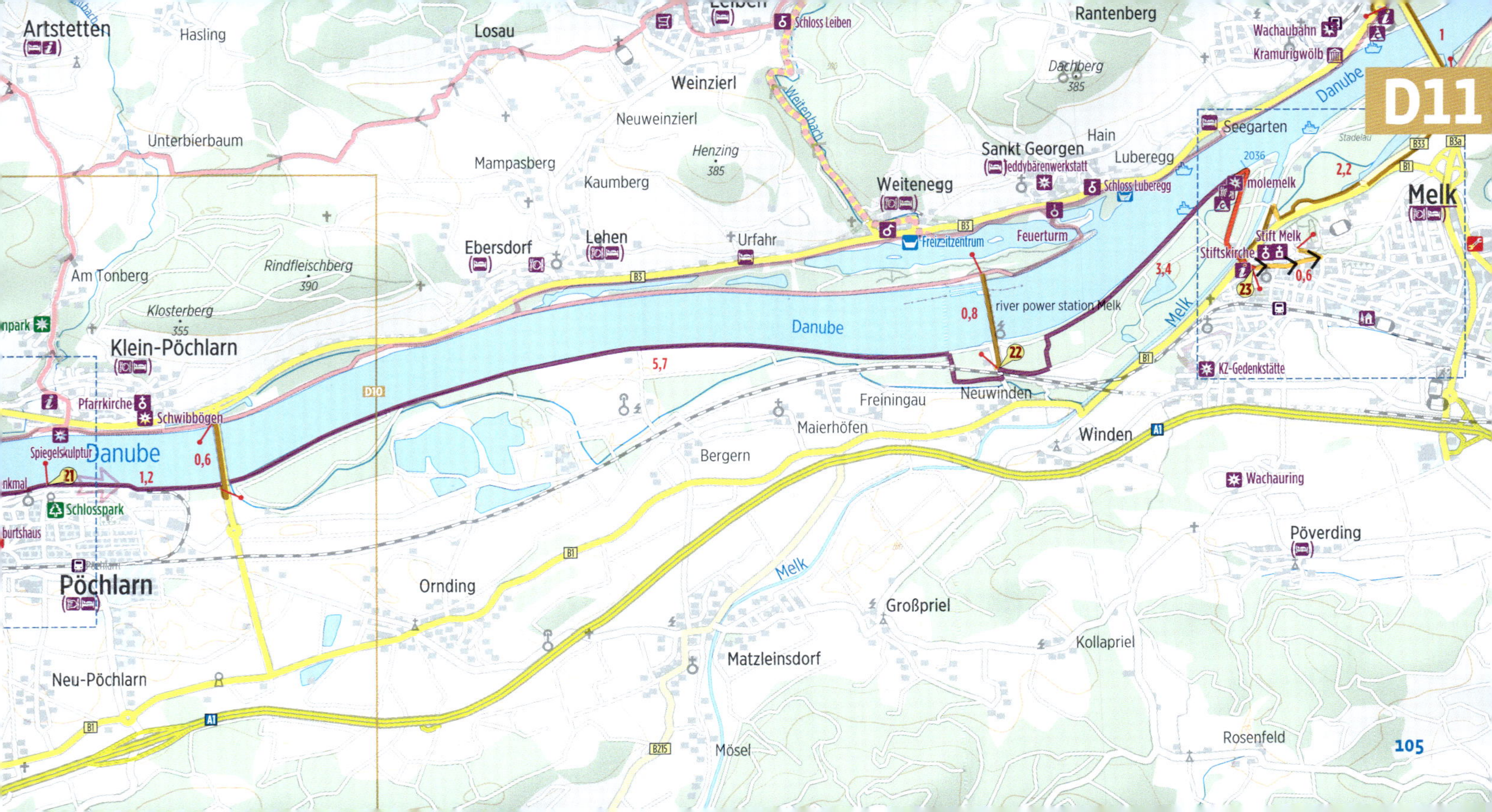

D11
105
Artstetten
Hasling
Losau
Leiben
Rantenberg
Schloss Leiben
Wachaubahn
Kramurigwölb
Danube
Unterbierbaum
Weinzierl
Dachberg
385
Neuweinzierl
Seegarten
Stadelau
Henzing
385
Sankt Georgen
Hain
Mampasberg
Teddybärenwerkstatt
Luberegg
2036
Imolemelk
Melk
Kaumberg
Weitenegg
Schloss Luberegg
2,2
B33  B3a
Lehen
Feuerturm
B1
Ebersdorf
Urfahr
Freizeitzentrum
Stift Melk
Am Tonberg
B3
3,4
Stiftskirche
Melk
Rindfleischberg
390
0,6
river power station Melk
0,8
23
Klosterberg
355
Danube
22
B1
Klein-Pöchlarn
5,7
Neuwinden
KZ-Gedenkstätte
npark
D10
Pfarrkirche
Freiningau
Winden
A1
Schwibbögen
Maierhöfen
Spiegelskulptur
Danube
0,6
Bergern
Wachauring
nkmal
21
1,2
Schlosspark
burtshaus
Pöverding
Pöchlarn
Melk
Pöchlarn
Ornding
Großpriel
Neu-Pöchlarn
Kollapriel
B1
Matzleinsdorf
A1
B1
B215
Mösel
Rosenfeld

### Pöchlarn to Melk              10.1 km

Along the Danube you head for Melk ~ shortly before the Melk power station leave the bank ~ cross under the railway tracks and continue left ~ at the priority road turn left and again pass under the railway **22** immediately afterwards turn right ~ after the power station entrance turn left ~ along the Danube bank to the Melk shipping centre ~ here the trail turns right and reaches the town of Melk via the Melk river ~ you can reach the centre of Melk straight ahead via **Kremser Straße**.



To visit the abbey, it is best to leave your bike at the Wachau Info Center in the bike shed (with lockers for your luggage) or parking area and walk up to the abbey. Then you save yourself the climb and simply continue along the shore afterwards.

## Melk

prefix: 02752

ℹ **Wachau Info Center (Info centre)**, Kremser Str. 5, ✆ 51160, ⓦ gbh486en

⛴ **Brandner Schiffahrt (Brandner shipping)**, Pionierstr., ✆ 07433/259021. Daily scheduled trips through the Wachau between Melk and Krems, bicycle transport approx. 2 Euro. ⓦ ylp658en

⛴ **DDSG Blue Danube (Shipping)**, Räcking 1, ✆ 01/58880. Daily scheduled trips through the Wachau between Melk and Krems, bicycle transport approx. 2 Euro. ⓦ cat118en

🛐 **Stiftskirche Hl. Peter und Paul (St. Peter and St. Paul abbey church)** The baroque building from the 1st half of the 18th c. contains a unique interior with ceiling frescoes by Johann Michael Rottmayr, a dome height of 64 m, sophisticated lighting effects, pictures of Troger in the side chapels and an impressive arrangement of columns, open space, crowns, canopy and medallion. ⓦ afx214en

🏛 **Stift Melk (Melk abbey)**, Abt-Berthold-Dietmayr-Str. 1, ✆ 555232 This magnificent baroque complex of European standing was built by master builder Jakob Prandtauer in place of the former monastery from 1702-38. The ceiling frescoes of the marble hall and the 100,000 volume monastery library represent the most impressive treasures of the complex. ⓦ ccw273en

✳ **molemelk**, Kolomaniau, ✆ 532 91. The new shipping centre at Hafenspitz in Melk is expected to be completed by 2024. In addition to the pier, the complex will include a modern restaurant, camping site, guest rooms, playground, toilet facilities and the ticket office of the shipping companies. ⓦ kqm678en

✳ **Rathausplatz (Town hall square)**. Besides the former Lebzelterhaus (1657) also medieval profane architecture. ⓦ xoa631en

✳ **Wachauring**, Am Wachauring 2, ✆ 0699/11510348. Covering an area of over 12 hectares, the Wachauring offers a wide range

Melk Abbey

of activities from safety training to rallycross, karting, racing events and seminars. @ hct415en

✷ **Zeithistorisches Zentrum - Melk Memorial (Contemporary History Centre),** Schießstattweg 2, ☎ 0681/10603349, ◷ Visits are possible at any time, keys can be borrowed from the Biragokaserne guardhouse, Prinzlstr. 22. In the course of the intensified armament efforts in the Third Reich, the camp in Melk was founded in 1944 as a subcamp of the Mauthausen concentration camp. A total of over 14,390 prisoners were interned here, who, in addition to building and expanding the camp, were also used, among other things, to build the tunnel system in Roggendorf. Since 1992, an exhibition on the history of the concentration camp subcamp has been on display in the former crematorium building. @ nrq178en

◡ **Wachaubad (Outdoor pool),** Fürnbergstr. 12, ☎ 21100-8144, @ icr577en

*The Benedictine monastery Melk painterly marks a rare interplay of landscape, building and electricity. After centuries of eventful his-tory, the monastery experienced a splendid bloom at the beginning of the 18th century under Abbot Berthold Dietmayer. The abbot had found a congenial and also economically thinking partner in Jakob Prandtauer, a master builder from St. Pölten. Prandtauer created the monumental Baroque magnificent building after the Turkish Wars and the successful Counter-Reformation as an expression of a new attitude to life, a strengthened will to rule on the part of both the Church and the Habsburgs.*

To reach the Melk Abbey by bike, continue uphill through the old town ⤳ into **Wienerstraße**, this one-way street is open to cyclists ⤳ at the intersection with **Jakob-Prandtauer-Straße**, turn left into **Abt-B.-Dietmayr-Straße** until you reach the barrier ⤳ push your bike to the covered bike parking area (with lockers).

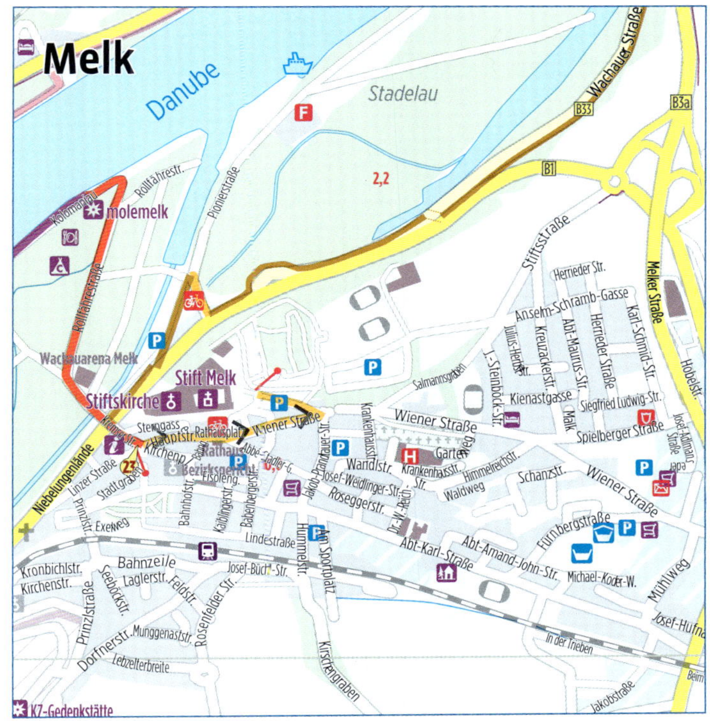

# Emmersdorf to Vienna along the north bank — 120.6 km

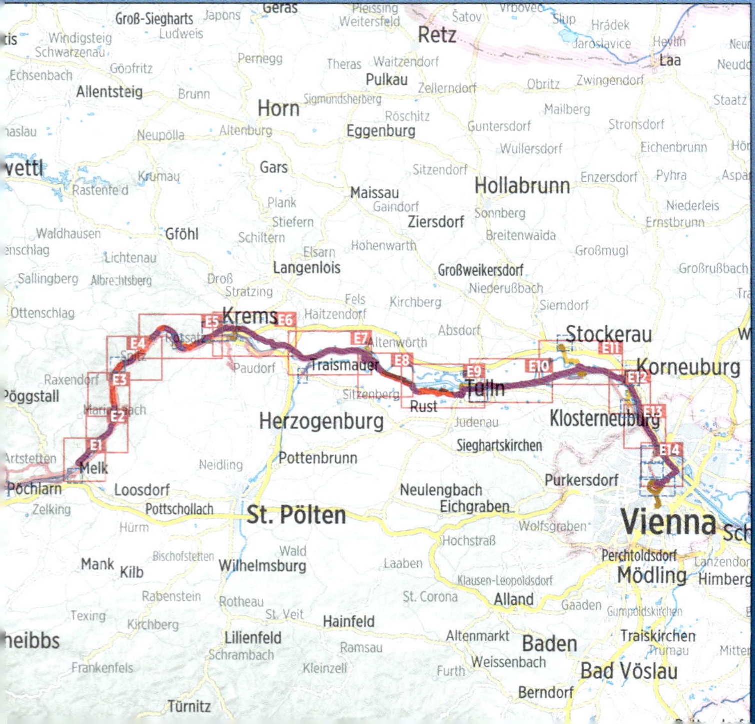

**m/km:** ⬀ 0.9 (112m) ⬂ 1.2 (139m)  **cycle path:** 71 %  **unpaved:** 0 %  **busy road:** 0 %

Many bicycle tourists will regard the final stage to Vienna as the highlight of the tour. The Wachau – one of Austria's best-known wine-growing regions – offers some of the most beautiful landscapes along the entire Danube River. A centuries-old tradition of producing wines has turned the steep south-facing slopes into terraced "stairs to the heavens" which give the valley its distinctive appearance. Downstream from Krems, the Danube valley then spreads into the expansive flood plains of the Tullner meadows, before reaching the Wiener Pforte. A few kilometres later the tour ends in Vienna, Austria's charming capital city.

From Emmersdorf to behind Krems near Altenwörth you cycle on cycle paths and quiet farm tracks. Between Altenwörth and Tulln the Danube bicycle route exists only on the southern bank, before returning to the northern side at Tulln.

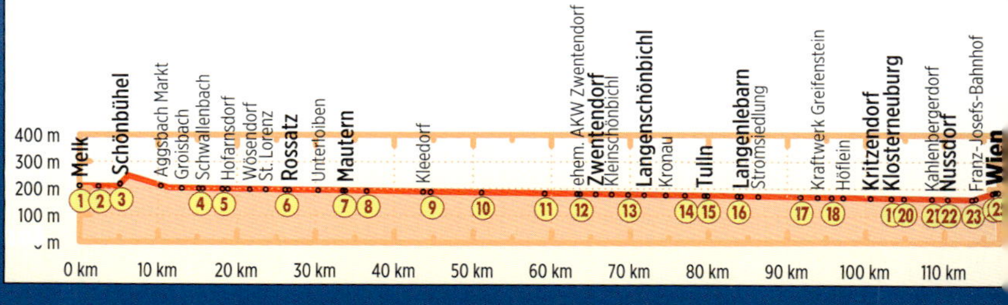

## Emmersdorf to Spitz · 15.6 km

**1** On the northern bank, ride under the Danube bridge between Emmersdorf and Melk and proceed along the bicycle path next to the road ⚠ after the **Schallemmersdorf** sign cross **Uferstraße** — continue on the service lane on the left side between the road and the railway tracks — at **Grimsing** the route departs briefly from the main road before returning to the main road 1.5 km later.

The route continues on the narrow bicycle path which runs between the road and the railway tracks — **2** in Aggsbach Markt bear left on **Dorfstraße**.

### Aggsbach Markt

pref x: 02712

ℹ **Marktgemeindeamt (Municipal office)**, Aggsbach 48, ☎ 214, @ ype663en

⛪ **Pfarrkirche (Parish church)**, Nr. 12, ☎ 213. Late Romanesque church from the 13th c.

After Aggsbach Markt continue down the bicycle path along the main road — **3** turn left into the side road towards **Groisbach** ride straight through the village to Willendorf.



To reach the Venus museum and the discovery site, turn left by the chapel. The museum lies next to the chapel, while the discovery site is reached to the right just after the railway underpass. However, the replica statue can also be seen from the route that crosses Willendorf straight ahead.

### Willendorf (Aggsbach Markt)

prefix: 02712

🏛 **Venusium**, Nr. 68, ☎ 214, ☎ 0676/5174546 ⊜ In the museum you will learn interesting facts about the finds of the excavations of the famous statuette. @ rjn261en

*When the Danube river railway was being built in 1908, workers found an 11-centimeter fertility figure in the ice-age loess near Willendorf. The limestone figure representing a plump naked female caused a sensation, and is regarded as an*

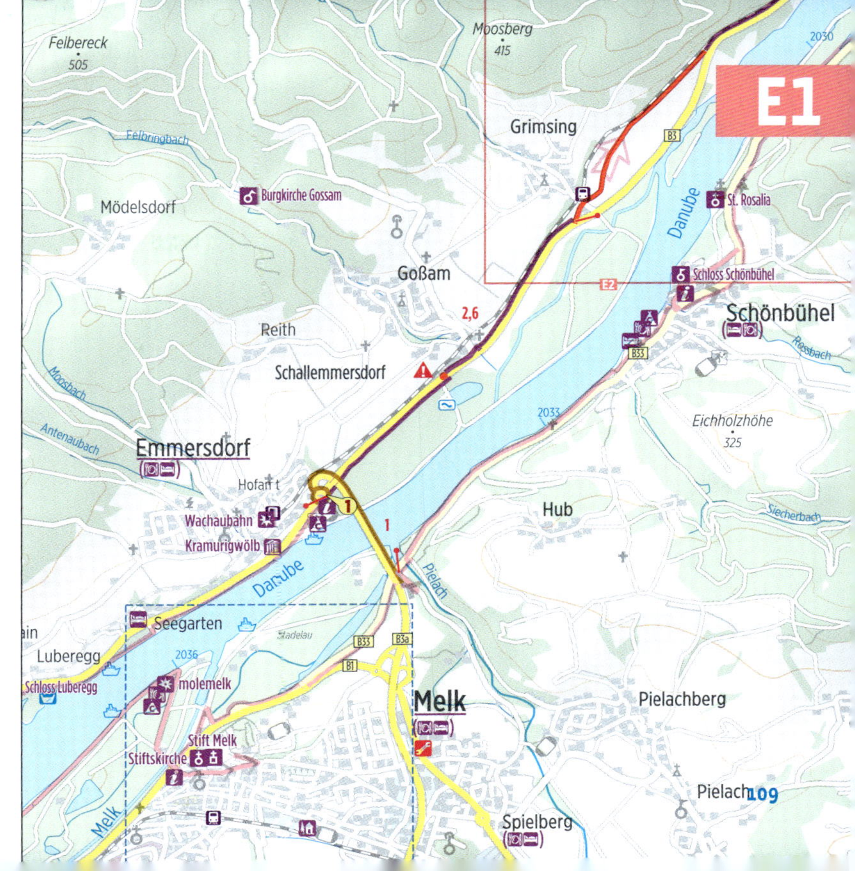

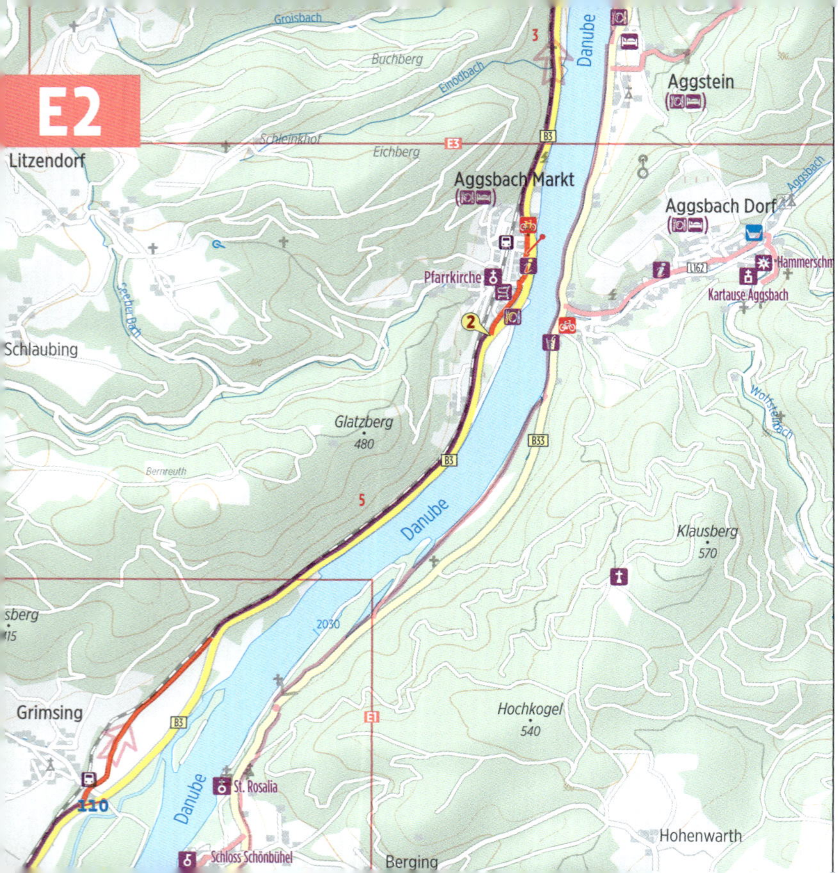

expression of female fertility, or a symbol of "magna mater." The Venus of Willendorf is considered the most aesthetically accomplished of more than 130 Paleolithic (old stone age) objects that have been found between southern France and Siberia.

Proceed straight ahead along a quiet lane through the vineyards ⁓ you pass straight through to **Schwallenbach** ⁓ at the end of the vineyards, continue on the bicycle path beside the main road ⁓ keep left into the side road, above you to the left lies the **Hinterhaus ruin** as you ride into Spitz ⁓ continue to the intersection, where you ride straight across into the **Hauptstraße** ⁓ at the fork keep right into the one-way street **Mittergasse** ⁓

 At the intersection with Rollfährestraße, it is possible to turn right towards the ferry to change to the south shore. To

*Monument at the site where the Willendorf Venus was found*

continue on the north shore, turn left here.

After the railway underpass turn right onto **Bahnhofstraße**, to reach the beautiful **Kirchplatz** ride straight ahead

## Spitz a. d. Donau

prefix: 02713

**ℹ Donau Niederösterreich Tourismus GmbH - Re (Tourist organisation of the Danube in Lower Austria)**, Schlossg. 3, ☎ 30060-60, @ vlf566en

**ℹ Tourist-Information (Tourist Info)**, Mitterg. 3a, ☎ 2363, @ iap632en

**⛴ Rollfähre Spitz-Arnsdorf (Ferry Spitz-Arnsdorf)**, ☎ 0650/2502103, ⏱ Apr, Oct Mon-Fri 6.15am-6pm, Sat, Sun/Fri 8.15am-6pm, May-Sept Mon-Fri 6.15am-7pm, Sat, Sun/Fri 8.15am-7.30pm. @ wnv613en

**⛴ Brandner Schiffahrt (Brandner shipping)**, Donau Bundesstr., ☎ 07433/259021. Daily scheduled trips through the Wachau between Melk and Krems, bicycle transport approx. 2 Euro. @ lfa716en

**⛴ DDSG Blue Danube**, Rollfährestr., ☎ 01/58880. Daily scheduled trips through the Wachau between Melk and Krems, bicycle transport approx. 2 Euro. @ qif331en

**🏛 Historischer Kaufmannsladen (Historical merchant's shop)**, Hauptstr. 2, ☎ 2074 © The trading house has housed a general store since 1736. The rooms are lovingly furnished with advertising materials, historical merchandise, detailed furnishings, documents and much more. @ vxy386en

**🏛♿ Schloss Erlahof - Schifffahrtsmuseum (Castle Erlahof - Shipping Museum)**, Auf der Wehr 21, ☎ 2246, ☎ 2187 The rich account of Danube navigation since Roman times goes into particular detail about the history of raftsmen, ship trains (or the "Hohe Nau") and Danube voyages. @ nga187en

**♿ Pfarrkirche Hl. Mauritius (St. Mauritius parish church)**, Kirchenpl., ☎ 2231. The late-gothic lower structure from the 14th/15th c. with a stately tower that is 100 years older. Interior mostly late-gothic architecture with baroque features like an altar by Kremser Schmidt (1799). @ hwv818en

**♿ Schloss Spitz-Niederhaus (Spitz-Niederhaus palace)**, Schlossg. 3. 17th c. Renaissance palace can be viewed only from the outside. Events. @ fvx571en

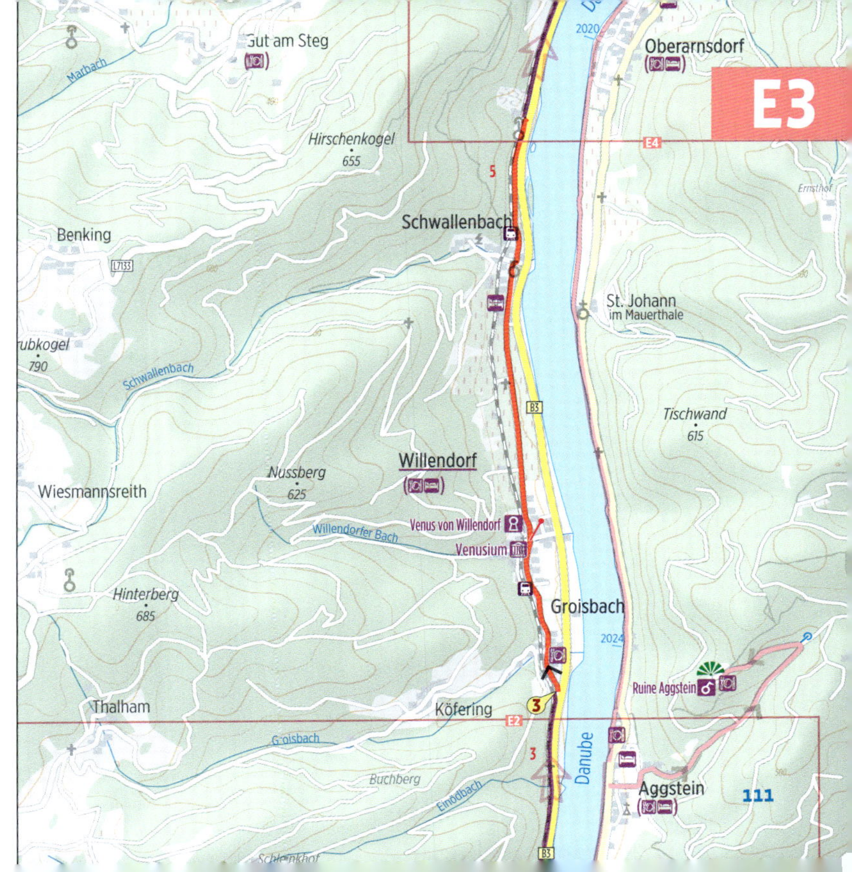

# Spitz

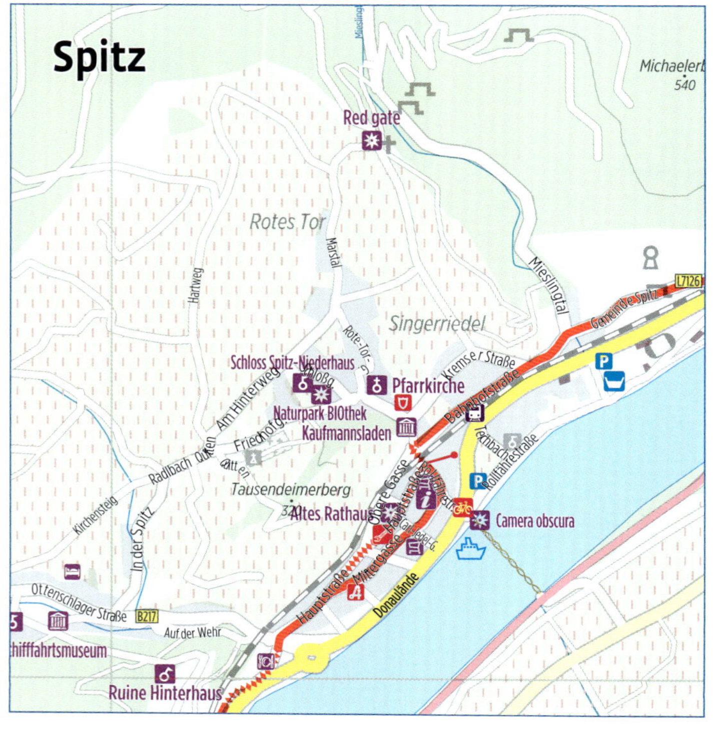



⚭ **Ruine Hinterhaus (Hinterhaus ruin)** ㉔ Built in the 13th c. on a rough outcropping, and extended in the 16th c. with round towers. The well-preserved ruin includes a large Romanesque keep, a Gothic yard, and Renaissance battlements. @ hno862en

✳ **Altes Rathaus (Old town hall)**, Hauptstr. 22. Part of a cluster of Gothic structures, including the Bürgerspital (hospital, from 1400), with a picturesque courtyard. @ qdn513en

✳ **Camera obscura auf der Rollfähre (Camera obscura on the ferry Spitz-Arnsdorf)**, ✆ 72935. Art installation by the Icelandic artist Olafur Eliasson creates a new and different way of looking at the Danube. @ lyy546en

✳ **Rotes Tor (Red gate)**. 20 min. walk north from the centre. Last of the seven defensive gates to be taken during the 30 years war. The name of the gate derives from the blood spilt here on both sides, but still proves to be a popular frame for romantic views of the Wachau. One of the best wine growing areas in the Wachau. @ oet683en

🛏 **Freibad (Outdoor swimming area)**, Mielingtal, ✆ 2289, @ olx648en

*Markt Spitz, population 2,000, lies at the foot of the Tausendeimerberg (thousand pails mountain), which is so named because the hill allegedly produces one thousand pails of wine (56,000 litres) in a good year.*

## Spitz to Krems      19 km

Follow **Bahnhofstraße** past the railway station ～ right on **Kremserstraße** past the Hotel Mariandl ～ after crossing the railway tracks continue along the left side of the main road ～ as you reach St. Michael, keep left into the lane before the church.

### St. Michael (Weißenkirchen in der Wachau)

⚭ **Wehrkirche St. Michael (St. Michael fortified church)**, St. Michael 7. The Gothic main church dates to around 1500, while the old parish building goes back another half a millennium, and is regarded as the oldest in the Wachau. The remarkable 7 rabbits on the presbytery's roof probably depict a hunt, but other fabulous explanations have also been proposed. @ eav317en

St. Michael fortified church

*The Wachau's best vineyards are located between Spitz and Dürnstein. The small Ritzlingbach stream is said to have lent its name to Riesling white wine. The local grape was then transplanted to the Rhine and later returned to the Wachau as the Rheinriesling.*

After the church the route takes you to the left along a quiet road between vineyards to Wösendorf. After the panoramic path along the Donaubreiten the route reaches **Wösendorf** — turn right at the church — **4** turn left at the next crossing street and follow the side street past **Joching**.

Continue along the street past vineyards and scattered houses to Weißenkirchen — ride straight across the crossroad — continue to the three-way intersection in the centre.

At the Rollfährestraße, turn right to the Danube ferry if you want to change to the south bank. Towards Dürnstein and Krems on the north bank, however, turn left.

Turn right after the railway crossing and ride up to the **Marktplatz** square at the foot of the fortified church.

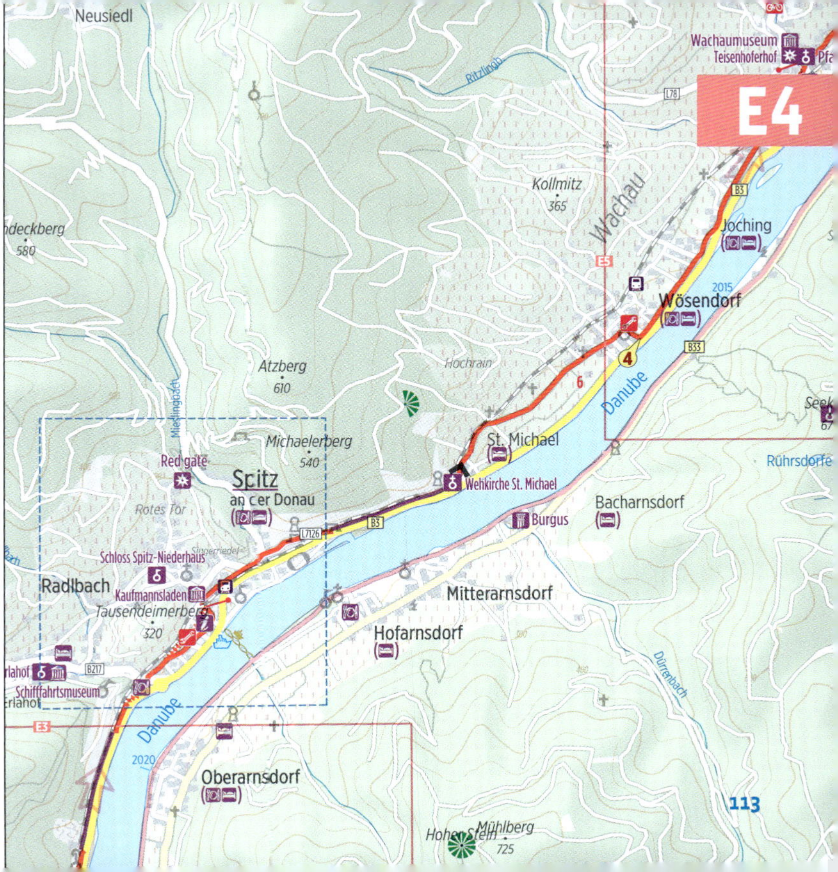

## Weißenkirchen in der Wachau

prefix: 02715

- **Tourist-Information (Tourist-Info)**, Wachaustr. 242, ✆ 2600, @ yst228en
- **Marktgemeindeamt (Municipal office)**, Rathauspl. 32, ✆ 2232, @ ghf256en
- **Rollfähre Weißenkirchen-St. Lorenz (Ferry)**, ✆ 2232, ⊘ April-Oct, Mon-Fri 8-11.45 and 13.30-18.45, Sat, Sun/Fri 8-18.45, @ qku122en
- **Wachaumuseum (Wachau museum)**, Weißenkirchen 177, ✆ 2268 ⊜ Part of the museum shows tools and equipment used by winemakers, and a historic wine-press, special exhibitions by various artists, @ aes612en
- **Pfarrkirche Mariä Himmelfahrt (Mariä Himmelfahrt parish church)**, Kremser Str. 3, ✆ 2203. The earliest parts of the church, which is situated above the town and surrounded by mostly-intact fortifications, were built around 1400. The interior combines late-gothic and baroque elements. @ dre831en
- **Teisenhofer- oder Schützenhof (Teisenhoferhof or Schützenhof)**, Marktpl. 177. An especially pretty arcaded courtyard in the Renaissance style dates to the second half of the 15th c. Seat of the Lower Austrian Wine Academy. @ snq518en
- **Naturbadestrand (Natural swimming beach)**

From the **Marktplatz** the route proceeds out of town past a pretty row of houses with several wine sampling and selling shops (Heurigenschenke) ⁓ **5** after the railway crossing ride on the bicycle path along the left side of the street ⁓ turn left after 1 km ⁓ onto a paved field road between the "Frauengärten" vineyards ⁓ after the vineyards back onto the bicycle path along the main road.

At the beginning of the village, the main route takes you right across the road and then down along the Danube bank on the

Treppelweg along Dürnstein. You can also stay on the left side of the road here and cycle through the village. This route is shown in orange on the map. Please note the push ban in the centre of the village due to the high pedestrian traffic. The best place to park your bike for a relaxed visit to this beautiful town is the car park by the boat landing stage a little south of the centre.

Before the village, turn right across the road and along the towpath below the village.

## Dürnstein

prefix: 02711

- **Gemeindeamt (Municipal office)**, Dürnstein 25, ✆ 219, @ sdn352en
- **Fremdenverkehrsverein Dürnstein/Loiben (Tourist office)**, Dürnstein 132, ✆ 200, @ ljv272en
- **Fähre Dürnstein-Rossatz (Ferry)**, ✆ 0676/3084750, ⊘ April/Oct, Fri-Sun/Fri 10am-5pm; May/Sept daily 9.30am-6pm; June-Aug Mon-Fri 9.30am-6pm, Sat/Sun 9am-6.30pm. @ boz554en
- **Brandner Schiffahrt (Shipping line)**, ✆ 07433/259021. Daily scheduled trips through the Wachau between Melk and Krems, bicycle transport approx. 2 Euro. @ gwq547en
- **DDSG Blue Danube (Shipping line)**, ✆ 01/58880. Daily scheduled trips through the Wachau between Melk and Krems, bicycle transport approx. 2 Euro. @ xof824en

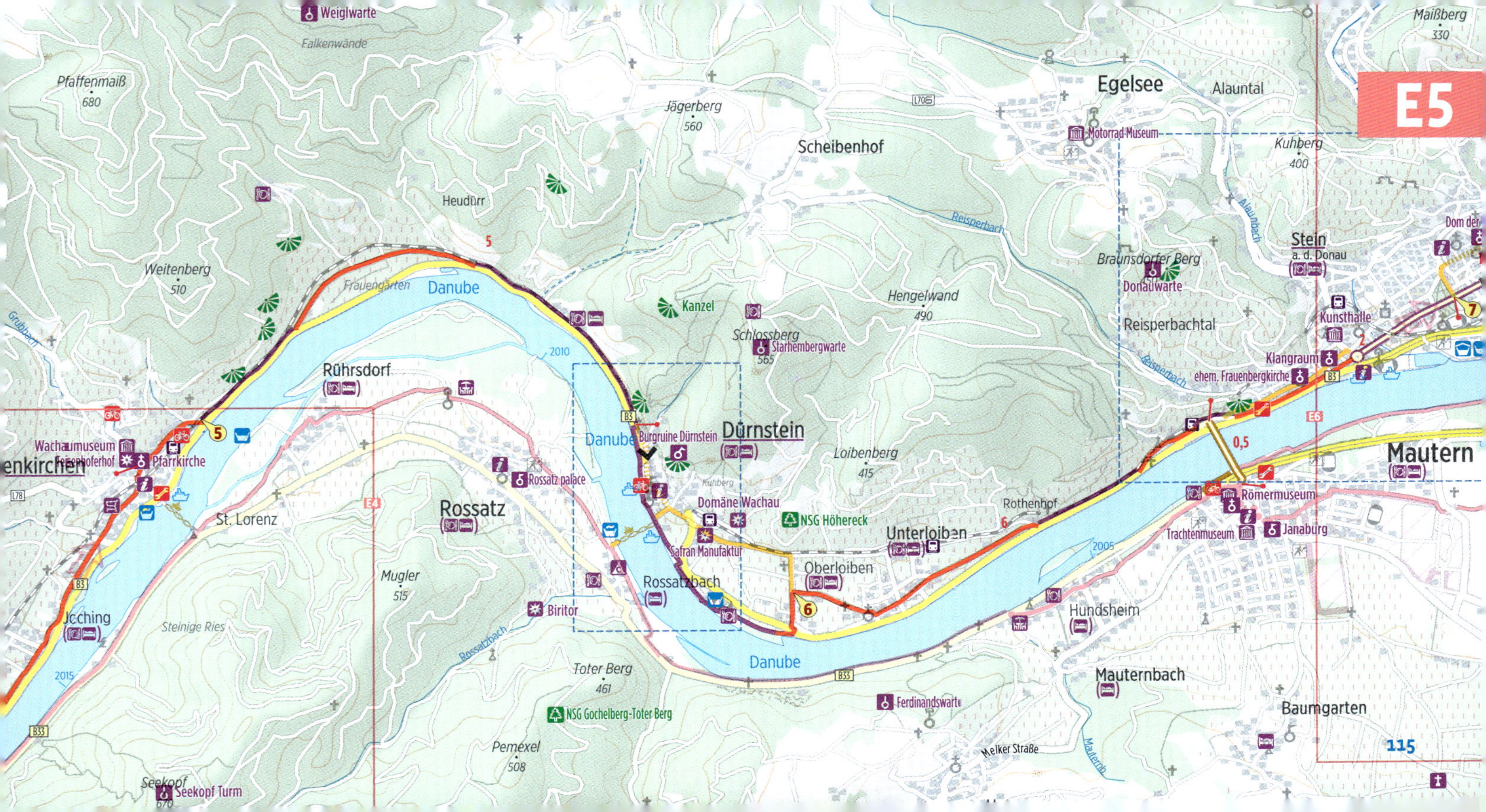

E5
Maißberg
330
Egelsee
Alauntal
Kuhberg
400
Scheibenhof
Jägerberg
560
L70
Motorrad-Museum
Weiglwarte
Falkenwände
Pfaffenmaiß
680
Heudürr
Reisperbach
Braunsdorfer Berg
Stein
a. d. Donau
Dom der
Weitenberg
510
Danube
Frauengärten
Kanzel
Hengelwand
490
Donauwarte
Reisperbachtal
Kunsthalle
5
2010
Schlossberg
565
Starhembergwarte
Klangraum
ehem. Frauenbergkirche
7
Rührsdorf
B3
Burgruine Dürnstein
Dürnstein
Loibenberg
415
E6
Wachaumuseum
Rosenhoferhof
5
Danube
Kuhberg
0,5
Mautern
Pfarrkirche
Rossatz palace
Domäne Wachau
NSG Höhereck
Rothenhof
Römermuseum
kenkirchen
St. Lorenz
Rossatz
E4
Safran Manufaktur
Unterloiben
6
Trachtenmuseum
Janaburg
L78
B3
Mugler
515
Rossatzbach
Oberloiben
2005
Jcching
Biritor
6
Hundsheim
B3
Steinige Ries
Toter Berg
461
Danube
B33
Mauternbach
2015
NSG Gochelberg-Toter Berg
Ferdinandswarte
Baumgarten
B33
Pemexel
508
Melker Straße
Seekopf
670
Seekopf Turm
115

**Stiftskirche Mariä Himmelfahrt (Mary's Assumption Abbey Church)**, ☎ 375. A masterpiece of Austrian baroque architecture, with its blue-white church tower (1733) is famous for how its complements the surrounding landscape. @ egu577en

**Stift Dürnstein (Dürnstein abbey)**, Nr. 1, ☎ 375 ⑦ Augustine abbey established in 1410 and converted to baroque style 1710-33 by significant artists. Includes one of the most beautiful abbey courtyards in Austria. Since 2019, the new exhibition on the themes of "the good", "the beautiful" and "the true" has also been showing spaces that have not been accessible to the public until now. @ fcr383en

**Schloss Dürnstein (New palace)**, Dürnstein 2, ☎ 212. Emperor Leopold was also a guest in this palace. September 1683 he received the news of the liberation of Vienna from the Turks right here. After the noble Starhemberg family sold the castle in 1937, it was converted into a hotel. @ rbc861en

**Burgruine Dürnstein (Dürnstein ruin)** ㉔ Built around the middle of the 12th century. Main hall and chapel added as the original for-tification was converted to a palace. King Richard the Lionhearted of England was held captive here in winter 1192-93. @ ixg835en

**Domäne Wachau**, Nr. 107, ☎ 371. Built 1714, with stucco interiors and ceiling frescos presumably by J. Prandtauer. A variety of wines can be tasted in the winery's vinotheque directly on the cycle path. Guided tours of the winery are offered. @ pev257en

**Wachauer Safranmanufaktur (Saffron manufactory)**, Dürn-stein 76, ☎ 0676/3322116. The saffron crocus, the most expensive spice in the world, is cultivated and harvested in abandoned wine terraces and then processed into delicious saffron products at the Wachau Saffron Manufactory. These can also be enjoyed in the saffron café at Dürnstein railway station. @ cof767en

**Kuenringerbad (Outdoor pool)**, Am Parkpl. 1, ☎ 320, @ rqp668en

*The romantic ruin of Dürnstein already heralds the most famous of all Wachau towns. King Richard the Lionheart of England was once held prisoner in the ruins, which have been abandoned since the Thirty Years' War. Some-what hidden away is Dürnstein Abbey, widely known for its blue church tower on the Danube.*

**You can cross over to the south bank below Dürnstein with the bicycle and passenger ferry.**

Take the cycle path past the boat landing stage and the **Kuenringerbad** on the right ⸺ at the height of Oberloiben, cross the main road at the pedestrian traffic lights ⸺ turn left across the car park and immediately right ⸺ straight on through Oberloiben.

### Oberloiben (Dürnstein)

**NSG Höhereck (Nature reserve Höhereck).** The nature reserve has been a conservation area since 2008 and is part of the flora-fauna habitat Wachau and the bird sanctuary Wachau-Jauerling. @ ilv147en

**6** Shortly before the end of the village, turn right at the crossroads – through the vineyards – in Unterloiben straight on – pass the church on the left – turn left into the village centre.

### Unterloiben (Dürnstein)

*After about 1 km there is a cliff marked with an odd inscription: I. Kyselak. That was the name of a travel-happy Biedermeier fellow who made a bet with friends that he would make himself known throughout the kingdom in the course of three years of travel. Armed with paint and a paint-brush, he scrawled his name in countless unlikely places throughout the land, and won his bet within a year-and-a-half. According to one anecdote, the early graffiti artist was summoned to the Kaiser to explain his actions. After he had chastised and dismissed Kyselak, the Kaiser was stunned to discover that Kyselak had managed to leave his name on the Kaiser's own desk.*

Follow the street straight out of the village and ride between the vineyards – the route returns to a bicycle path along the main road – you pass a sign marking the end of the Wachau – keep left onto the street through **Förthof** – continue on the bicycle path past the end of the bridge.

**TIP** Take the bridge across the Danube if you wish to continue on the south bank or reach the village of Mautern or the excursion to Göttweig Abbey.

To cycle along the north bank to Stein and Krems, stay straight ahead at the height of the Mautern bridge on the left-hand cycle path – on the **Steiner Donaulände** right next to the main road along the town centre.

**TIP** Where the Steiner Landstraße turns left into the old town of Stein, the cycle path ends and you continue on the Steiner Donaulände between the main road and the old town. A traffic-calmed alternative is to cycle through the old town on Steiner Landstraße. This is open to cyclists. However, the cobblestone road is a bit bumpy and you will encounter many pedestrians.

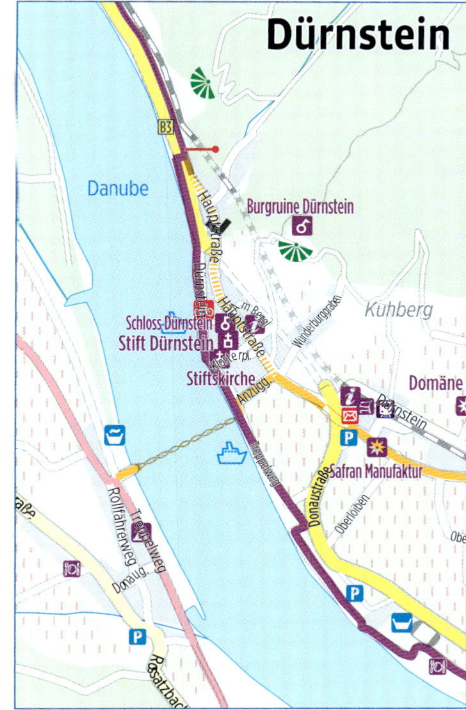

Stein a. d. Donau

### Stein (Krems a. d. Donau)

prefix: 02732

- **Kunstmeile Krems Besucherzentrum (Tourist Information)**, Museumspl. 5, ☎ 908010, @ tnj681en
- **Schifffahrts- u. Welterbezentrum Wachau (Shipping and World Heritage Centre)**, Welterbepl. 1, ☎ 78282, @ hlj775en
- **Brandner Schiffahrt (Brandner shipping)**, Welterbepl. 1, ☎ 07433/259021. Landing stages of the Wachau route: Krems (Station 24), Weißenkirchen (Station 17), Spitz (Station 15), Emmersdorf (Station 38) and Melk (Station 10). Bicycle transport approx. 2 Euro. @ trc728en
- **DDSG Blue Danube (Shipping line)**, Welterbepl. 1, ☎ 58880, ☎ 01/78282, @ tfh575en
- **Karikaturmuseum (Cartoon museum)**, Museumspl. 3, ☎ 908010 The Museum of Caricature is Austria's first museum for satire, caricature and political art. Includes an evolving exhibition of about 200 works by Manfred Deix on the first storey. @ jca871en
- **Kunsthalle (Art Gallery)**, Museumspl. 5, ☎ 908010 The international exhibition venue shows contemporary art since 1945. A second location is in Krems in the former Dominican Church. @ hrb216en
- **Landesgalerie Niederösterreich (State Gallery Lower Austria)**, Museumspl. 1, ☎ 908010 The architecturally spectacular new museum building sees itself as a dynamic centre for Austrian art. A combination of Lower Austrian state and private collections. Exhibitions will give space to the present and its themes. @ xgk541en
- **Ehem. Frauenbergkirche (Former Frauenberg church)**, Frauenberg 23 Built in 1380. The tower has a large network of arches. Renovated as a war memorial in 1963. @ iwd852en
- **Pfarrkirche St. Nikolaus (St. Nikolaus parish church)**, Steiner Landstr. 55, ☎ 21190. The 3-nave church dates from the 15th c. Ceiling frescos and altar paintings by Martin Johann (Kremser) Schmidt were retained during a re-gothicization of the church in 1901. @ bqq743en
- **Klangraum Krems Minoritenkirche (Soundspace Minorites church)**, Minoritenpl. 4, ☎ 908030, ☎ 908033. The 3-nave pillar-basilica is among the earliest arched-roof constructions built by the German mendicant order (1264). Noteworthy: The 14th c. frescos. Today the church serves as a gallery for modern art projects as well as international renowned concerts. @ ruh888en
- **Stadttore Krems-Stein (City gates)**. The town was surrounded by a protective wall, a ring of walls, until the 19th century. Krems Gate: was built in 1470 and renewed around 1600. Reben Tor: offers a magnificent view of the old town and is not far from the Frauenberg church. Linzer Tor: with a high, massive gate and was built in the 15th century.
- **Steiner Landstraße**. The well-preserved old buildings and the inserted squares with baroque statues and columns give the street a rare charme.

Shortly before the large roundabout, the left-hand cycle path becomes a bidirectional cycle path and thus leads left along the roundabout directly right past the Kunsthalle Krems then right across the road and on the right-hand cycle path to Krems — you will reach the Stadtpark (city park) **7**.

To reach the historic centre of Krems, turn left on Utzstraße after the city park, then keep right at the intersection before turning right through the large town gate into the pedestrian zone. Follow the Obere and Untere Landstraße, then turn right at the regulated crossing by the Krems River. You rejoin the main route on Austraße after the next intersection.

# Krems a. d. Donau

prefix: 02732

- **ℹ Wachau Info-Center (Tourist Info Wachau)**, Körnermarkt 14, ℂ 82676, @ jhd686en
- **🏛 Kunsthalle Krems - Dominikanerkirche (Art Gallery - Dominican Church)**, Körnermarkt 14, ℂ 908010 ⓦ Second location of the Kunsthalle Krems with exhibitions of contemporary art after 1945 in the former Dominican Church from the 13th century. @ lhb234en
- **🏛 museumkrems**, Körnermarkt 14, in the former Dominican monastery, ℂ 801567 ⓦ The exhibitions in the historic building take you through 30,000 years of cultural history of the wine town. Some secrets from the production of the famous Krems mustard are revealed and exhibitions of contemporary art are shown in the gallery. @ qdt467en
- **⛪ Bürgerspitalkirche (Hospital church)**, Obere Landstr. 5, ℂ 83285, ℂ 0676/826633192. Based on the system of inward facing buttresses erected in 1470. Worth seeing are the sweeping window measurements and the multiform iron doors of the Gothic sacrament niche. @ aiq557en
- **⛪ Dom der Wachau (Wachau cathedral)**, Pfarrpl. 5, ℂ 83285. The parish church of St. Vitus, which appears massive from the outside, was completed by Cypriano Biasino in 1630. Along with the collegiate church of Göttweig, it is one of the first examples of baroque church construction in Austria. @ ohx856en
- **⛪ Dominikanerkirche (Dominican church)**, Körnermarkt 14, ℂ 801567. The basilica was completed around 1265 and is one of the early vaults of the German mendicant orders. After the dissolution of the monastery (1785), the building was used as a button factory, granary or theatre, and since 1891 it has housed the town museum, which today operates under the name museumkrems, @ uby328en
- **⛪ Piaristenkirche Unsere liebe Frau (Piarist church)**, Piaristeng. 1, ℂ 82092, ℂ 0664/75125204. Built 1475-1515 under the influence of Viennese architectural trends, with a handsome staircase and a 3-nave main hall. As in the Viennese style, the pillars are

decorated with statues. All altar paintings by Martin Johann Schmidt. @ ktp525en
- **🏛 Kloster Und (Und Monastery)**, Undstr. 6, ℂ 0664/9112121. Begun 1614, rebuilt after a fire in 1656 and dissolved 1796, Fresco by Daniel Gran von 1756. Restored in 2002 and 2007, now used for events. @ irb224en
- **🏰 Gozzoburg (Gozzo castle)**, Hoher Markt 11, ℂ 801-571, ⏱ Visits only as part of guided tours: Sat, Sun & Fri 2pm. Built 1260-70 in the style of an Italian town palace by Gozzo, a wealthy magistrate and citizen of Krems. The especially beautiful hall and the high quality frescos, discovered 2006, make this the most significant secular structure of this period in Austria. @ anm778en
- **✳ Bürgerhäuser (Town houses)**, Untere und Obere Landstr./ Körnermarkt/Margarethenstr. The townscape is mainly dominated by 16th century buildings with oriels, reliefs and sgraffiti on the façades, which are occasionally covered with attractive baroque stucco.
- **✳ Rathaus (Town hall)**, Pfarrpl., ℂ 801540. Donated to the town by Ulrich von Dachsberg in 1453, beautiful Renaissance columns from 1549 in the entrance hall. The oriels with rich coat-of-arms reliefs and decorative ornamentation are particularly worth seeing and date from the same period.
- **✳ Steiner Tor (Steiner Gate)**, Stadtgraben. Built 1480 with 4 Gothic towers, baroque additions 1754. One of Krems' old city gates, today the town's best-known landmark.

*Krems, Steiner Tor*

✳ **Winzer Krems (Winemaker Krems)**, Sandgrube 13, ☎ 85511-33 ⓦ During the wine experience tour of the traditional Krems winery, you will enjoy a unique wine sensation for all senses along the eight stations. ⓦ epi646en

🛁 **Badearena (Bathing arena)**, Strandbadstr. 5, ☎ 801636, ☎ 801638, ⓦ grp131en

*Krems is regarded as the oldest city in Lower Austria. Its unique character is shaped by the confusion of baroque town houses with Renaissance courtyards, Gothic baywindows and chapels nestled into a maze of narrow medieval streets and alleys that crisscross the old city centre. The Steiner Tor (Gate) is the town's best-known landmark, with its tall baroque tower surrounded by pointed little medieval spires. Behind the gate rises the Wachtberg, on which stands one of Krems' most beautiful churches, the Piarist Church. The church can be reached via the partly roofed ancient Piarist staircase. It was built in 1475 in the Gothic style and houses a high altar by Martin Johann Schmidt, known as Kremser Schmidt. In addition to the excellently maintained old town, Krems today also enjoys the reputation of an innovative city with novel scientific institutions and artistic projects.*

### Krems to Altenwörth power station      21.2 km

For the main route, continue straight along the **Ringstraße**, past the nearby railway station ⟿ turn right after the Krems and past the cycle shop ⟿ after a while, cross the Krems by means of a pedestrian and cyclist bridge and continue cycling along the right-hand side of the **Rechte Kremszeile** on a cycle path that runs alongside the road.


Just before the road bridge a bicycle path leads away to the right. This path will take you onto the bridge across the Danube to connect with the main route along the south bank.


Just north of Krems lies the wine village of Rohrendorf.

### Rohrendorf bei Krems

✳ **Kellergasse (Cellar lane)**, Lindobelg. The longest cellar lane in Austria, with 72 press houses and cellar tubes, extends over a length of 1,650 m. Some of the cellars date from the 14th/15th century, but most of them date from after 1848. ⓦ xrr875en

Now straight ahead on the footpath and cycle path along the Krems.


**8** At the next intersection, cross the road with a lot of caution due to the high traffic density and the difficult turning situation of car traffic.

Continue straight ahead on the bicycle path beside the Krems river ⟿ you pass an industrial area and transport terminal ⟿ cross the Krems just before the next road bridge and continue on the other river bank ⟿ after another 2.5 km cross the river again as you reach a small road coming from Theiß ⟿ follow the path as

# Krems

Krems
Kamp-Thaya-March-Radweg
Kunberg
400
Wachbergstraße
St.adtgraben
Piaristenkirche
Dom der Wachau
museumkrems
Gozzoburg
Rathaus
Hoher Markt
Dominikanerkirche
Bürgerspitalkirche
Steiner Tor
Dreifaltigkeitspl.
Hafnerplatz
Südtiroler Platz
Wiener Straße
Hohensteinstraße
Wachaustr.
Linke Kremszeile
Rechte Kremszeile
Rechter Kremszeile
Mitterweg
Hohensteinstraße
Wilhering
Missongasse
Sankt-Paul-Gasse
Pointgasse
Hafenstraße
Weinzierl
Klomserstr.
Mazzettistraße
Am Rosenhügel
Kögelweg
Kögelweg
orfer Berg
auwarte
Alauntalstr.
Reißgasse
Gewerkgasse
Wiedeng.
Alauntalstraße
Gerlg.
Am Goldberg
Philosophensteig
Donauniversität Krems
Kloster Und
Kunsthalle
Karikaturmuseum
Landesgalerie Niederösterreich
Steiner Donaulände
Kremser Tor
Welterbe-Platz
Klangraum
Rebentor
ehem. Frauenbergkirche
St. Nikolaus
Linzer Tor
Steiner Landstr.
Steiner Donaulände
Sepp-Puchinger-Promenade
Reisperbachtalstraße
Hintere Fahrstr.
Rathausplatz
Mautener Brücke
Dr.-Karl-Dorrek-Straße
Meyereckstraße
Kaiser-Friedrich-Str.
Schillerstr.
Ringstraße
Ringstraße
Ringstraße
Bahnhofplatz
Bahnhof
Martin-Luther-Platz
Kerschbaumerstraße
Strandbadstraße
Badearena
Dr.-Franz-Riel-Promenade
Fritz-Landertinger-Promenade
Am Schutzdamm
Treppelweg
Danube
Edmund-Hofbauer-Straße
Am Frachtenbahnhof
W.-Gause-Str.
Dr.-J.-M.-Eder-Gasse
Dr.-A.-Nagl-G.
Bertschingerstraße
Göttweigergasse
Dr.-Gschmeidler-Straße
Mitteraustraße
Austraße
Exerzierplatz
Am Exerzierplatz
Beethovenstr.
Langenloiser Straße
Wiener Straße
Sigleithenstraße
Lehnergasse
Antonig.
Florianig.
Schießstattgasse
Pulverturmg.
Stiftgasse
Kremsstr.
Wienerstr.
Ringstr.
0,5
121
2,5
1,2
7
2
E6
E5
B33
B3
H
F

E6
Maißberg
330
210
Am Steindl
In der Leithen
Winzer Krems
Kellergasse
Lindoe-Ig.
L45
Oberer Mitterweg
Rohrendorf
Krems
a. d. Donau
Kamp-Thaya-March-Radweg
B35
Landersdorf
Neuweidling
Stratzdorf
Grunddorf
Wiener Straße
B37
Lerchenfeld
Neustift
a.d. Donau
S5
Dom der Wachau
1,2
1,2
8
Ringstraße
Altweidling
S5
0,8
7
Schlickendorf
Badearena
S5
Krems harbour
Theiß
Danube
2,5
2000
5,5
Donaudor
Treppelweg
E5
B33
Krems
E7
Stockgraben
3,2
Fahrbh2
9
L100
Palt
Danube
Brunnkirchen
Thallern
Wurmsaumlacke
Treppelweg
S33
1995
1990
122
Angem
B37a
Sprinzenberg
280
Marillen Erlebnisweg
Pfarrkirche
Hollenburg
Furth
bei Göttweig
Natura Trail Löss und Wein
Oberfucha

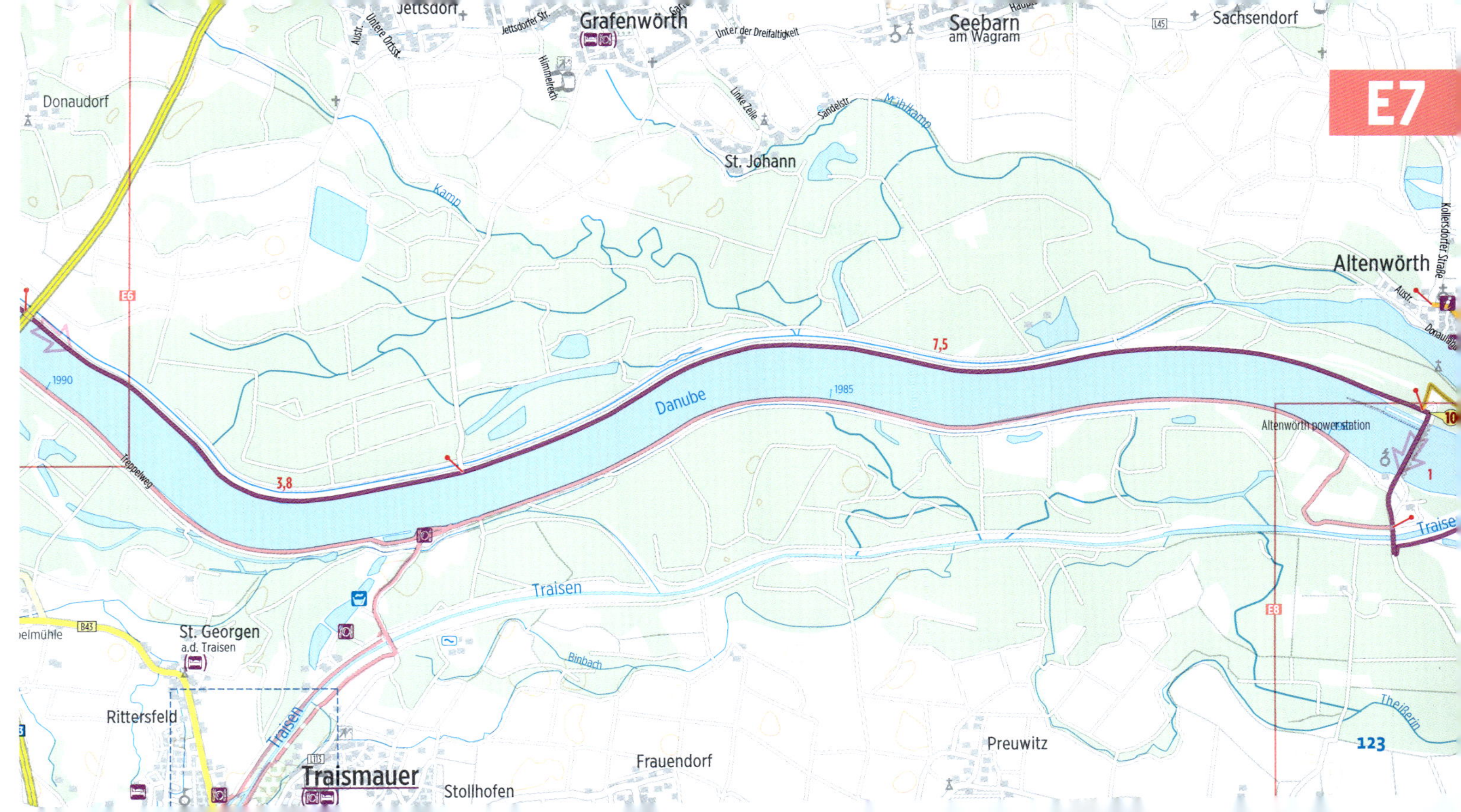

E7
Jettsdorf
Grafenwörth
Seebarn am Wagram
Sachsendorf
Donaudorf
Unter der Dreifaltigkeit
St. Johann
Mühlkamp
Sandelstr.
Linke Zeile
Jettsdorfer Str.
Untere Ortsst.
Himmelreich
Kamp
Altenwörth
Kollersdorfer Straße
Austr.
Donaulänge
E6
7,5
1990
1985
Danube
Altenwörth power station
Treppelweg
3,8
1
10
Traisen
Traisen
Traisen
E8
Binbach
St. Georgen
a.d. Traisen
B43
B43
Theißerin
Rittersfeld
Preuwitz
L113
123
Traismauer
Frauendorf
Stollhofen

it winds its way through riparian forest and crosses two small river arms ~ after 700 m you reach the towpath on the Danube **9** ~ the towpath offers a smooth asphalt surface for fast and easy kilometres to the **10** Altenwörth hydroelectric power station.


> **TIP** Those wishing to take a break in quiet surroundings can turn left by the power station and follow the path into the nearby village.

### Altenwörth (Kirchberg am Wagram)

**ℹ** Heimat- und Fremdenverkehrsverein Altenwörth/Gigging (Tourist Office), Hauptstr. 4, ☏ 0681/10277829, @ sha167en

### Altenwörth power station to Tulln          21.4 km

The bicycle route between Altenwörth and Tulln only runs along the southern (right) bank of the Danube. To cross the river ride up to the bridge across the power station barrage.

> **TIP** You can get across the power plant through the side door of the power plant gate, which is not locked during the day. At other times, use the intercom.

After crossing the Danube, ride straight ahead ~ turn left immediately after crossing the bridge over the river Traisen ~ follow the tributary back out to the Danube.

*Two power generating stations now dominate the landscape as the route proceeds downstream: the waste incinerating thermal plant at Dürnrohr and the never-completed nuclear power plant at Zwentendorf. In the background the northern fringes of the Vienna Forest can be seen.*

The path branches off to the right and leads you away from the Danube through the shady floodplain forest ~ after the footbridge over a branch of the Danube, keep left and return to the Danube to immediately turn right again into the floodplain forest ~ at the asphalt road on the left and past the nuclear power plant ~ after this, the path joins an access road and leads over a bridge ~ **11** turn left onto the towpath after crossing a bridge ~ ride along the river past the town of Zwentendorf.

### Zwentendorf an der Donau

prefix: 02277

**ℹ** Marktgemeindeamt (Municipal office), Rathauspl. 4, ☏ 2209, @ oxk668en

**⛪** Wallfahrtskirche Maria Ponsee (Maria Ponsee pilgrimage church), Maria Ponsee 1, Maria Ponsee (Zwentendorf an der Donau). It was built in the 12th century from a chapel and has some special features: High altar with a life-size statue of the Virgin Mary, which was washed ashore in 1720, a unique defensive tower made of Roman quarry stones and an early Baroque extension designed by Jakob Prandtauer. @ ylv613en

**✳** Atomkraftwerk Zwentendorf (Nuclear power plant), Sonnenweg 1, ☏ 02236/2000 Ⓒ Austria's only nuclear power plant that never went into operation is, along with Hainburg, a symbol of success for the domestic environmental protection movement after it was shut down by referendum in 1978. @ jwp444en

**▱** Badesee Dürnrohr (Swimming lake), Dürnrohrer Hauptstr., ☏ 0699/10700022, @ ekg358en

**▱** Hallenbad (Swimming hall), Schlossg. 5, ☏ 2255, @ bxp755en

## Shipping on the Danube

*Navigation of the Danube began with "naufahren" – the art of guiding heavy, freight-loaded flat-bottom barges downriver on the Danube's current. Most of these ships never returned to their harbours of origin, and instead landed with the "plättenschinder" who chopped them into firewood. But first they had to survive the journey downstream with its many hazards. Many merchants even unloaded their cargoes and transported them overland past the dangerous narrows in the Greiner Struden.*

*A growing commerce in grains and wine from eastern regions created a demand for transports upriver, in which the barges where hauled against the current by teams of horses. The arduous trip from Vienna to Linz took more than 3 weeks; and another 8 days to reach Passau from Linz. The craftsmen who built the vessels that plied the Danube were called "schopper." Every river develops its own kinds of vessels. The Danube's boat and barges originally consisted of various simple "plätten" and "mutzen." Then came the "gamsen" that were used especially on the Inn river to haul gravel before being sent downriver to the "plättenschinder" when they were too worn out for heavy loads. Around 1850 the Danube's most elegant type of ship was developed, the sleek "siebnerin."*

Follow the path along the Danube past Zwentendorf — turn right before a concrete building — after a short distance left towards **Kleinschönbichl** — you pass between the village and the harbour — the path takes you to the right by the small stream — cross the stream at the next bridge and follow the bicycle path next to the main road to Pischelsdorf — turn left by the first houses of the village.

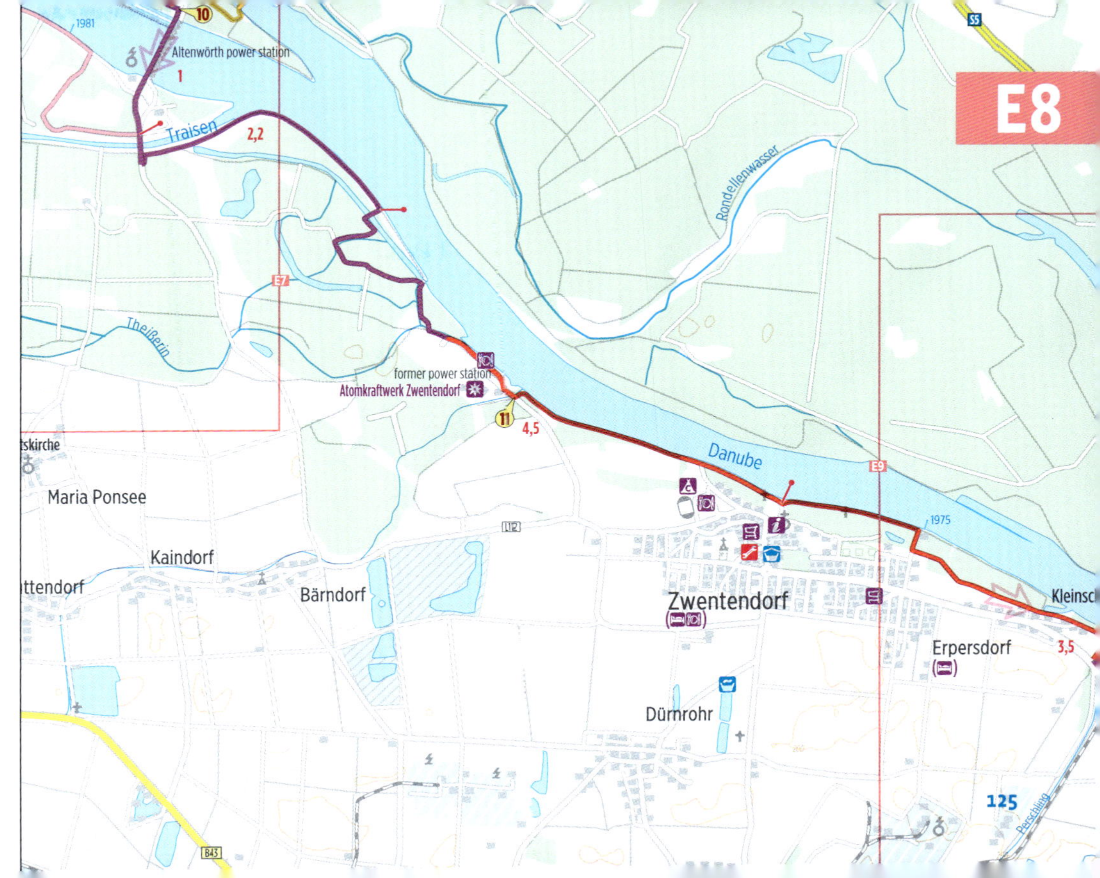

Tulln

## Pischelsdorf (Zwentendorf an der Donau)

Along the outskirts of Pischelsdorf ~ turn left at the T-junction before the stream ~ then right over stream **12** ~ immediately left ~ underpass the L 112 state road ~ now follow the path with a winding course ~ in Langenschönbichl at the main road straight ahead ~ straight through the village

## Langenschönbichl

At the end of the village turn left towards **Kronau** ~ follow the quiet road past fields

and forest to Kronau ~ continue straight ahead through Kronau ~ straight ahead into the cul-de-sac and residents' road, which later becomes a cycle path ~ follow the cycle path through the underpass ~ keep left and up to the embankment path along the river Große Tulln ~ turn left on the bank ~ pass under the B 19 ~ after the next bridge undercrossing, turn left to the bridge and over the Große Tulln ~ **13** immediately left again.


From here you can ride directly to the Tulln gardens, simply continue straight from the bridge and turn left at the roundabout.

The main route follows the path along the Große Tulln to the Danube where it follows the river bank into the "garden city" of Tulln.


S-Bahn trains to Vienna depart from Tulln train station.

## Tulln an der Donau

prefix: 02272

**Donau Niederösterreich Tourismus GmbH - Regionalbüro Tullner Donauraum-Wagram (Tourist Info)**, Minoritenpl. 2, ☎ 67566-0, @ dbq487en

**Egon Schiele Geburtshaus (Egon Schiele Birthplace)**, Bahnhofstr. 69, ☎ 690135 @ The birthplace of the world-famous artist is designed as a walk-in world of experience. In stylishly furnished rooms, visitors can feel how a family lived at the end of the 19th century. The family history of the Schieles is illuminated with the use of numerous media. @ akm452en

**Egon Schiele Museum (Egon-Schiele-Museum)**, Donaulände 28, ☎ 64570 @ On display are around 60 original oil paintings, watercolours and drawings from the first creative phases of the artist of the century. The exhibition documents Schiele's development up to the founding of the Neukunstgruppe in 1909. @ nyf113en

**Österr. Zuckermuseum (Sugar museum)**, Minoritenpl. 1, ☎ 0664/1106133 @ Located in the attic of the Minorite monastery, Austria's sweetest museum documents the development of sugar production from the cane sugar mill to the modern sugar factory. @ yvx624en

**Römermuseum (Roman museum)**, Marc Aurel Park 1b, ☎ 690189 @ Original artefacts and exhibits about military and civilian life in the Roman encampment "Comagenis" between about 90-488 AD. @ shu416en

**Minoritenkirche (Minorite church)**, Minoritenpl. 1, ☎ 6900. The abbey church was built 1732-39, with stylistically unified interior decoration and excellent altar statuary, baroque crypt and an old hermitage with walls decorated with shells, stones and bones. @ tnk116en

**Stadtpfarrkirche St. Stephan (St. Stephan parish church)**, Wiener Str. 20, ☎ 623380. With its Ottonian-Romanesque core,

E9
Trübensee
Mollersdorf
S5
B19
E8
1975
Plackenwasser
Danube
Kleinschönbichl
Danube
1970
Erpersdorf
3,5
Donau-Chemie
E10
14
B19
1966
1,4
Schiff Regentag
Nibelungendenkmal
Stadtpfarrkirche
Langenschönbichl
3,2
3
Die Garten Tulln
Wasserpark
12
L2148
Pischelsdorf
Messegel.
4
Kronau
13
Neusiedl
L112
Asparn
Große Tulln
Alter Perschlinglauf
Perschling
319
P
P
127

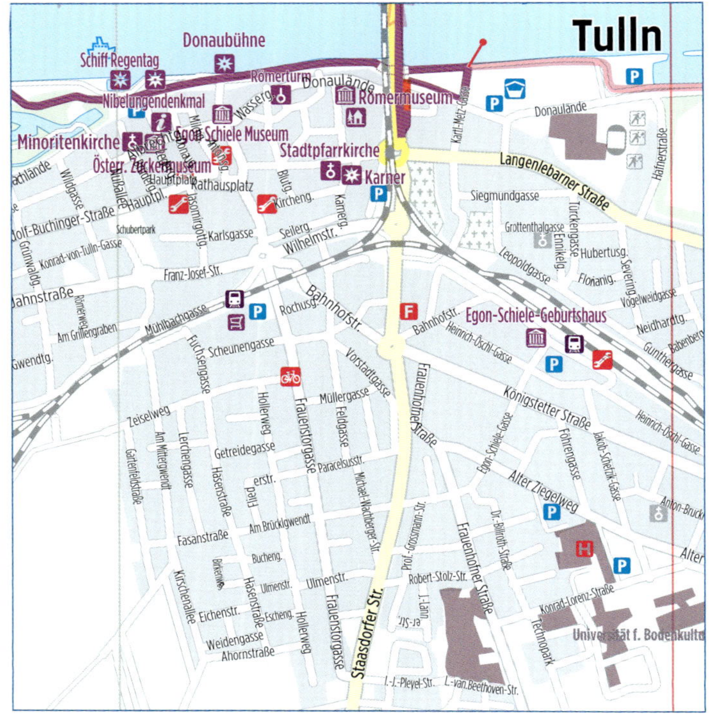


Gothic choir, Baroque towers and interior decoration, the church combines several architectural styles. It is unusual that the two church towers have different owners: The parish owns the south tower, but the north tower belongs to the municipality. This was the home of the city watchman, who used to ring bells to warn the people of Tulln of fires in the city area. @ bnb835en

**Römerturm (Roman tower)**, Donaulände 38, ☎ 62338. Inspection only possible from the outside. The Roman tower was the flanking tower of the Roman camp Comagena and dates back to around 300 AD. The Roman walls have been preserved up to the base of the roof, making the tower one of the few fully preserved ancient buildings north of the Alps. @ ceb356en

**Hauptplatz (City centre)**. The most striking buildings on the main square are the district administration built in 1891 in the style of the Vienna Ringstrasse buildings and a Renaissance building with Venetian battlements. In the middle of the square a baroque Trinity column can be seen.

**Schiff „Regentag" (Ship "Regentag" ("rainy day"))**, Gästehafen, ☎ 690135 © The Aus-

trian artist Friedensreich Hundertwasser lived and painted on the 100-year-old wooden sailing motor ship for more than 10 years. @ dgp462en

**Tullner Karner**, Kircheng., ☎ 62338. The Karner with his eleven corners lies directly behind the city parish church St. Stephan and is a jewel of the late Romanesque architecture, which looks for its equals in whole Europe. The magnificent funnel portal literally draws the visitor inside and thus into times long past. @ vlg712en

**Nibelungendenkmal (Nibelungen monument, Egon-Schiele monument, Marc Aurel monument)**. The monument is located along the Donaulände. @ gvb881en

**Die Garten Tulln (The Tulln Gardens)**, Am Wasserpark 1, ☎ 68188 (7d) 70 show and model gardens, ecological garden ideas, barrier-free treetop path, adventure and nature playground, events, seminars and children's programme. @ isa522en

**Wasserpark mit Bootsverleih (Boat rental in the Waterpark)**, Seerosenbrücke, ☎ 0664/80690440 (7d) The natural floodplain forest was created in the course of the Danube

E10
E11
E9
Perzendorf
Neumühle
Zaina
Schmida
Schmida
Stockerauer Alm
S5
Danube
6,5
1955
4,2
Alte Naufahrt
Donau
14
1,4
Stromsiedlung
Muckendorf
a.d. Donau
Zeiselmau
Danube
1960
1962
Unteraigen
Langenlebarn
Schiff Regentag
Nibelungendenkmal
Stadtpfarrkirche
Rafelswörth
Kleine Tulln
Oberaigen
Rainbow's End
B14
B19
L2152
Tulln
Wipfing
Fliegerhorst
P
P
P
L2134
129
Wolfpassing

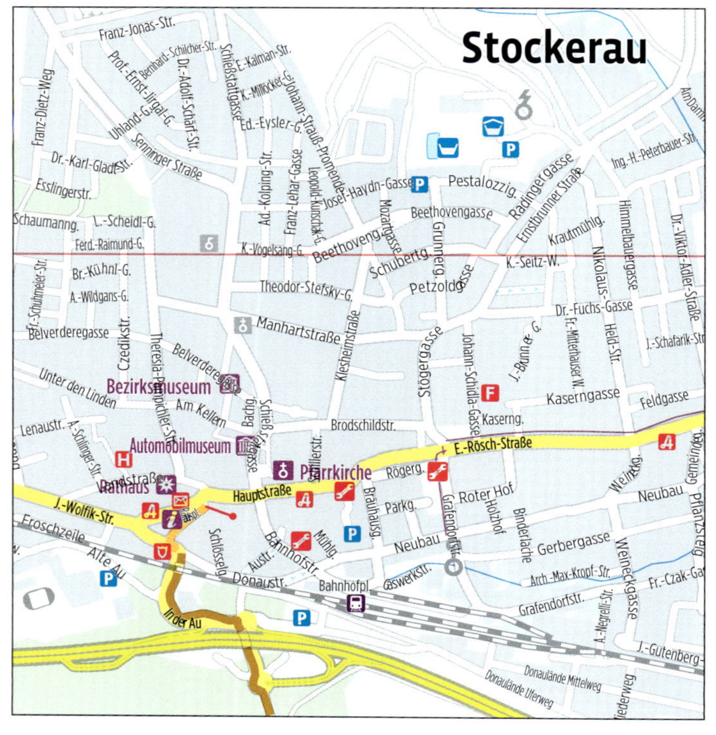




regulation at the end of the 19th century and was later revitalised for public use. @ cow45len

- **Aubad und Erholungspark (Aubad with recreation area)**, Donaulände 78, ☎ 68667, @ pkl357en
- **DonauSplash**, Karl-Metz-G. 1a, ☎ 690480. Sports pool, adventure pool, sauna, solarium, @ yuy626en

*The district capital Tulln is an economic, cultural and leisure centre with the highest leisure quality. As a trade fair city, Tulln is known far beyond its borders. The Danube city is interwoven by green spaces from the water park to the Danube lands to the Aubad and has made a name for itself nationally and internationally as a garden city. As the birthplace of Egon Schiele, with the imposing Danube stage and the Roman past, Tulln is also closely linked to the theme of art.*

## Tulln to Korneuburg 22.4 km

Cross under the Danube bridge on the Danube promenade ~ then immediately turn right into **Karl-Metz-Gasse** ~ at the crossroads turn right onto the cycle path ~ before the bridge turn left, **Mauthausgasse** ~ turn sharp right onto the bridge ~ **14** after crossing the Danube turn right back to the river bank ~ proceed down the smoothly-paved towpath to the hydroelectric power station at Greifenstein ~ turn away from the shoreline about 300 m before reaching the dam ~ **15** turn right on the service road.

**EXCURSION** Turn left on the service road if you wish to take the excursion to Stockerau.

## Stockerau Excursion

Follow the service road over the Krumpenwasser stream ~ after 500 m turn left on a forest path ~ follow the signs through the environmentally-protected flood plain ("Au") ~ you reach Stockerau after 4 km ~ follow the bicycle

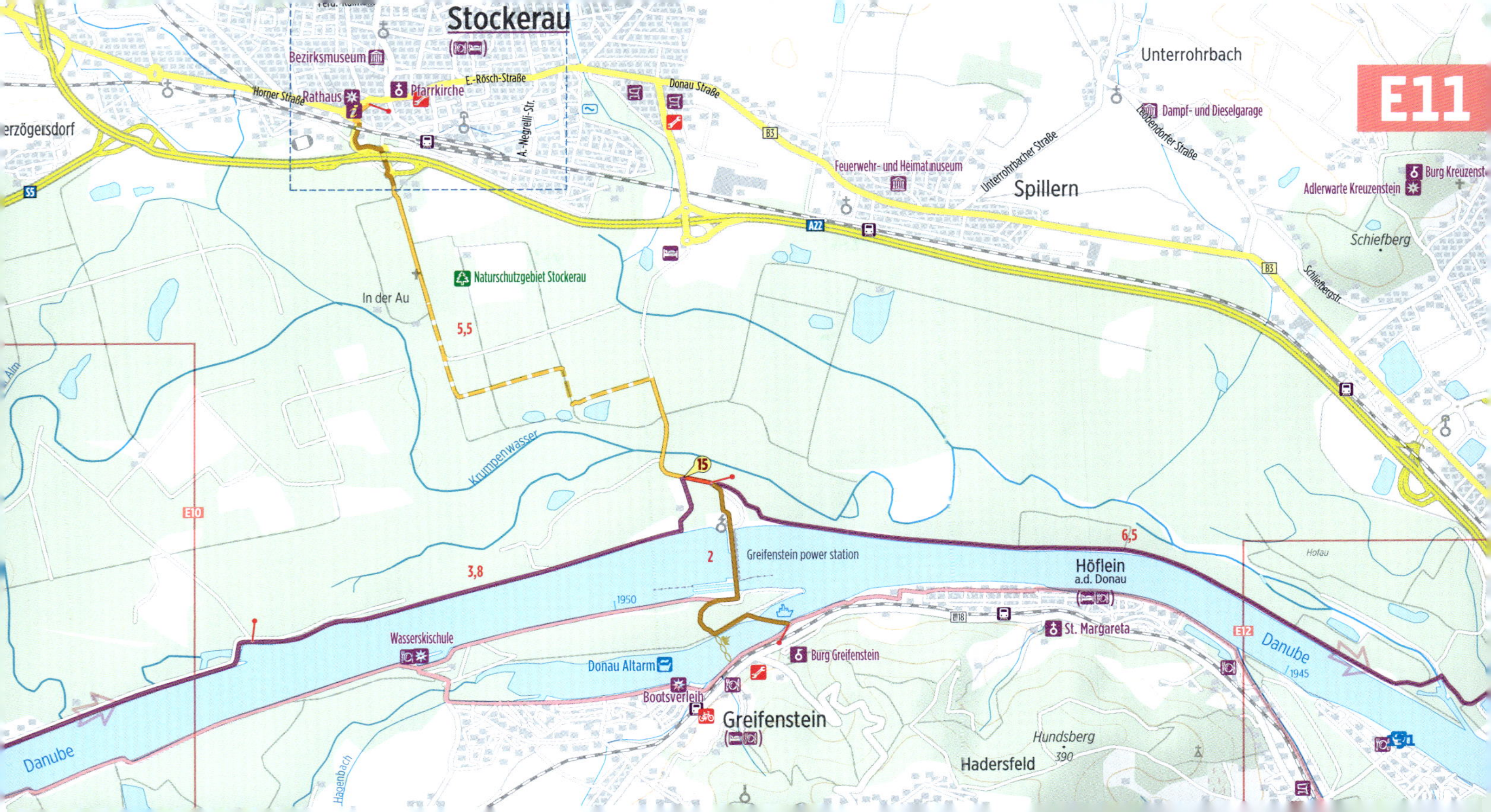

E11
Stockerau
Bezirksmuseum
Horner Straße
Rathaus
Pfarrkirche
E.-Rösch-Straße
A.-Negrelli-Str.
Donau Straße
B3
Feuerwehr- und Heimatmuseum
Unterrohrbach
Dampf- und Dieselgarage
Teßdendorfer Straße
Unterrohrbacher Straße
Spillern
Adlerwarte Kreuzenstein
Burg Kreuzenst
Schießbergstr.
Schiefberg
B3
A22
S5
erzögersdorf
Naturschutzgebiet Stockerau
In der Au
5,5
Krumpenwasser
15
E10
3,8
2
Greifenstein power station
6,5
Höflein
a.d. Donau
Hofau
1950
Wasserskischule
Donau Altarm
St. Margareta
E12
Danube
1945
Bootsverleih
Burg Greifenstein
Danube
Greifenstein
Hagenbach
Hundsberg
390
Hadersfeld

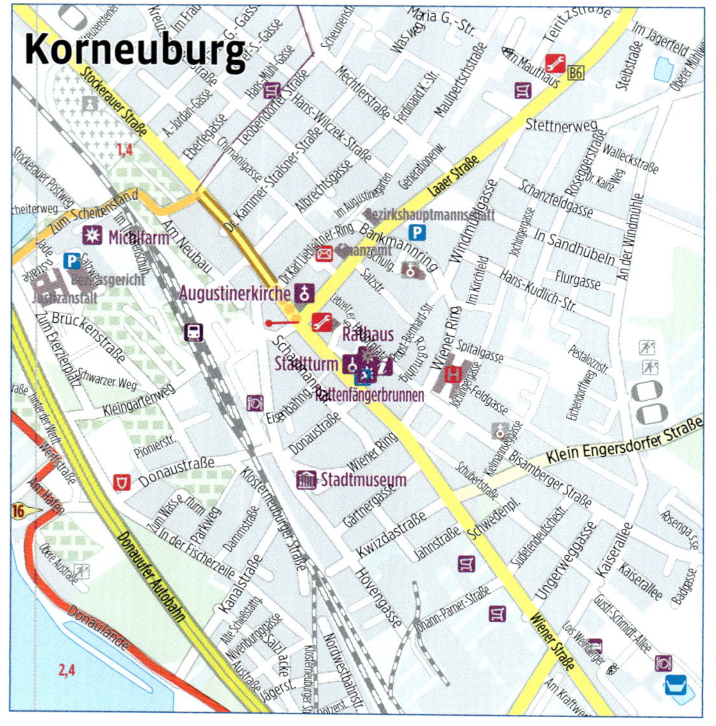


path past the first roundabout and through the underpass ~ after the second roundabout take the path to the left ~ after the railway underpass turn left and immediately right to reach the main square, **Rathausplatz**.

## Stockerau

prefix: 02266

**Stadtgemeindeamt (Municipal office)**, Rathauspl. 1, ☎ 69518, ⓦ gyg173en

**Automobilmuseum (Automobile museum)**, Schießstattg. 9, ☎ 0676/3582719 ⟳ Collection of historical and classic automobiles from Austrian, German and English production. ⓦ puj214en

**Bezirksmuseum (District museum)**, Belvedereg. 3, ☎ 6955200 ⟳ ⟲ Prehistoric and early historical collections, exhibits from folklore and natural history as well as sacral objects document the history of the city. Complemented by changing exhibitions and the memorial to the poet Nikolaus Lenau, who lived in Stockerau from 1818-22. ⓦ avb113en

**Pfarrkirche Hl. Stephan (St. Stephan parish church)**, Kirchenpl. 3, ☎ 62771. The 88 m tower is the tallest steeple in Lower Austria, built 1725. The early-classical church has a cross-shaped nave. ⓦ yoj278en

**Belvedereschlössl**, Belvedereg. 3, ☎ 6955201. The baroque jewel from the 16th century is today the centre of cultural life north of the Danube with around 60 events a year. Originally, it served as a knight's estate, machine factory and residential building. ⓦ ups377en

**Rathaus (City Hall)**, Rathauspl. 1. The former Puchheim Castle is a stately 17th century Baroque building with a remarkable pilaster structure, designed by Fischer von Erlach the Younger. ⓦ nuj534en

**Schlössl**, Donaustr. 6. The town house from the 16th century served as a state caste office from 1804-1824. In the 18th century, the building was baroqueised and redesigned in a romantic-historical style in 1832. The cornered tower shows a relief of St. George. Today it is a residential building.

**Naturschutzgebiet Stockerau (Stockerau nature reserve)**. Since construction of the Greifenstein power station, the floodplain only receives water during floods. In spite of this the area supports at least 27 swamp and water plants that are on the red list of endangered plants. ⓦ ulq463en

**15** Proceed towards the Greifenstein power station until you come to a fork in the road.

 From here you can cross the river on the Greifenstein power station bridge during daylight hours to reach Greifenstein.

On the north bank, pass the power station entrance on the left and after a right-hand bend continue on the towpath — proceed straight ahead towards Korneuburg — the path finally turns left into the forest — over the Krumpenwasser branch of water — after the wooden bridge, pass the barrier — at the crossroads, turn left — at the next junction, turn right into **Werftstraße**.

 If you wish to visit Korneuburg, proceed straight ahead under the road bridge and then across the railway line to the main street. Turn right and follow the bicycle path 600 m to the main square.

## Korneuburg

prefix: 02262

**Stadtgemeindeamt (Municipal office)**, Hauptpl. 39, 770, @ lue473en

**Rollfähre (Cable ferry)**, Tuttendörfl 10, 0664/2155443, End of March – 2 Nov, Mon-Fri 7 a.m. until dusk, Sat, Sun & Fri 8 a.m. until dusk, @ xhr171en

**Stadtmuseum (City Museum)**, Dr.-Max-Burckhard-Ring 11, 72553 In the building erected in 1908 as a bath for common people, you can see the exhibition: From prehistory to the present and changing special exhibitions. @ vdc743en

**Augustinerkirche (Augustine church)**, Laaer Str. 1. A former monastery church built 1745-48 with grand rococo altar and a painted faux architecture with a depiction of Christ's last meal, by F. A. Maulpertsch (1770). @ acc423en

**Stadtturm (City tower)**, Hauptpl. 39 The tower was built in 1444-47 as a defence and watchtower above the former Nikolai Church. It is the town's landmark and offers a beautiful view over the town. @ kmp367en

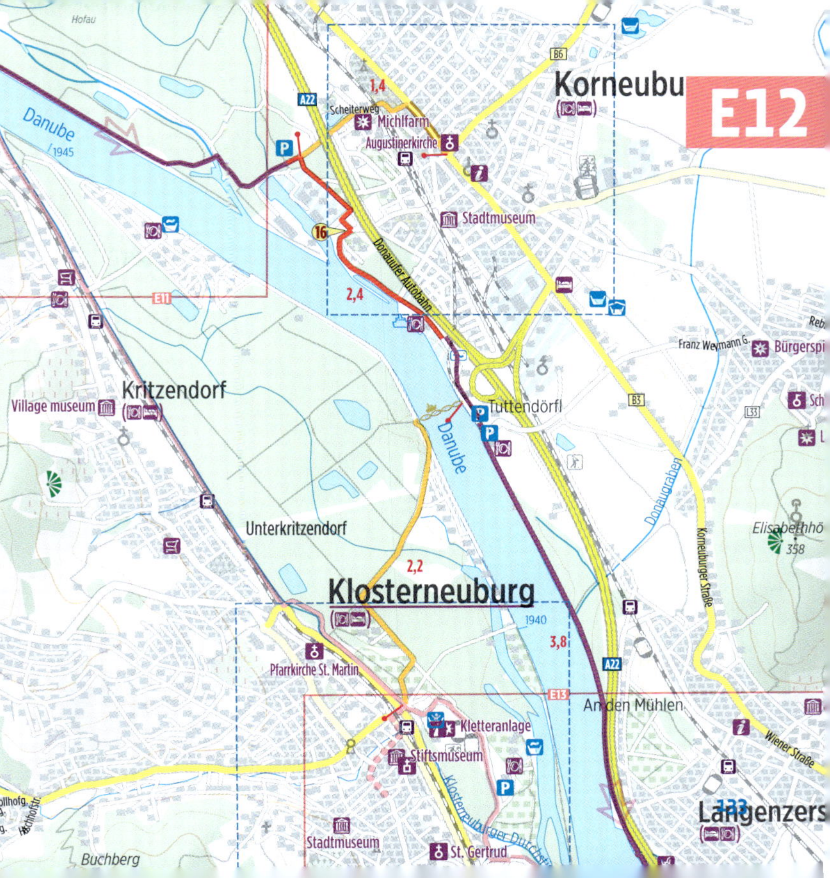

Town Hall Korneuburg

* **Rathaus (Town hall)**, Hauptpl. 39. The neo gothic building was built 1894-96 and seamlessly incorporates the medieval city tower. Noteworthy the magnificent ceiling, restored wooden staircases and hearing rooms. @ vqk852en
* **Rattenfängerbrunnen (Rat catcher´s fountain)**, Hauptpl. A beautiful well built in 1898 by the Viennese sculptor Emanuel-Pendl. Depicts a rat catcher who is part of the folklore of the city of Korneuburg. @ nxg328en
* **Florian-Berndl-Bad**, Gustl-Schmidt-Allee 1, Bisamberg, ℰ 72134. Outdoor and indoor swimming pool with sauna world, @ jkd635en


Just north of Korneuburg lies Leobendorf with Kreuzenstein Castle.

## Leobendorf

* **Burg Kreuzenstein (Kreuzenstein Castle)**, ℰ 02264/7291, ℰ 0664/1632700 ⓝ Originally destroyed by the Swedish armies, it was rebuilt as a typical 15th c. castle by Graf Wilczek in 1879, using original parts and components collected from throughout Europe. Today, the castle is a popular film location for feature films, including "The Three Musketeers" (1993) and "The Last Knight Templar" (2011) with Nicolas Cage. @ wte573en
* **Adlerwarte Kreuzenstein (Falconry)**, Kreuzensteiner Str., ℰ 0664/8998325 ⓔ The birds of prey can be observed up to three times a day during their free flights by falconry. @ wcf161en

## The Rat Catcher of Korneuburg

*Like many other cities in Medieval Europe, the people of Korneuburg suffered from numerous plagues of rats. According to local lore, once when rats threatened to overwhelm the city, the high council set a bounty for the elimination of the pests.*

*A short time later a man appeared and promised to free the city of its rats. Playing a flute, he attracted the rats into the open and down to the Danube where they drowned. The mayor then refused to give the man his full payment, offering only one-quarter of the agreed amount. The piper refused the payment and left.*

*He returned, however, and again began playing his flute. But this time, he lured the city's children to a ship on the Danube. The ship then sailed down the river and disappeared. The children were never seen again. Only two children were left behind – a mute child who had not heard the piper, and another who missed the ship because he returned home for a jacket.*

Kreuzenstein Castle

see page 154

### Korneuburg to Vienna     19.7 km

Follow **Werftstraße** to the end ▸ turn right into **Schiffwerftstraße** ▸ turn left again at the next opportunity ▸ **16** turn right at the T-junction and follow **Donaustraße** onto **Donaulände** ▸ you pass a marina and a small commercial warf before reaching the ferry to Klosterneuburg.

▎**TIP** You can use the ferry to connect with the main route along the south bank and the centre of Klosterneuburg, where you can visit the abbey and several museums. see page 154

After the Korneuburg-Klosterneuburg ferry, change to the towpath at the "Tuttendörfl" inn ▸ **17** ride up onto the bridge on the barrage and cross the Neue Donau (New Danube) onto the **Donauinsel (Danube island)** ▸ follow the path along the island into Vienna ▸ you pass below several bridges on the way ▸ after 9 km you reach the **Reichsbrücke** by the small marina and lighthouse ▸ just before the white lighthouse, keep to the right and ride up the cycle and pedestrian ramp below the bridge to the Reichsbrücke.

▎**TIP** If you turn left on the bridge, you will come to the metro station. To get into the city by bike, turn right on the lower edge of the bridge towards the city centre.

▎**CONNECTION** The Danube bicycle route does not end in Vienna, you can simply continue along the Danube to Bratislava and Budapest.

Continue straight ahead at the end of the bridge ▸ follow the bicycle path along **Lassallestraße** to the **18** **Praterstern**, where one can consider a visit to the world famous Prater park and its giant Ferris wheel ▸ proceed down **Praterstraße** over

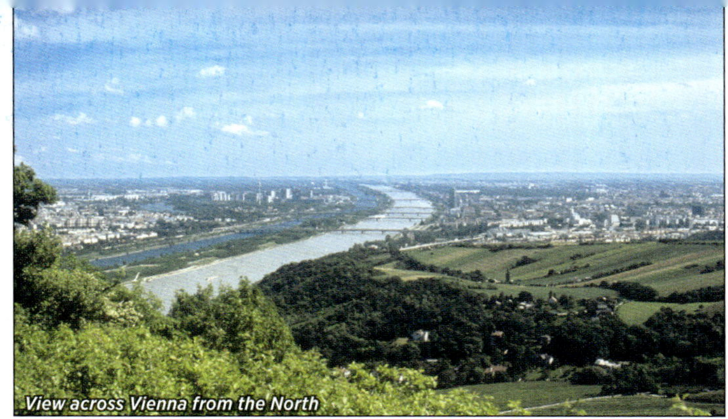

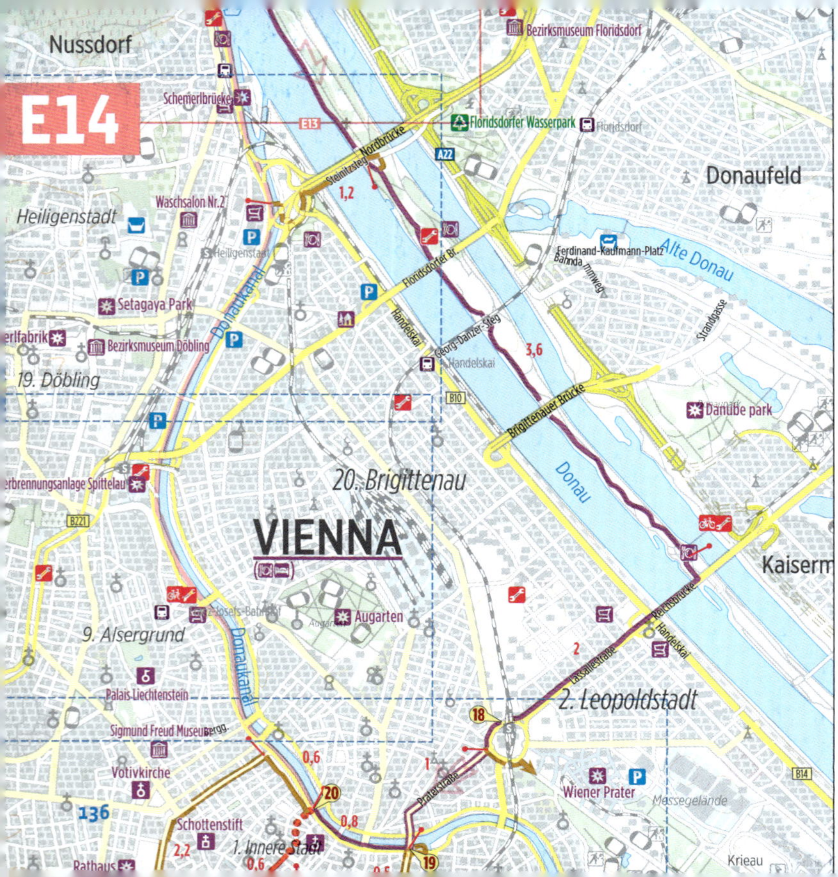


*View across Vienna from the North*

the **Aspernbrückengasse** to the **19 Urania**.

**TIP** Straight ahead you connect with the Ring-Rund-Radweg, a bicycle route that encircles the old city and connects some of the most important sights in Vienna. It is shown in orange on the city map.

After the bridge turn right follow the bicycle path **20** by the **Salztorbrücke (bridge)** left into **Salztorgasse** follow the road into **Vorlaufstraße** and **Tuchlauben** turn left into **Brandstätte** and proceed to **Stephansplatz**.

*You have now reached the centre of Vienna and in front of you stands one of Vienna's landmarks, the Stephansdom (cathedral), which is also the landmark of Austria.*

**Vienna** see page 158

# Melk to Vienna along the south bank



**m/km:** ↗ 1.1 (128m) ↘ 1.3 (151m) **cycle path:** 75 % **unpaved:** 0 % **busy road:** 1 %

Turning downstream from the Benedictine Abbey at Melk, the Danube bicycle route enters Austria's best-known wine producing region, the Wachau. The river valley is especially beautiful in the spring, when the apricot orchards blossom. The route passes under the ruins of the castle at Aggstein and past the valley's little jewels: Spitz, Weißenkirchen and Dürnstein. The Wachau region ends just before the old city of Krems, where the Danube enters the expansive flatlands of the Tulln plain. The river narrows once more upstream from Vienna, where it passes the "Wiener Pforte" (gate) at the feet of the Viennese woods before flowing past Klosterneuburg and into Austria's capital city, Vienna.

The route down the south bank mostly follows bicycle paths and quiet country lanes and side streets. The only steep climbs are on the excursions to Aggstein ruin and Göttweig abbey.

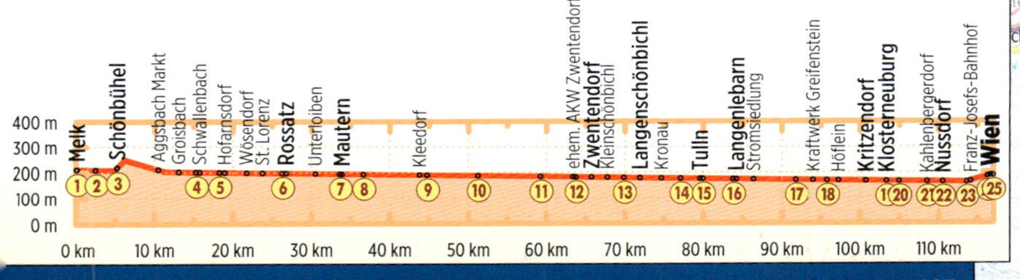

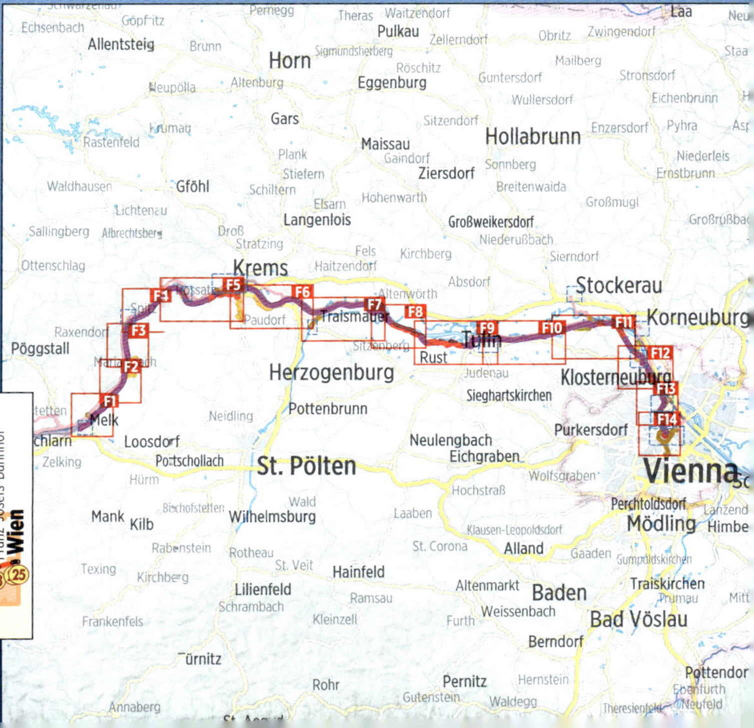

### Melk to Oberarnsdorf     17.3 km

**1** Follow the cycle path to the left of the main road ～ turn right at the crossroads and then left again into the cycle path alongside the road ～ cross over to the other side of the road through the subway ～ pass under the bridge **2** ～ the cycle path takes a right turn under the B 33 ～ you will reach Schönbühel with its castle of the same name ～ cross the road in front of the Amtshaus Schönbühel.

### Schönbühel (Schönbühel-Aggsbach)

prefix: 02752

**Gemeindeamt (Municipal office)**, Nr.48, ✆ 8619, @ pij423en

**Servitenkloster u. Pfarrkirche Hl. Rosalia (St. Rosalia parish church)**, Nr. 49, ✆ 0650/4080958. The church was built as a simple, single-nave building together with the monastery in 1666-74. The chapel of St. Peregrine, which was added to the side in 1737, contains a dome with a fresco by Johann Bergl (1767). The Grotto of the Nativity of Christ, based on a model from Bethlehem, was reproduced in the rocks. The imposing monastery was built by master builder Christoph Schachinger. @ oan823en

**Schloss Schönbühel (Schönbühel Palace)**. The complex dates back to the 12th c., although the rectangular buildings visible today were built 1819-21. Private property, closed to the public. @ pxo511en

**3** Continue right along the B 33 uphill towards Aggsbach-Dorf ～ at the Schönbühel cemetery follow the cycle path on the right ～ approx. 500 m after the cemetery cross the road and continue on the left ～ turn left onto the towpath, which has been upgraded to a cycle path ～ continue to Aggsbach-Dorf.

**TIP** From the village, you can also take a short detour to the Aggsbach Charterhouse, the Hammerschmiede (approx. 100 m from the Charterhouse) and the Mineral Centre. To do this, leave the main road to the right 500 m after the former boat station and cycle through the valley.

*Schönbühel Palace*

## Aggsbach-Dorf (Schönbühel-Aggsbach)

prefix: 02753

- **Marktgemeindeamt (Municipal office)**, Nr. 48, ☎ 8269, @ qsk874en
- **Geozentrum Steinstadel (Steinstadel mineral centre)**, Aggsbach-Dorf 3, ☎ 8269, ☎ 0664/9370444 ☯ Exhibits with various minerals, rocks and fossils from the area including the Pyrop red gem. @ fwo316en
- **Hammerschmiede (Forge)**, Hauptstr. 24, ☎ 0676/5268661 ☯ The show force with three water wheels shows past times of a high craftsmanship. Only with a guided tour. @ cdp487en
- **Kartäuserkirche Maria Himmelfahrt (Carthusian church Maria Himmelfahrt)**, ☎ 0664/9370444. The narrow single-nave church was consecrated in 1392. Noteworthy the figured keystone, the baroque pulpit with the four evangelists and the altar paintings (17th c.). @ rsu443en
- **Kartause Aggsbach (Charterhouse).** In 1380 Heidenreich von Maissau, cupbearer and land marshal of Austria, founded the monastery with 12 Carthusian monks. After its decline during the Reformation, it was dissolved by

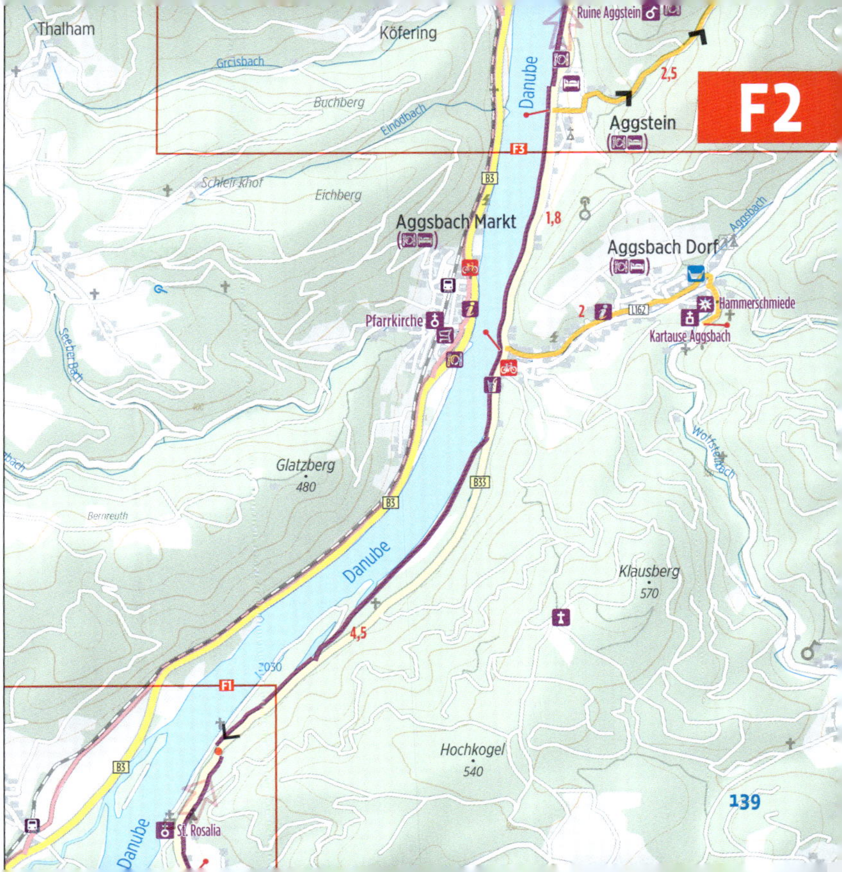

**F2**

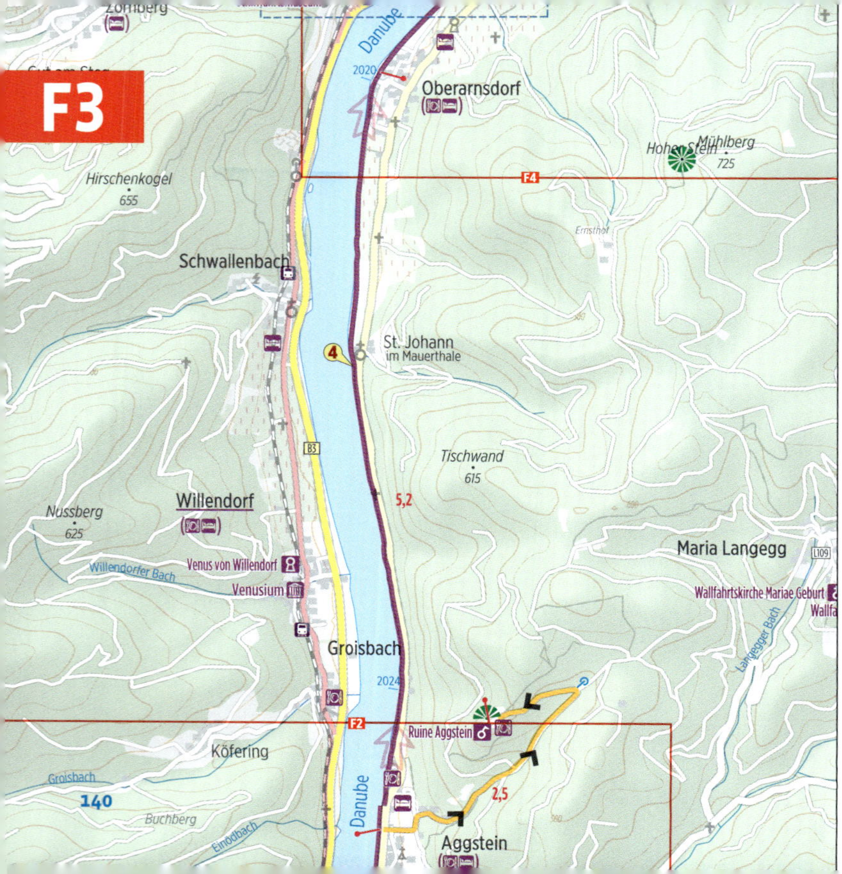

*Aggstein ruin*

Joseph II in 1782. Today there is a parish here with monastery and economic tracts from the 16th-17th centuries with a remarkable meditation garden. ⓦ jvd652en

**Waldbad (Forest bath)**, Nr. 112, ☎ 8232, ⓦ vwv281en

Continue on the bicycle path along the river bank to Aggstein.

**EXCURSION** A steep road with grades of up to 20% leads up to the ruin, so you must dismount and push. Nevertheless, the 2 km detour is strongly recommended for all who love old castles and spec-tacular views. The view from the 300 m plateau extends deep into the Wachau and as far as the Alps.

**Aggstein** (Schönbühel-Aggsbach)

prefix: 02753

**Ruine Aggstein (Aggstein ruin)**, ☎ 82281 On a steep rock 300 metres above the Danube lies the legendary ruins of Aggstein Castle, where the Kuenringers already ruled. During a tour, you can also climb the highest walls on wooden viewing platforms. ⓦ wrh613en

*Aggstein castle was established in the 13th century. Devastated by the Turks, it was rebuilt in 1606*

After Aggstein continue on the path along the river – after 3.5 km you reach **St. Johann im Mauerthale** 4 here the path veers away from the road to follow the river – continue along the river to Oberarnsdorf.

## Oberarnsdorf (Mitterarnsdorf)

prefix: 02714

- **Marktgemeindeamt (Municipal office)**, Rossatz 29, Rossatz (Mitterarnsdorf), ✆ 6217, @ yuu828en

- **Rollfähre Spitz-Arnsdorf (Ferry Spitz-Arnsdorf)**, Spitz a. d. Donau, ✆ 0650/2502103,

⏱ Apr, Oct Mon-Fri 6.15am-6pm, Sat, Sun/Fri 8.15am-6pm, May-Sept Mon-Fri 6.15am-7pm, Sat, Sun/Fri 8.15am-7.30pm. @ wnv613en

### Oberarnsdorf to Mautern   16.2 km

After a short distance you reach the ferry landing to Spitz 5.


Spitz is well worth a visit, and from there it's only a short ride along the north bank route to Weißenkirchen, another jewel of the Wachau.

Continue on the path along the river past the wine villages of **Hofarnsdorf**, **Mitterarnsdorf** and **Bacharnsdorf**.


Wine growers offering samples can be recognized by the "ausg'steckten" (hanging) bunches of twigs or wreaths next to the road.

Continue down the bicycle path beside the steep forested slopes to St. Lorenz.

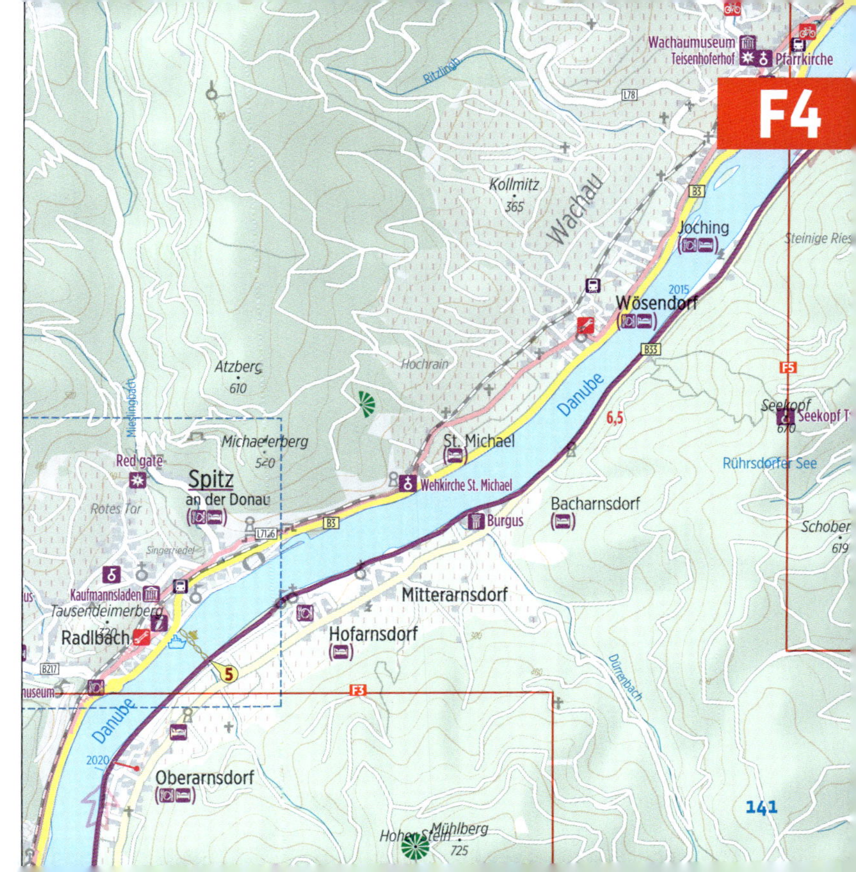

### St. Lorenz (Mitterarnsdorf)

🚢 **Rollfähre Weißenkirchen-St. Lorenz (Ferry)**, Weißenkirchen in der Wachau, ✆ 02715/2232, 🕒 April-Oct, Mon-Fri 8-11.45 and 13.30-18.45, Sat, Sun/Fri 8-18.45, @ qku122en

The route continues between vineyards along a quiet field road ～ in Rührsdorf ride straight ahead onto the village street, which you follow through the right and left bends.

### Rührsdorf (Mitterarnsdorf)

Turn left by the fork at the end of the village and continue between vineyards and orchards ～ **6** turn left after a right and left bend, keep right if you wish to ride through the village of Rossatz.

### Rossatz (Mitterarnsdorf)

prefix: 02714

ℹ️ **Marktgemeindeamt (Municipal office)**, Rossatz 29, ✆ 6217, @ yuu828en

🏰 **Schloss Rossatz (Rossatz castle)**, Nr. 74, ✆ 6218. The former castle of Count Schönborn has been owned by the Rossatzer since 1859 and with its three-storey arcades is a popular venue for events. @ ukk542en

The route passes to the left of Rossatz and reaches the river at the campground at Rossatzbach, where the passenger ferry to Dürnstein docks.

### Rossatzbach (Mitterarnsdorf)

prefix: 02714

🚢 **Fähre Dürnstein-Rossatz (Ferry)**, Dürnstein, ✆ 0676/3084750, 🕒 April/Oct, Fri-Sun/Fri 10am-5pm; May/Sept daily 9.30am-6pm; June-Aug Mon-Fri 9.30am-6pm, Sat/Sun 9am-6.30pm. @ boe554en

📧 **Donaustrand (Danube beach)**, Donaulände, ✆ 6217. The idyllic sandy beach offers all kinds of leisure activities.

Past the campsite ～ on the cycle path alongside the road to Hundsheim ～ at the first opportunity turn right into the village.

### Hundsheim (Mautern a. d. Donau)

Ride through Hundsheim, going straight at the intersection and take the farm lane through the vineyards ～ soon the route again approaches the main road ～ ride across the parking lot at the Römerhalle to reach the Danube river bridge.



**Cross the Danube now if you wish to visit Krems. If you want to continue directly towards Tulln, stay on the main route along the right bank. Additionally, after about 3 km the excursion to the imposing Göttweig abbey begins from this route.**

Ride past the Roman hall and the palace on **Kremser Straße** into the centre.

### Mautern a. d. Donau

prefix: 02732

ℹ️ **Stadtgemeindeamt (Town office)**, Rathauspl. 1, ✆ 83151, @ bha821en

🏛️ **Römermuseum (Roman museum)**, Schlossg. 12, ✆ 83151, ✆ 0664/9233058 🕒 Information about life in the former Roman fort of Favianis-Mautern and its surrounding civilian settlement. The museum is also dedicated to the life of St. Severin. @ ocd682en

🏛️ **Wachauer Goldhauben- und Trachtenmuseum (Museum of traditional costumes)**, Frauenhofg. 5, in the Margaret Chapel, ✆ 72643 🕒 🕒 The multifaceted exhibition ranges from typical Wachau gold bonnets to furniture and everyday and festive costumes of the region. @ glc314en

🏰 **Pfarrkirche St. Stephan (St. Stephan parish church)**, Kirchenpl. The Gothic church with polygonal choir dates to around 1400

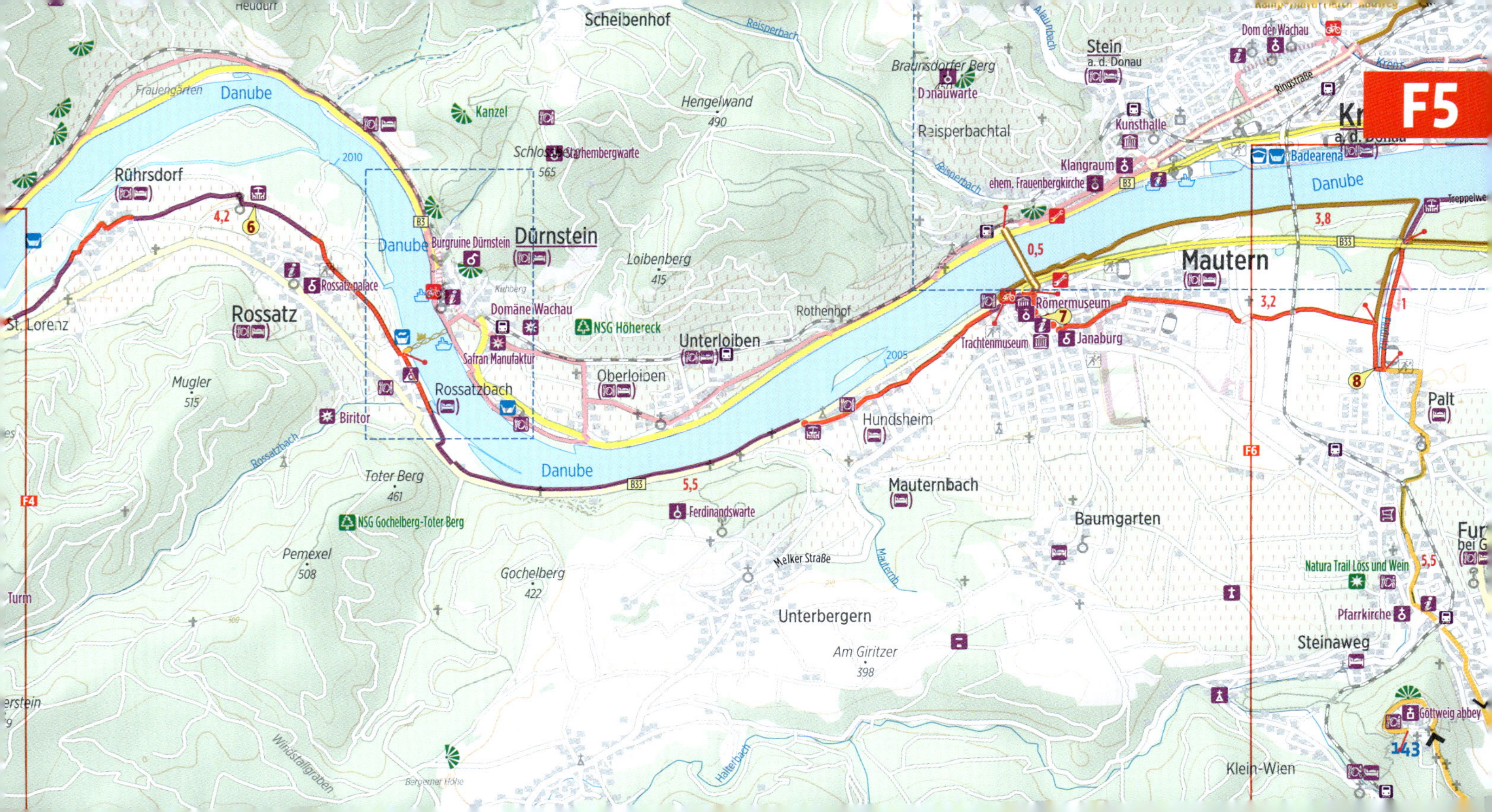

F5
Heudorf
Scheibenhof
Reisperbach
Alaubach
Dom der Wachau
Stein a. d. Donau
Kr
a. d. Donau
Braunsdorfer Berg
Donauwarte
Kunsthalle
Krems
Ringstraße
Frauengärten
Danube
Kanzel
Hengelwand
490
Reisperbachtal
Reisperbach
Klangraum
ehem. Frauenbergkirche
B3
Badearena
Danube
2010
Schloss Starhembergwarte
565
Treppelwe
Rührsdorf
3,8
Danube
4,2
6
B3
Danube
Burgruine Dürnstein
Dürnstein
Loibenberg
415
B33
Mautern
0,5
Rossatz palace
Kuhberg
Römermuseum
3,2
Rossatz
Domäne Wachau
Rothenhof
7
1
St. Lorenz
NSG Höhereck
Unterloiben
Trachtenmuseum
Janaburg
Safran Manufaktur
Oberloiben
2005
8
Mugler
515
Rossatzbach
Palt
Biritor
Hundsheim
Danube
B33
5,5
F6
Toter Berg
461
Mauternbach
NSG Gochelberg-Toter Berg
Ferdinandswarte
Baumgarten
F4
Pemexel
508
Melker Straße
Mauternb
Natura Trail Löss und Wein
5,5
Gochelberg
422
Fur bei G
Turm
Unterbergern
Pfarrkirche
Am Giritzer
398
Steinaweg
Göttweig abbey
143
Klein-Wien
Windstallgraben
Bergener Höhe
Rossatzbach

and is especially noted for the stations of the cross paintings by Martin Johann Schmidt (1770). @ riq853en

- **Margarethenkapelle (Margarethe chapel)**, Frauenhofg. 5. Already mentioned in 1083 and built along the Roman city wall. Today it houses the Wachau Goldhauben and Trachten Museum. @ mpo643en
- **Janaburg**, Südtirolerpl. 5. A 16th c. building with a triumphal arch portal and a Renaissance fountain in the courtyard.
- **Schloss (Castle)**, Schlossg. 6-8. The four-winged building includes 15th c. Renaissance elements and once served as administrative offices of the Passau bishopric. @ rgy376en

Göttweig Abbey

- **Bürgerhäuser (Town houses)**, St. Pöltner Str. The closed row of massive houses with portals, round core and Renaissance-style entrance halls mostly dates from the 16th century.

*In the first millennium, the Roman city was one of the most important centres on the Danube. In connection with the construction of the Danube Limes as the northern border of the empire, "Favianis", a military camp, and shortly afterwards also a civilian town, was built here. In the 4th and 5th centuries, St. Severin worked at this site and founded a monastery. The walls of the mighty watchtower of the fort and the Roman Museum still bear impressive witness to Mautern's Roman history.*

### Mautern to Altenwörth power station    25.5 km

**7** Turn left on **St. Pöltner Straße** ~ pass the Rathausplatz and continue to **Südtiroler Platz** ~ turn left to the Landhaus Bacher and then turn right on **Grüne Weg** ~ pass the Raabkaserne (barracks) and ride out of Mautern ~ cross the road and under the railway ~ turn right when you reach the embankment along the Fladnitz River ~ cross the river at the next bridge **8**.



Now you must decide whether to turn left and return to the Danube and the south bank route or make the side-trip to the Göttweig abbey, in which case you continue straight ahead.

## To Göttweig Abbey    11 km

**8** After crossing the Fladnitz river go straight ~ turn right at the end of the street and ride into **Palt** ~ turn right at the T-intersection and then left before the bridge ~ follow the path along the Fladnitz to

### Furth bei Göttweig
prefix: 02732

- **Marktgemeindeamt (Municipal office)**, Obere Landstr. 65, ✆ 846220, @ yvd283en

At the T-intersection with the **Obere Landstraße** you turn left away from the river ~ follow the street under the railway line and uphill out of the town ~ after about 1 km you reach an intersection, where you turn right and follow the road up the wooded hill to the abbey.

### Stift Göttweig (Furth bei Göttweig)
prefix: 02732

- **Stift Göttweig (Benedictine monastery)**, Stift Göttweig 1, ✆ 855810 @ The magnificent monastery, visible from afar, was built according to the (not fully executed) plans of Johann

F6
dearena
Krems harbour
Danube
Treppelweg
2,5
2000
3,8
F33
3
Theiß
Donaudorf
Krems
Stockgraben
1
8
Palt
Brunnkirchen
L100
Thallern
Danube
2,6
Wurmsaumlacke
S33
B37a
Treppelweg
3,8
1995
9
Furth
bei Göttweig
Sprinzenberg
280
F5
Angem
Marillen Erlebnisweg
6
Pfarrkirche
Hollenburg
1990
Natura Trail Löss und Wein
5,5
Oberfucha
Am Glockenberg
Kleedorf
Treppelweg
3,5
Pfarrkirche
Steinaweg
Göttweig abbey
Tiefenfucha
Würbelmühle
B43
St. Georgen
a.d. Traisen
Krustetten
Wagram
ob der Traisen
Rittersfeld
F7
Paudorf
Ried
Neusiedl
Eggendorf
Nußdorf
ob der Traisen
145
Höbenbach
Runde Heide
Urzeitmuseum
0,4
Schloss Traismauer

Traismauer, Roman Gate

Lucas von Hildebrandt after a fire at the beginning of the 18th century. Particularly worth seeing: the imperial staircase with the ceiling fresco by Paul Troger, the Altmannisaal and the collegiate church of the Assumption of the Virgin Mary. This forms the centre of the monastery complex and houses the high altar designed by Hermann Schmidt. The relics of the monastery founder Altmann von Passau and the pilgrimage picture are kept in the crypt. @ jta342en

**Stiftskirche Mariä Himmelfahrt (Mariä Himmelfahrt abbey church).** The abbey church with its magnificent two-tower façade forms the centre of the monastery complex. The elevated late Gothic presbytery with the elegant east choir and the early Baroque nave with the side chapels create a special impression. The choir room is dominated by the high altar painting by

the Munich court painter Andreas Wolff showing the Assumption of Mary (1694). @ hhh872en

*From the panorama terrace you have an impressive view of the Danube valley.*

From Göttweig return to the main route the way you came.

**8** To continue on the main route, turn left after the bridge over the Fladnitz ～ follow the paved field road beside the embankment along the river ～ keep left at the end of the fields and ride under the road bridge ～ the bicycle path soon comes to follow the bank of the Danube ～ ride under the Danube bridge and past the little harbour ～ the path comes to follow the top of the dike along the Danube.


After another 300 m you reach a turnoff. From here you have the option of a sightseeing detour of the small wine villages of Thallern, Angern and Hollenburg. Follow the green-white signs. This route is shown on map F6 in orange.

**Angern** (Krems a. d. Donau)
prefix: 02739

**Wachauer Marillen Erlebnisweg (Wachau Apricot Experience Trail)**, Dorfstr. 34, ☎ 2205 ㉔ The 4.5-kilometre-long, well-

signposted circular hiking trail leads through the picturesque wine landscape and old apricot gardens. @ qov174en

**Hollenburg** (Krems a. d. Donau)
prefix: 02739

**Pfarrkirche (Parish church)**, Untere Hollenburger Hauptstr. 4, ☎ 2565. Three-nave pillar basilica with distinctive west tower and a noted Gothic Madonna from around 1420. @ qin122en

The main route continues along the bank of the Danube and follows the freeway a short distance ～ **9** you pass a turnoff to the right, where the excursion route from Hollenburg rejoins the main route ～ continue along the Danube ～ the route now takes you into an increasingly flat and open landscape.


After 6 km the route passes a marina, where there are information boards next to the inn.
**10** From here the nearby town of Traismauer is only a short detour and well worth a visit.

**Traismauer**
prefix: 02783

**Tourismusinfo (Tourist information)**, Hauptpl. 1, ☎ 8555, @ ixr815en

**Stadtmuseum-Hungerturm (Town Museum)**, Florianig. 11, ☎ 86510, ☎ 8555 ⓒ The town and local history museum is housed in the Hunger Tower, which was once a fortification tower of the Roman cavalry fort. Finds of a mammoth tooth, Roman vessels

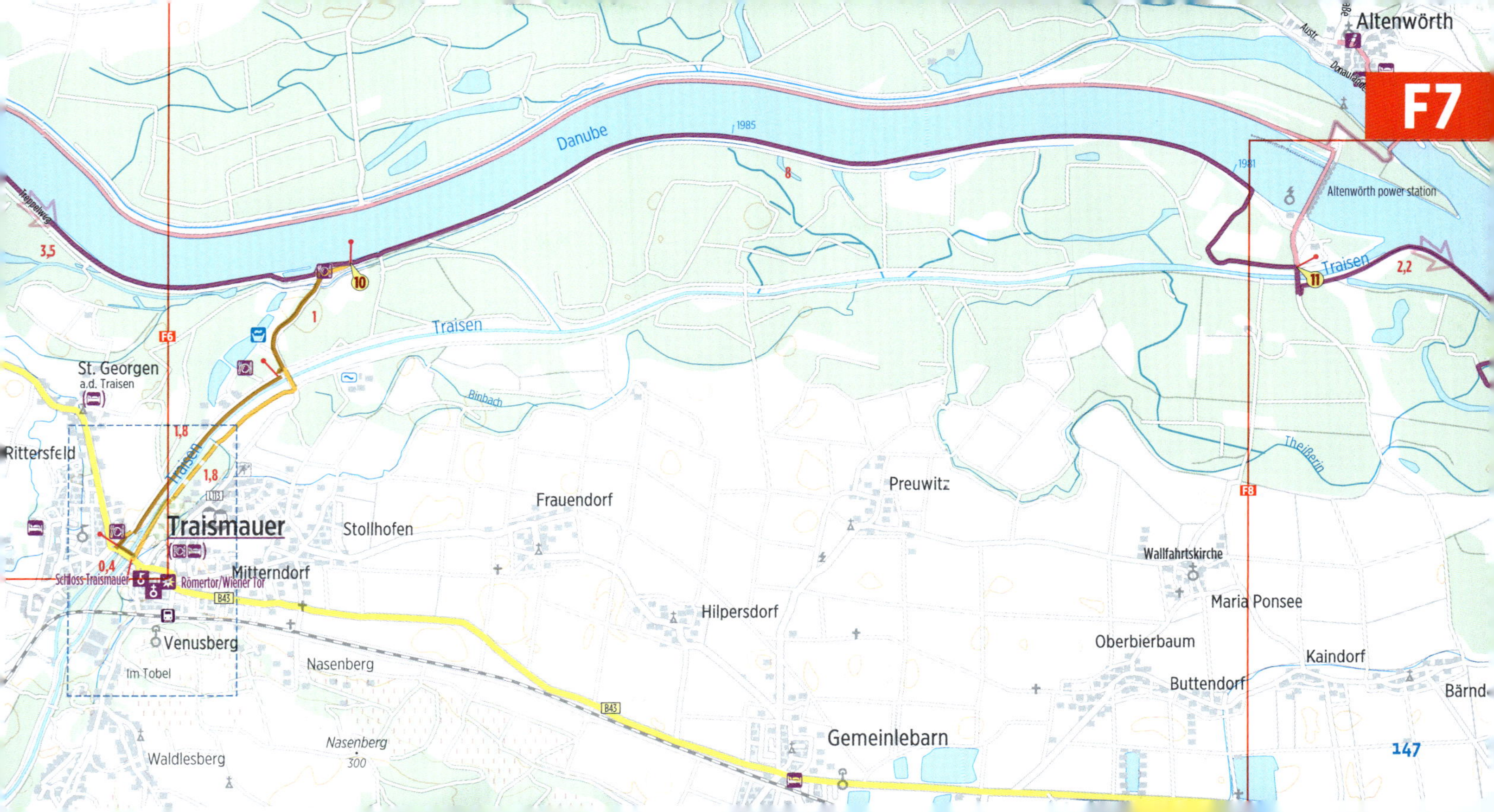
F7
Altenwörth
Altenwörth power station
Danube
1985
1981
Traisen
2,2
8
10
11
1
3,5
Teppelweg
Traisen
F6
St. Georgen
a.d. Traisen
Binbach
Rittersfeld
1,8
1,8
Traisen
L113
Traismauer
Frauendorf
Stollhofen
Preuwitz
Theißerln
F8
Wallfahrtskirche
0,4
Schloss Traismauer
Mitterndorf
Römertor/Wiener Tor
B43
Maria Ponsee
Venusberg
Hilpersdorf
Oberbierbaum
Im Tobel
Kaindorf
Nasenberg
Buttendorf
Bärnd
Waldlesberg
Nasenberg
300
B43
Gemeinlebarn
147

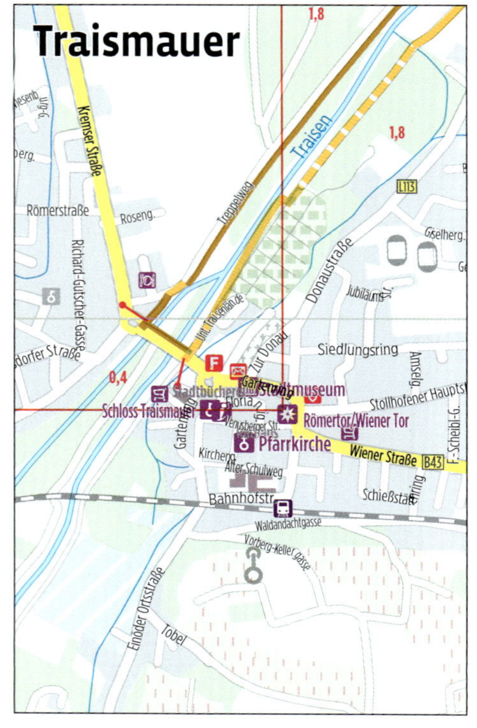


Continue past the Marina and along the bank of the Danube ~ after almost 7 km the route veers away from the river just before the barrage of the **Altenwörth hydroelectric power station** ~ keep to the right and follow the cycle path to the bridge over the Traisen **11**.

## Altenwörth power station to Tulln  20.4 km

Turn left immediately after crossing the bridge over the river Traisen ~ follow the tributary back out to the Danube.

*Two power generating stations now dominate the landscape as the route proceeds downstream: the waste incinerating thermal plant at Dürnrohr and the never-completed nuclear power plant at Zwentendorf. In the background the northern fringes of the Vienna Forest can be seen.*

The path branches off to the right and leads you away from the Danube through the shady floodplain forest ~ after the footbridge over a branch of the Danube, keep left and return to the Danube to immediately turn right again into the floodplain forest ~ at the asphalt road on the left and past the nuclear power plant ~ after this, the path joins an access road

and medieval documents and marksmen's targets are on display. Currently closed for rehabilitation. ⓦ hju772en

**Pfarrkirche und Unterkirche (Parish church)**, Kirchenpl. 1, ☎ 6356. During the renovation of the Baroque church, the remains of the Roman military camp Augustianus from the 1st century A.D. and the burial chamber of the border count Cadaloc were uncovered. Cadaloc was killed in 802 by an arrowhead near Güns in defence against the Avars. ⓦ yrq861en

**Schloss Traismauer (Traismauer palace)**, Hauptpl. 1, ☎ 8555, ☎ 0676/4000237. With its Renaissance-style staircase tower and Gothic lift tower, the castle is definitely worth a visit. The foundation walls were built in the 1st century AD. The original castle at the site is mentioned in the Nibelungenlied. ⓦ jva681en

**Römertor/Wiener Tor (Roman Gate/Viennese Gate)**, Wiener Str. 16, ☎ 0664/4351828. Today the former main gate of the Roman fort with its two horseshoe towers is the landmark of the city.

**Auf den Spuren der Römer (Culture Trail "Speaking Romans")**, Hauptpl. 1, ☎ 8555 ㉔ Along the early border wall, five Roman figures tell about the buildings and history of the Romans in Traismauer, who had their equestrian camps here for 500 years. Information at the tourist office, ⓦ bcp358en

**Naturseen (Nature bathing lakes)**, In der Traisenau, ☎ 865111. The three natural bathing lakes offer cooling in the summer months as well as enough shady spots on the large sunbathing lawn. ⓦ hfx237en

and leads over a bridge — **12** turn left onto the towpath after crossing a bridge — ride along the river past the town of Zwentendorf.

## Zwentendorf see page 124

Follow the path along the Danube past Zwentendorf — turn right before a concrete building — after a short distance left towards **Kleinschönbichl** — you pass between the village and the harbour — the path takes you to the right by the small stream — cross the stream at the next bridge and follow the bicycle path next to the main road to Pischelsdorf — turn left by the first houses of the village.

## Pischelsdorf (Zwentendorf an der Donau)

Along the outskirts of Pischelsdorf — turn left at the T-junction before the stream then right over stream **13** — immediately left — underpass the L 112 state road — now follow the path with a winding course — in Langenschönbichl at the main road straight ahead — straight through the village

## Langenschönbichl

At the end of the village turn left towards **Kronau** — follow the quiet road past fields and forest to Kronau — continue straight ahead through Kronau — straight ahead into

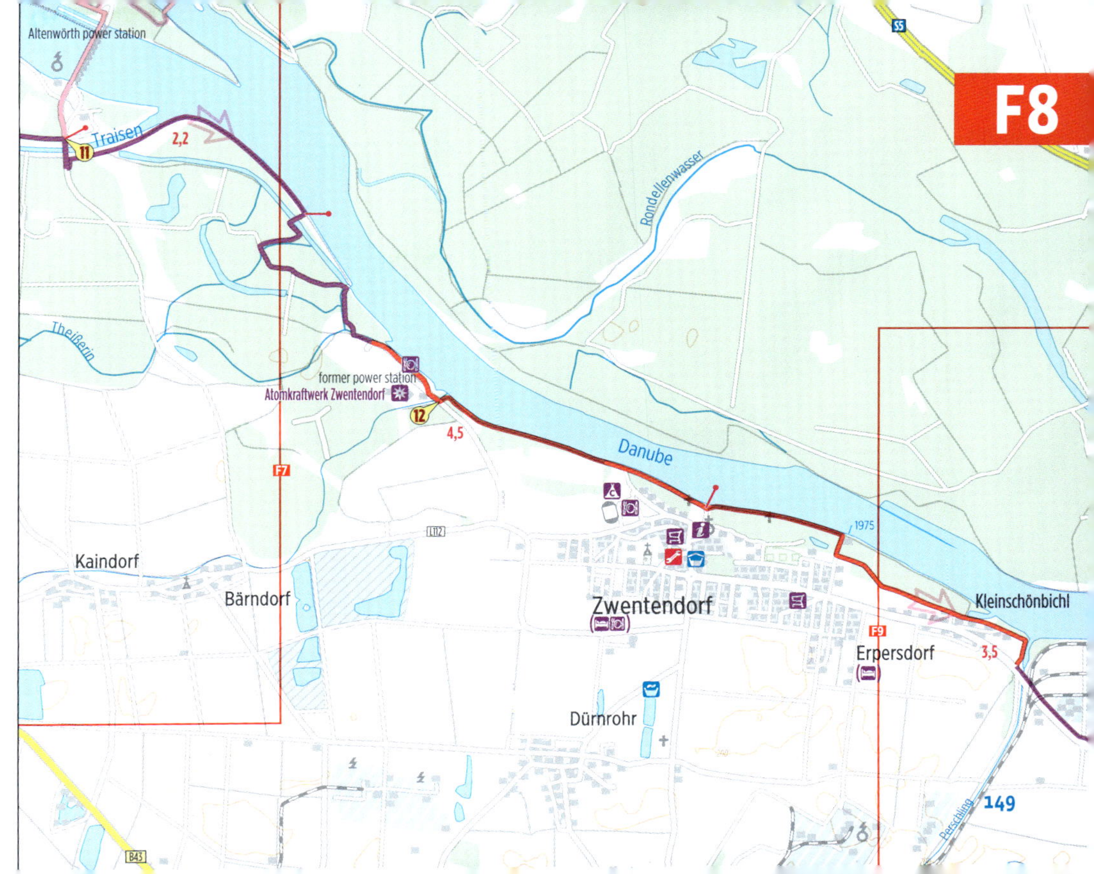

F9
Plackenwasser
Kleinschönbichl
F8 Danube
1970
3,5
Donau-Chemie
1966
Langenschönbichl
3,2
Schiff Regentag
Die Garten Tulln
Wasserpark
Nibelungendenkmal
Stadtpfarrkirche
1,4
15
3
13
Pischelsdorf
L2148
4
Kronau
14
Messegel.
Neusiedl
L112
F10
Alter Perschlinglauf
Asparn
Große Tulln
Tulln
Perschling
L2152
150
B19
B19
B19
B213
Rust
im Tullnerfeld
Langenrohr
Josef-Reither-Museum

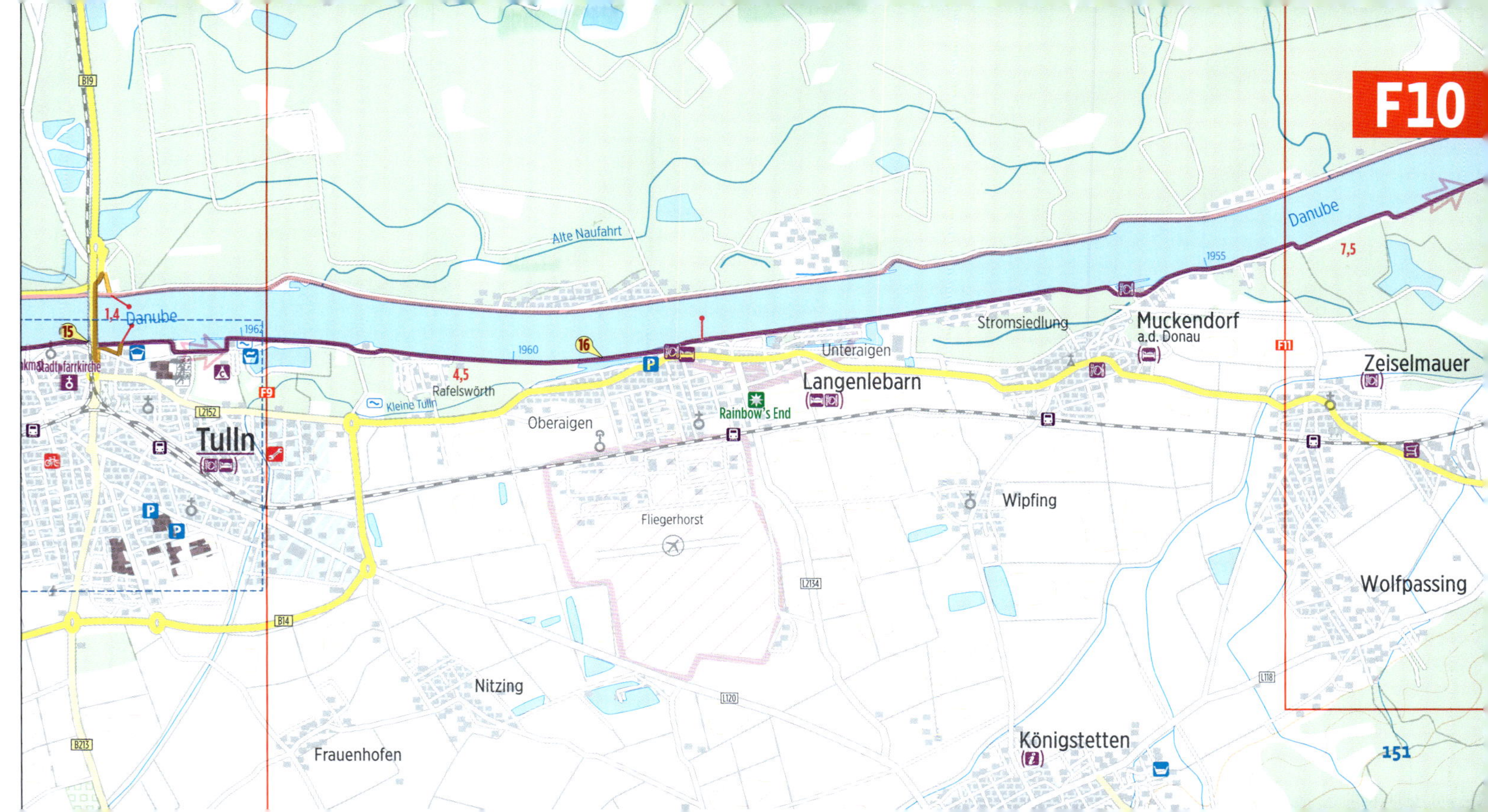

F10
B19
Danube
Alte Naufahrt
1955
7,5
1.4 Danube
15
Stadtpfarrkirche
Denkmal
F9
L2152
Tulln
1960
1962
Kleine Tulln
4,5
Rafelswörth
16
P
Unteraigen
Stromsiedlung
Muckendorf
a.d. Donau
F11
Zeiselmauer
Langenlebarn
Oberaigen
Rainbow's End
Wipfing
Fliegerhorst
L2134
Wolfpassing
B14
L120
L118
Nitzing
Königstetten
B213
Frauenhofen
151

the cul-de-sac and residents' road, which later becomes a cycle path ~ follow the cycle path through the underpass ~ keep left and up to the embankment path along the river Große Tulln ~ turn left on the bank ~ pass under the B 19 ~ after the next bridge undercrossing, turn left to the bridge and over the Große Tulln ~ **14** immediately left again.

> From here you can ride directly to the **Tulln gardens,** simply continue straight from the bridge and turn left at the roundabout.

The main route follows the path along the Große Tulln to the Danube where it follows the river bank into the "garden city" of Tulln.

> S-Bahn trains to Vienna depart from Tulln train station.

## **15** Tulln

see page 126

### Tulln to Greifenstein
15.2 km

From the Danube promenade in Tulln follow the towpath to the Danube river bridge ~ ride under the bridge and follow the shoreline ~ ride around the harbour ~ then on the bicycle path along the river towards Greifenstein ~ after about 3 km you pass

Langenlebarn and the **16** little lake of the Kleinen Tulln stream.

### Langenlebarn

* **Rainbow's End**, Bahnstr. 19, ☏ 0664/3070711 ⓒ The 13 m wide and 90 m long show garden is divided into several themes, such as a rose garden, a sweet tooth garden or a water garden. @ muk261en

Continue along the river to the marina of **Muckendorf** ~ after passing around the marina you ride another 4 km along the Danube to the marina of Greifenstein.

**17** From here you have a choice of two routes. The main route continues straight along the Danube, where you can also use the power station to cross to the north bank. The dam is open during the day, after dark use a speaker-phone to ask the guard to open the gate. The alternative route takes you along the south of the old river arm into Greifenstein.

To ride via Greifenstein, turn right by the marina and then keep right by the intersection ~ after crossing a stream turn left into the lane **Treppelweg** ~ follow the path past the old harbour and a sunbathing lawn ~ pass the ferry pontoon ~ continue to the causeway, where you return to the main route.

To take the main route, proceed to the sluices by the barrage of the **Greifenstein hydroelectric power station** ~ turn right before the barrage ~ follow the left bend to the bank of the oxbow ~ across the oxbow ~ on the right is the village of Greifenstein and the bathing meadow, the route continues to the left.

### Greifenstein
prefix: 02242

ℹ **Marktgemeindeamt St. Andrä-Wördern (Municipal office)**, Altg. 30, St. Andrä-Wördern, ☏ 31300, @ jdh561en

⛴ **MS Gernot (Motor shipping Gernot)**, Rechtes Donaualtarmufer, ☏ 38079. Crossings, round trips, boat rentals, etc. @ lus348en

🏰 **Burg Greifenstein (Greifenstein Castle)**, Kostersitzg. 5. Rebuilt in the 19th c. by Prince Johann Liechtenstein, on the site of an older fortification. The typical small castle with walls, keep, and main hall includes squire's room and gate room from the 12th c. @ cwv745en

▭ **Donau Altarm (Danube oxbow lake)**

* **Bootsverleih (Boat rental)**, Am Alten Hafen 1, ☏ 33837, @ usm588en

* **Wasserskischule (Water skiing school)**, Am Hafen 1, ☏ 32955. Waterski, Wakeboard, Fun Tubes, Gastronomy. @ rgi361en

F11
Greifenstein power station
2
1950
3,2
Wasserskischule
Donau Altarm
3
Bootsverleih
17
Hagenbach
Donaustraße
Greifenstein
Burg Greifenstein
18
L118
Höflein
a.d. Donau
St. Margareta
Danube
1945
4,1
A22
P
Hofau
Hundsberg
390
Hadersfeld
Altenberg
7,5
F10
Zeiselmauer
St. Andrä-Wördern
Sonnberg
420
Weißer Hof
Village museum
Kritzendorf
Freiberg
393
F12
3,5
Unterkritzendorf
Lourdesgrotte
Wolfpassing
B14
Kulturhaus St. Andrä
B14
Maria Gugging
Kierling
Dettenbrunn
Hagenbachklamm
L2118
Pfarrkirche St. M
153

### Greifenstein to Vienna  21.5 km

Continue back out to the Danube ~ **18** turn left at the first intersection ~ follow the street beside the houses of Höflein.

#### Höflein (Klosterneuburg)
prefix: 02243

- St. Margareta, Schulg. 9, ☎ 80141. The Romanesque fortified church (12th century) houses a Baroque high altar from 1725.

Keep left into the path where the street turns to the right ~ ride along the Danube until you reach the mouth of a small canal (Klosterneuburger Durchstich).

Stift Klosterneuburg

From here the route turns south and follows the small lane between the canal and the railway line. You now enter the **Wiener Pforte** (Vienna gate), which is the name given to the passage carved between the hills by the Danube.

#### Kritzendorf (Klosterneuburg)
prefix: 02243

- **Rollfähre (Cable ferry)**, Tuttendörfl 10, Korneuburg, ☎ 0664/2155443, ⊙ End of March - 2 Nov, Mon-Fri 7 a.m. until dusk, Sat, Sun & Fri 8 a.m. until dusk, @ xhr171en
- **Dorfmuseum (Village museum)**, Hauptstr. 56-58, ☎ 24666, ☎ 0664/4389425 ⊙ The museum informs about the history of wine making, the history of Kritzendorf, the church, and more. @ obn552en
- **Strombad (River bath)**, Neue Badstr.1, ☎ 444276

Keep left at the intersection and ride straight ahead into the side street **Durchstichstraße** ~ you pass the **Kritzendorf train station** ~ at the end of the street continue straight ahead into the bicycle path ~ after 2 km ride under the road overpass and turn left across the canal ~ continue on the other side of the canal as far as the intersection **19**.

 Do not miss the opportunity to visit the impressive monastery complex or one of the museums in Klosterneuburg before setting off on the final kilometers into Vienna.

The abbey dominates the town nestled between the forests of the Kahlenberg and the Leopoldsberg.

To reach the abbey, turn right and ride across the bridge and straight through the railway underpass ~ turn left on **Niedermarkt** ~ turn right and follow the street **Hundskehle** up to the Rathausplatz and the abbey.

#### Klosterneuburg
prefix: 02243

- **Tourismus Klosterneuburg (Klosterneuburg tourism)**, In der Au 2-4, ☎ 32038, @ fws563en
- **Archäologische Sammlung (Archaeological collection)**, Martin-str. 38, ☎ 32568 ⊜ Documents 1,000 years of church history. The oldest traces at the site are from a Frankish wooden church from around 900. Also noteworthy: a late-Gothic baptismal. @ grm411en
- **Stadtmuseum (Town museum)**, Kardinal Piffl-Pl. 8, ☎ 444299 ⊙ History of Klosterneuburg and changing special exhibitions. @ grx133en
- **Stiftsmuseum (Abbey Treasury and Museum)**, Stiftspl. 1 ⊙ The collections in the Abbey Museum include major works of painting, sculpture and craftsmanship from Middle Ages to modern times. The Treasury contains works of art of European standing - the Austrian Archduke's Hat, the veil monstrance, major works of medieval goldsmithing, sacred textiles and works of art made

of ivory. Audioguide available in 14 languages. @ wav852en

- **Pfarrkirche St. Martin (parish church)**, Martinstr. 38. The parish dates back to before the middle of the 11th century. Inside, the 16 larger-than-life, gilded wooden statues on wall consoles stand out. @ ybx387en
- **Stiftskirche Unsere Liebe Frau (Abbey church)**, Stiftspl. 1. The Romanesque building dates from 1114-1136, the interior was given its present form in the 18th century. In the Leopold Chapel there was the famous Verdun Altar, perhaps the most magnificent enamel work of the Middle Ages, consisting of 51 biblical panels. Today, this jewel can be seen in the monastery's museum. @ rdk626en
- **Stift Klosterneuburg (Abbey)**, Stiftspl. 1, ℓ 411212 (7d) The medieval collegiate building (1108) was erected on the site of a Roman fort and further expanded from the 15th to the 19th century. Under Charles VI, the new baroque monastery building was erected from 1730-1755 to demonstrate the unity of church and imperial state. However, the beginning of secularisation put an early end to the gigantic project. The guided tours include the

imperial rooms with their outstanding stucco work and the Gobelin Hall. @ mym713en

- **Kletteranlage (Climbing facility)**, In der Au 1, ℓ 0664/2012100 (7d) The climbing centre with indoor, outdoor areas, bouldering area, walls up to 14 m height and much more, offers 200 routes from the third to the tenth degree. @ fwr535en
- **Strandbad (Outdoor pool and beach)**, Strandbadstr. 16, ℓ 44276, @ ojf811en
- **Happyland (Adventure pool)**, In der Au 1, ℓ 217000, @ gwv543en

Ride straight ahead across the intersection into the bicycle path — follow the path to the left around the water park and parking area — the path takes you beside the street past a sporting complex — follow the bicycle path to the right.


By the large car park you can turn left to reach the outdoor pool.

Over the bridge across the canal and the Weidlingbach — **20** turn left into the next side street **Donaustraße**.

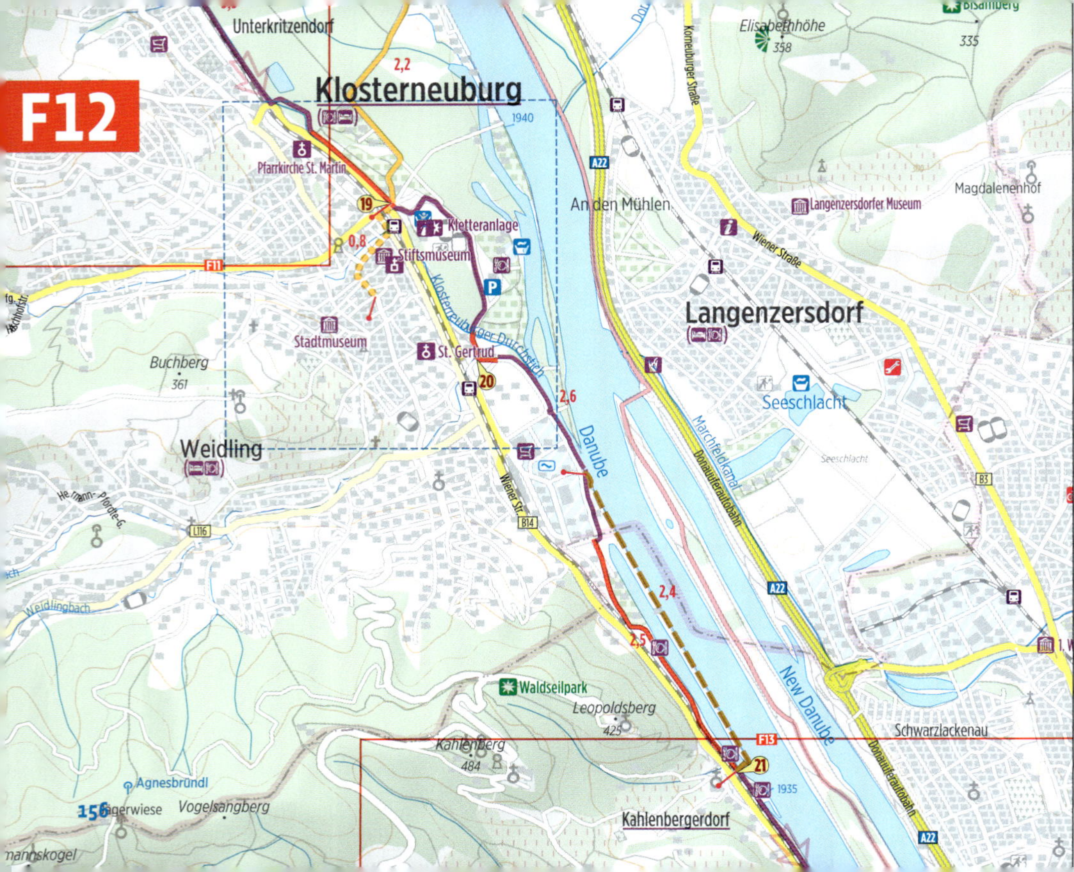




To the right you can see the Kahlenberg and the Leopoldsberg, the southern exposures of which are covered with vineyards. The wines from these hills can be tasted at the famous "Heurigen" in Grinzing, Nußdorf and Kahlenbergerdorf. Wine is also produced on the left flank of the Pforte, on the Bisamberg.

Follow the bicycle path along the **Donaustraße** — the cycle path ends, here continue left on **Kuchelauer Hafenstraße** — soon the outskirts of Vienna are reached.

## Kahlenbergerdorf (Wien)

**21** The route continues on the bicycle path that runs to the left of the railway tracks — from this point on the route into the centre of Vienna is virtually impossible to lose — ride through a park and for a short time along the Danube — you pass Nußdorf as the route comes to follow the Danube canal into the city. To reach **Nußdorf**, go under the railway line before the barrage.

The main route crosses the Danube canal here and then over the Danube onto the Danube island, which it follows towards Lobau. The route we have chosen takes you into the centre of Vienna.

**22** You ride over a small rise as you pass the barrage, designed by Otto Wagner, on the Danube canal — keep left before the railway underpass.


The signs now point you towards Urania as you follow the "Donaukanal-Radweg", the bicycle path along the Danube canal.

Ycu pass under numerous bridges — on the right note the **23** colourful waste incinerator beautified by the artist Friedensreich Hundertwasser — keep going along the Danube canal into the city until ycu see the Rossauer Kaserne, the large red and white brick building, to the right.


From here you can connect with the Ring-Rund-Radweg, a bicycle route that encircles the old city and connects some of the most important sights in Vienna. Take the upramp and cross the street in front of the Rossauer Kaserne, then turn left across the Maria-Theresien Straße and the Schottenring to the bicycle path. The Ring-Rund-Radweg is shown in orange on the city map.


Vienna's main train station can best be reached from the Ring

## To the main railway station     2,1 km

Opposite the **Vienna Opera House**, turn right onto the left-hand cycle path along **Operngasse**. Turn left before the large crossing with traffic lights and immediately after the underground exit. The cycle path ends briefly, then continue on the cycle path to the crossroads Canovagasse. Here turn right on the cycle crossing over the multi-lane road. Continue through the **Resselpark** towards the Karlskirche. Turn right in front of the **Karlskirche** and then left into **Argentinierstraße**. Follow the

Viennese Prater with Ferris Wheel

cycle paths to the main entrance of the main station.

To reach the centre of the old city, continue beside the Danube canal under the second bridge by the Rossauer Kaserne to the **24 Salztorbrücke (bridge)** – take the upramp and turn right into **Salztorgasse** – follow the street into **Vorlaufstraße**, then right along **Marc-Aurel-Straße** and straight onto **Tuchlauben** – turn left into **Brandstätte** and proceed to **25** **Stephansplatz**.

*You have now reached the centre of Vienna and in front of you stands one of Vienna's landmarks, the "Stephansdom" cathedral, which is also the landmark of Austria.*

## Wien (Vienna)

prefix: 01

- **Tourist-Information (Tourist information)**, Albertinapl./Mayederg., 1. Bezirk (Wien), 24555, @ yjw785en
- **DDSG Blue Danube**, Handelskai 265, 58880 Sightseeing Cruises in Vienna. Locations: Schwedenplatz, Marina Wien, Reichsbrücke, @ qyb267en
- **Albertina**, Albertinapl. 1, 534830 One of the world's most important art museums. Artists represented range from Michelangelo to Rubens, Dürer to Picasso. Significant special exhibitions about various artists and photographers. Archives include more than 60,000 drawings and about 1 million printed pages from the late Gothic period to the present. @ wpa636en
- **Heeresgeschichtliches Museum (Military History Museum)**, Ghegastr., 05020/11060301 Occupies an oriental-classical building from 1857, which was Vienna's first building planned as a museum. Contains valuable Austrian military items from the 30 Years War to World War I. Among other things, the car is exhibited in which Archduke Franz Ferdinand and his wife Sophie Chotek were shot by Gavrilo Princip on June 28, 1914 in Sarajevo. The assassination triggered a European crisis that led to the First World War. @ ksl841en
- **Kunsthistorisches Museum (Art history museum)**, Burgring 5, 525240 One of the most renowned art collections in the world. The core collection includes works by Dürer, Rubens, Titian and Bruegel the older (largest Bruegel collection in the world). Also noteworthy: the Egyptian/Oriental collection, antiquity collections and numismatics collection. @ jbg576en
- **MAK - Museum für angewandte Kunst (Museum of Applied Arts)**, Stubenring 5, 711360 Furniture, textiles or glass and ceramics - how art influences everyday life and how everyday life influences art can be explored in the MAK. The exhibits range from East Asian and Islamic art, art prints, metalwork and works by the Wiener Werkstätte to a collection of carpets and the works of modern artists. @ mlt288en
- **Mozarthaus Vienna (Mozart House)**, Domg. 5, 5121791 Wolfgang Amadeus Mozart lived in this house for three years, from 1784 to 1787. The exhibition deals with his work and life. @ ewy774en
- **Naturhistorisches Museum (Natural History Museum)**, Burgring 7, 521770 The museum displays minerals, rare uncut diamonds and meteorites, a fossil collection and 15,000 skeletons (including dinosaurs). Prehistoric items include the original "Willendorf Venus" and anthropological items from the early-Paleolithic period to the present. @ umu572en
- **Oberes Belvedere (Upper Belvedere)**, Prinz-Eugen-Str. 27, 795570 A survey of Austrian painting from Biedermeier through the Ringstraße Period to art nouveau. Large collections

of works by Klimt, Schiele and Kokoschka, plus Waldmüller, Romako, Makart, Wotruba and others. @ cpu853en

🏛 **Österreichische Nationalbibliothek (Austrian National Library)**, Josefspl. 1, 📞 53410 🕗 The baroque main hall was created by Fischer von Erlach and son 1723-37. Ceiling painting by Daniel Gran. Holds the 15,000 gold-printed volumes collected by Prince Eugene of Savoy. Also worth seeing: State Hall, Literature Museum, Globe Museum, Papyrus Museum and Esperanto Museum. @ xhe814en

🏛 **Kaiserliche Schatzkammer (Imperial Treasury)**, Hofburg-Schweizerhof, 📞 525240 ⊜ One of the world's great treasures, includes the Holy Roman Emperor's crown (ca. 962), the Austrian Emperor's crown, the Burgundy treasure and the treasures of the Order of the Golden Fleece. @ ytp216en

🏛 **Albertina Modern**, Karlspl. 5, 📞 53483540 🕗 The Museum of Modern and Contemporary Art shows Austrian art history of the last 80 years, with a focus on the Essl Collection. Additionally, an insight into collections of international art is provided. @ kbl828en

🏛 **Belvedere 21**, Arsenalstr. 1, 📞 795570 ⊜ The museum shows Austrian art from the 20th and 21st cs. and is housed in a remarkable building designed by star architect Karl Schwanzer as an Austrian pavilion for the 1958 World Exhibition. @ eje228en

🏛 **Dritte Mann Museum (Third Man museum)**, Pressg. 25, 📞 0676/4757818 ⊙ Here everything revolves around the film classic "The third man" and post-war Vienna. @ isf382en

🏛 **Haus der Geschichte Österreich (House of History Austria)**, Heldenpl., 📞 53410805. Museum dedicated to the history of the country since the founding of the Republic in 1918. It shows the political and social upheavals that Austria has experienced since then. @ hvu573en

🏛 **Haus der Musik (House of music)**, Seilerstätte 30, 📞 5134850 🕗 All about music, with many interactive exhibits that visitors can try. @ gtx815en

🏛 **Haydnhaus (Haydn house)**, Haydng. 19, 📞 5961307 ⊜ Information about the last years of the composer's life. @ okk657en

🏛 **Jüdisches Museum (Jewish Museum)**, Dorotheerg. 11, 📞 5350431 ⊜ Opened 50 years

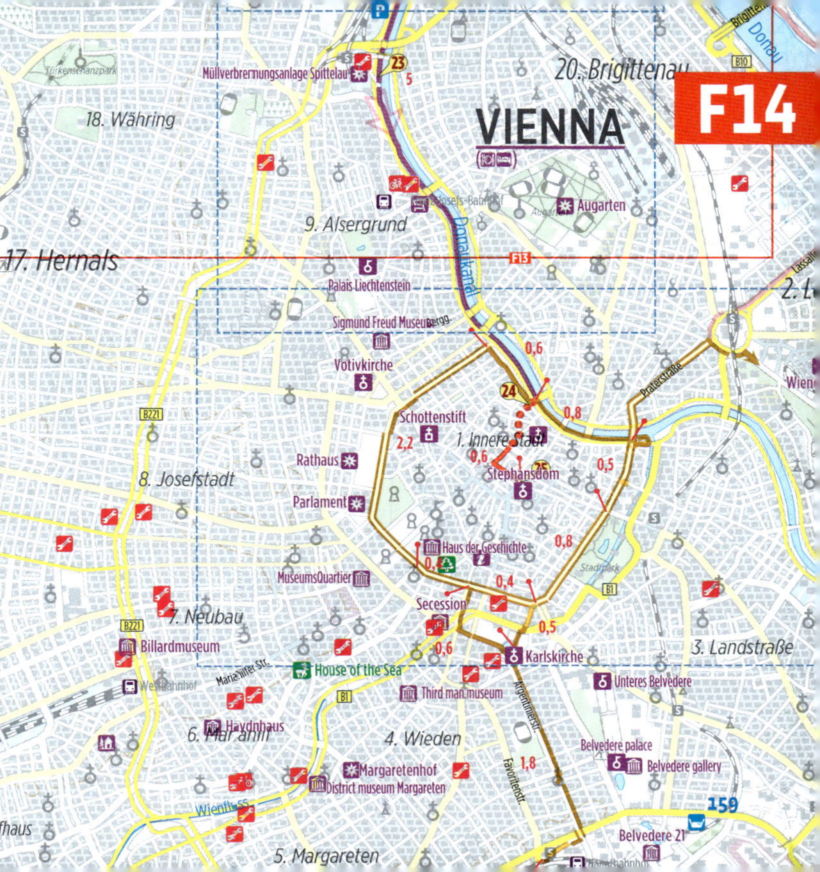

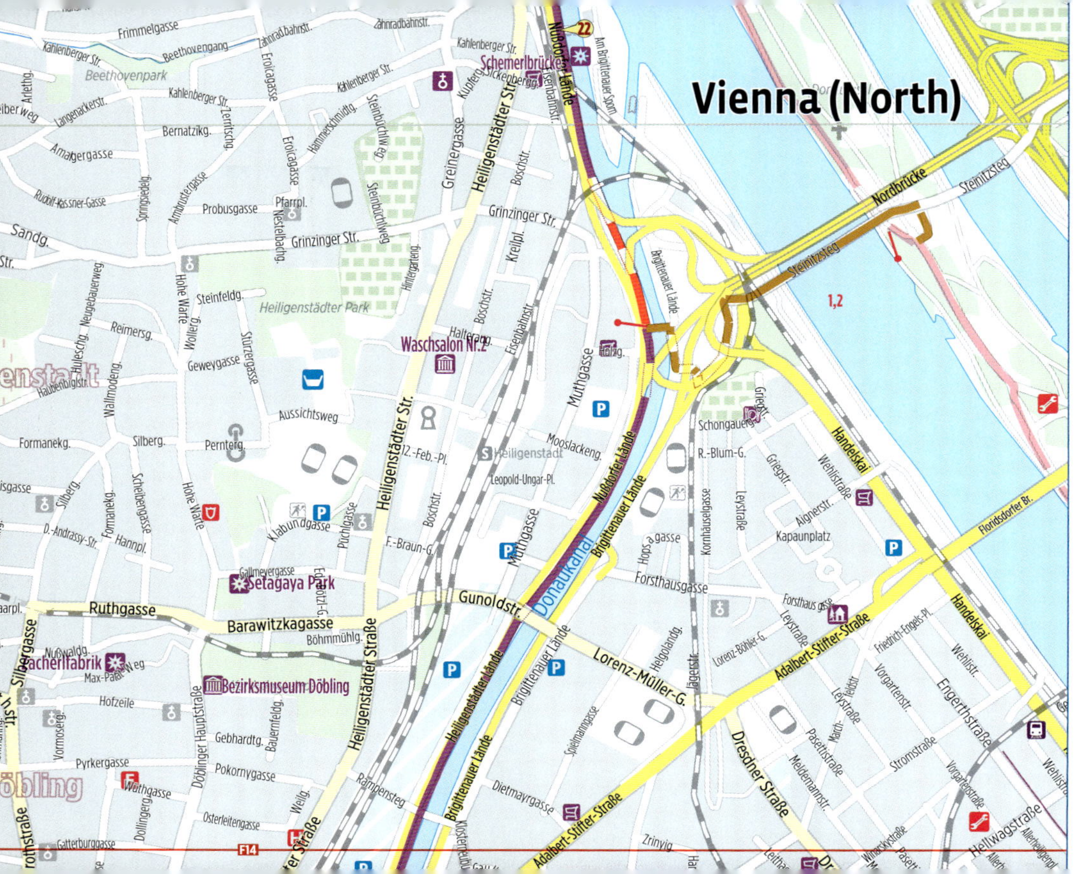


after the end of World War II. Changing exhibitions illustrate Jewish cultural history, art, literature and photography. Another location: 1., Judenpl. 8. @ erc481en

**Kaffeemuseum (Coffee Museum)**, Vogelsangg. 36, 5. Bezirk (Wien), ☎ 0664/1441406 od. 0676/4068728 The collection highlights everything about coffee, from coffee beans to antique coffee machines and Viennese coffeehouse culture. @ xvr684en

**Klimt Villa**, Feldmühlg. 11, 13. Bezirk (Wien), ☎ 8761125 Gustav Klimt created many influential works in the largely neo-baroque villa from 1911 until his death in 1918. The exhibition shows exhibits from Klimt's studio. @ ghf743en

**Kunst Haus Wien (Museum Hundertwasser)**, Untere Weißgerberstr. 13, ☎ 7120491 Paintings, architecture, sculptures by Friedensreich Hundertwasser, plus exhibitions featuring other 20th c. artists. @ puh754en

**Kunsthalle Wien (Vienna Art Hall)**, Treitlstr. 2, ☎ 521890 Changing exhibitions featuring contemporary art and masterpieces of classic modernism. @ jxq341en

**Leopold Museum**, Museumspl. 1, ☎ 525701584 Houses the art collection of Rudolf und Elisabeth Leopold, one of the world's most important collections of modern Austrian art, including Schiele, Klimt, Moser, Gerstl, Kokoschka and Waldmüller. @ njb763en

**Madame Tussauds**, Riesenradpl. 5-6, ☎ 8903366 The world-famous wax museum in Vienna's Prater features more than 80 wax figures and an interactive Sisi experience. @ dgv245en

🏛 **mumok - Museum moderner Kunst (Museum of modern Art)**, Museumspl. 1, ☎ 525000 ➲ Modern and contemporary art. Extraordinary collection with works of classical modern art, pop art, Viennese actionism, contemporary film and media art. ⓦ tel748en

🏛 **Museum der Illusionen (Museum of Illusions)**, Wallnerstr. 4, ☎ 5322255 ⑦ The small museum displays a remarkable collection of optical illusions, holograms and stereograms. ⓦ wyb146en

🏛 **MuseumsQuartier (MuseumQuarter)**, Museumspl. 1, ☎ 5235881 ⑦ Spectacular cultural area on the edge of Vienna's Old Town and the eighth largest museum district in the world. ⓦ xfd527en

🏛 **Narrenturm (Fool's Tower)**, Spitalg. 2, ☎ 52177606 ➲ The so-called Narrenturm (Fool's Tower) was built 250 years ago as the first psychiatric clinic under Emperor Joseph II., it houses the world's largest pathological-anatomical collection. ⓦ rrq563en

🏛 **Römermuseum (Roman museum)**, Hoher Markt 3, ☎ 5355606 ➲ Interactive exhibition about the history of the legionary camp Vindobona. ⓦ pka174en

🏛 **Secession**, Friedrichstr. 12, ☎ 5875307 ➲ Built 1897-98 according to plans by Joseph Olbrich for the "Viennese Secession" group of progressive artists. Rotating exhibitions of modern art plus the 34-meter Beethoven frieze by Gustav Klimt. ⓦ tyg288en

🏛 **Sigmund-Freud-Museum**, Bergg. 19, ☎ 319159611 ➲ The founder of psychoanalysis lived here from 1891 until he was

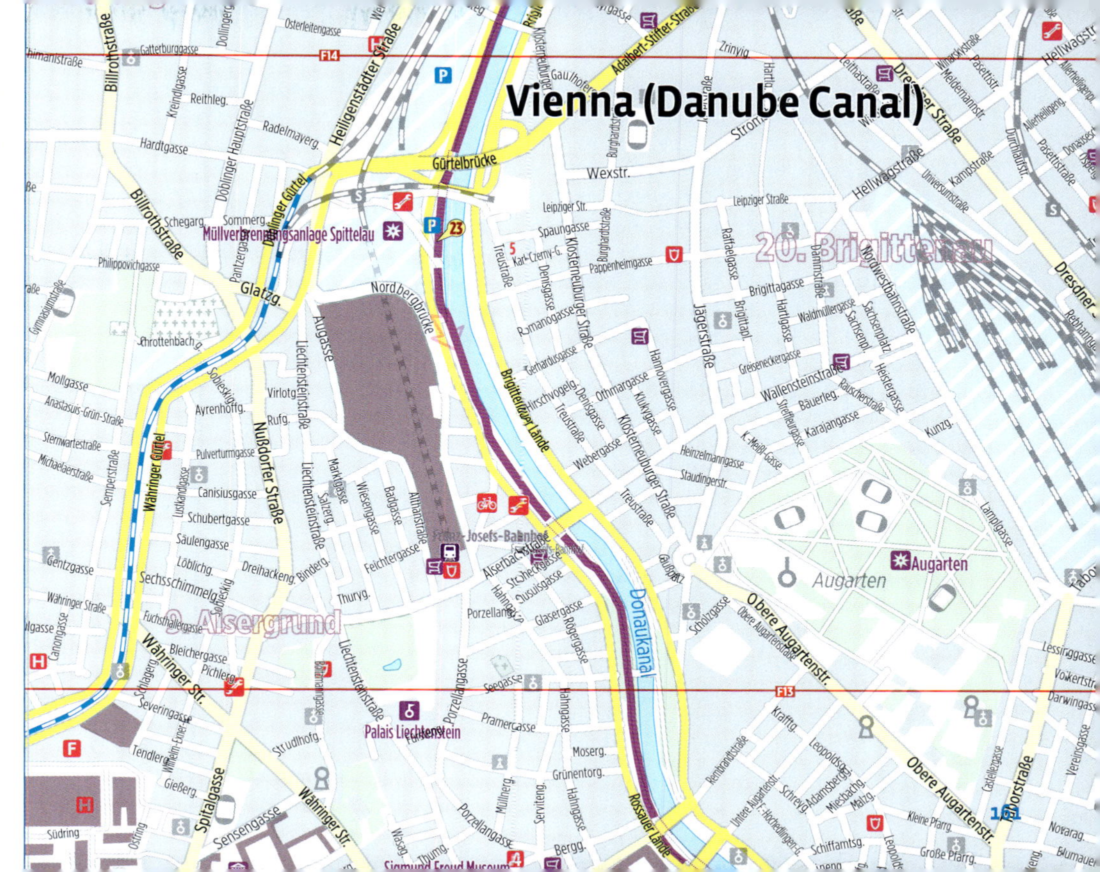

forced to leave in 1938. Freuds former ordination is now a museum. @ eua627en

🏛 **Sisi Museum**, Michaelerkuppel, ✆ 5337570 🕖 Central themes in the impressively and sensitively designed Sisi Museum are the carefree girlhood in Bavaria, the surprising engagement to the emperor and her official role as Austrian empress. @ sxb461en

🏛 **Theatermuseum (Theatre museum)**, Lobkowitzpl. 2, ✆ 525242729 🚇 The museum includes mainly stage settings, costumes and props as well as photos and drawings. @ kea186en

🏛 **Time Travel**, Habsburgerg. 10A, ✆ 5321514 🕖 In the vaults of the St. Michael monastery, visitors can embark on a virtual journey through the history of Vienna. @ oxl671en

🏛 **Verkehrsmuseum Remise (Transport Museum Remise)**, Ludwig-Koeßler-Pl. 109, ✆ 790946803 🚇 More than 80 historical vehicles since 1871 as well as buses and cars of the former Vienna light rail system. @ ysc885en

🏛 **Waschsalon Nr. 2 (Washhouse No. 2)**, Halteraug. 7, Karl-Marx-Hof, ✆ 0680/2267601 🔄 In the historical Karl-Marx-Hof four thematic areas show the history of the Red Vienna of the First Republic. Waschsalon means laundrette and describes the exhibition space. Here the early inhabitants of the Karl-Marx-Hof, built in 1926, did their laundry in round 30 washingspaces, there were also bathes and showers for the hygienic cleaning. @ tsr184en

🏛 **Weltmuseum Wien (World Museum)**, Heldenpl., ✆ 534305052 🚇 Ethnographic museum with unique cultural treasures from all over the world and exciting stories to go with them. @ bkd354en

🏛 **Wien Museum**, Karlspl. 8, ✆ 5058747 🚇 Historical Museum of the City of Vienna. A fascinating mixture of art and history from the Neolithic to the middle of the 20th century. The Wien Museum can be experienced in the MUSA (Felderstr. 6-8) until 2024. @ uam287en

🏛 **Stephansdom (St. Stephen's Cathedral)**, Stephanspl. 3, ✆ 5137648 🕖 Austria's most important Gothic structure and, along with the Prater Ferris-wheel, a Vienna landmark. Noteworthy: the red marble gravestone for Kaiser Frederick III, Anton Pilgram's pulpit (1514/1515), the Viennese "Neustädter Altar" (1447). Guided tours of the extensive catacombs under the cathedral. Below the cathedral there is an extensive system of catacombs with valuable historical testimonies. @ usi533en

🏛 **Votivkirche (Votive Church)**, Rooseveltpl., ✆ 4061192 🕖 The church was built 1856-79 by the architect Heinrich Ferstel, it is one of the most important Neo-Gothic religious buildings in the world. With a height of 99 m it is the second tallest church in Vienna. @ lwi661en

🏛 **Schottenstift (Scottish abbey)**, Freyung 6, ✆ 53498600 🚇 In the year 1155, when Duke Heinrich II. Jasomirgott moved his residence from Klosterneuburg to Vienna, he summoned Irish monks to found a monastery in Vienna. In the same year, construction of the Schottenkirche began. In 1418 Duke Albrecht V. withdrew the monastery from the Irish in the course of the Melk Reform and handed it over to German-speaking Benedictines, but the name "Schotten" was retained. The former abbot's flat of the Schottenstift houses a museum. @ wqf356en

🏛 **Hofburg**, Michaelerpl., ✆ 5337570 🕖 Until 1918 the magnificent castle complex in the centre of Vienna was the centre of the former monarchy, today it fulfils the same function for the Republic of Austria. The Hofburg also houses the Spanish Riding School, the Austrian National Library, the Sisi Museum and the Imperial Apartments. @ cai462en

🏛 **Schloss Belvedere (Belvedere Palace)**, Prinz-Eugen-Str. 27, ✆ 79557134 🕖 The palace is regarded as one of the most beautiful baroque structures. Built 1700 by Lukas von Hildebrandt as a summer residence for Prince Eugene of Savoy. Includes an elegant terraced garden with cascades and sculptures. @ jeh616en

🏛 **Schloss Schönbrunn (Schönbrunn Palace)**, Schönbrunner Schlossstr. 47, ✆ 811130 🕖 Original plans by Fischer von Erlach proposed a palace that would be larger and more magnificent than Versailles. Built 1696-1730, with 1.441 rooms and chambers. Served as Habsburg summer residence and venue of the congress of Vienna. @ spo121en

🏛 **Hermesvilla**, Hermesvillaweg, in the Lainzer Tiergarten, 13. Bezirk (Wien), ✆ 8041324 🚇 Emperor Franz Joseph gave his wife Elisabeth the "Palace of Dreams" (1882-1886) in the middle

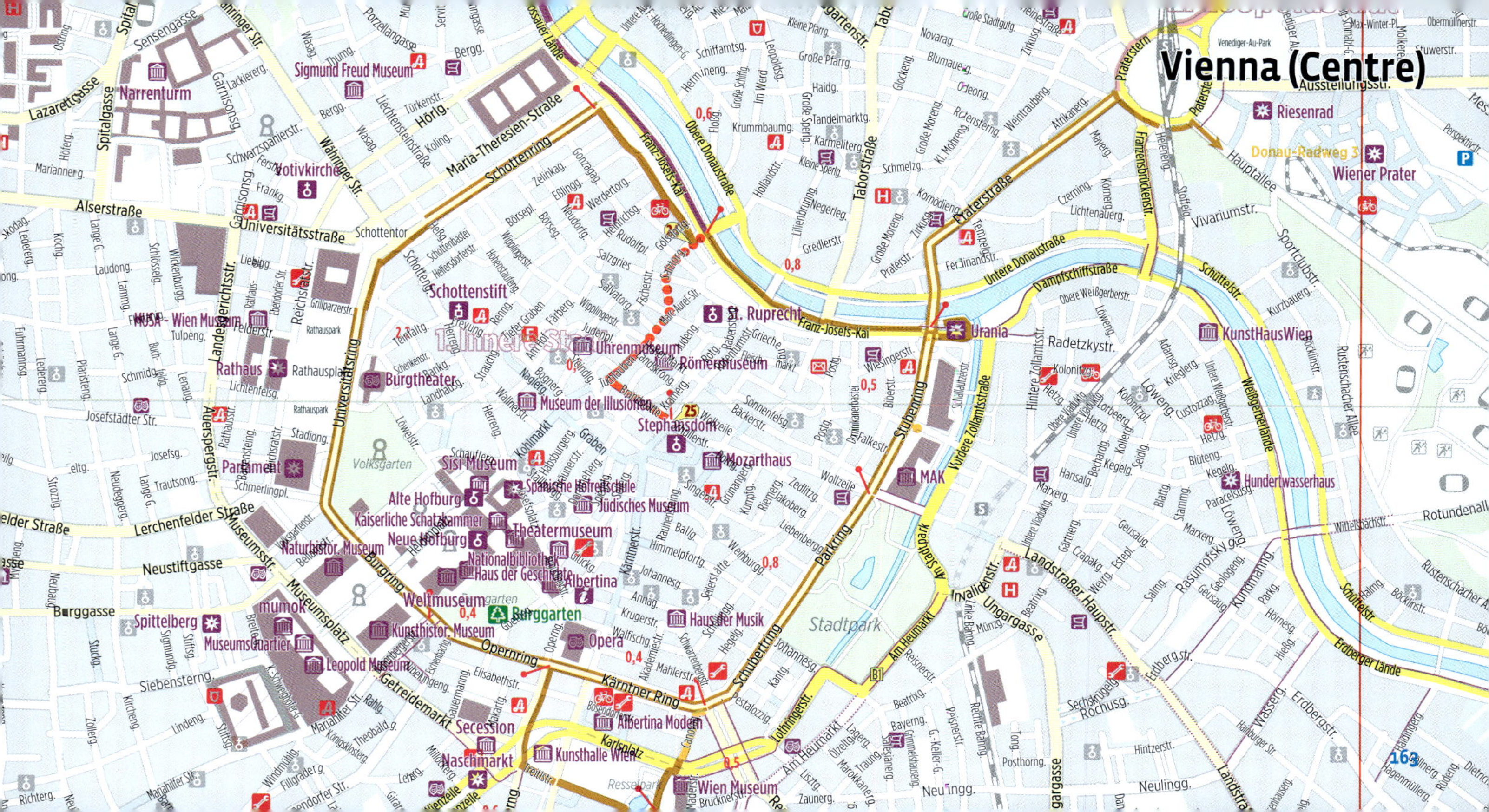

Vienna (Centre)
Narrenturm
Sigmund Freud Museum
Votivkirche
Universitätsstraße
Schottenstift
Schottentor
MUSA - Wien Museum
Rathaus
Burgtheater
Maria-Theresien-Straße
Schottenring
Uhrenmuseum
Römermuseum
St. Ruprecht
Urania
KunstHausWien
Museum der Illusionen
Stephansdom
Mozarthaus
MAK
Parlament
Sisi Museum
Alte Hofburg
Spanische Hofreitschule
Jüdisches Museum
Kaiserliche Schatzkammer
Neue Hofburg
Theatermuseum
Naturhist. Museum
Nationalbibliothek
Haus der Geschichte
Albertina
Hundertwasserhaus
mumok
Welt museum
Burggarten
Kunsthistor. Museum
Haus der Musik
Stadtpark
Leopold Museum
Opera
Spittelberg
MuseumsQuartier
Secession
Albertina Modern
Naschmarkt
Kunsthalle Wien
Wien Museum
Riesenrad
Wiener Prater
Donau-Radweg 3
Venediger-Au-Park
Franz-Josefs-Kai
Maria-Theresien-Straße
Volksgarten
Rathauspark
Ringturm
Stubenring
Parkring
Schubertring
Kärntner Ring
Opernring
Burgring
Museumsplatz
Karlsplatz
Praterstern
Praterstraße
Untere Donaustraße
Obere Donaustraße
Taborstraße
Franzensbrückenstr.
Hauptallee
Dampfschiffstraße
Landstraßer Hauptstr.
Ungargasse
Invalidenstr.
Am Heumarkt
Rennweg
Lothringerstr.
Resselpark
163

Vienna, Schönbrunn Palace

of the former imperial hunting grounds as a gift to keep her in Vienna more often. An exhibition on the first floor shows the history of the house. @ yyj734en

**Palais Liechtenstein**, Fürsteng. 1, ☏ 31957670 ⊘ In the Garden- und Townpalais, works and furniture from five centuries from the collection of the Princes von Liechtenstein are shown. Only with guided tours in German. @ odi284en

**Burgtheater**, Universitätsring 2, ☏ 514444545. The Austrian National Theatre with its excellent theatre performances is also Europe's largest acting theatre. @ lie188en

**Wiener Staatsoper (Vienna State Opera)**, Opernring 2, ☏ 514442250. Today's Vienna State Opera evolved from the Vienna Court Opera founded by the Habsburgs. It was ceremoniously opened in 1869 in the presence of Emperor Franz Joseph and Empress Elisabeth. Today, the Vienna State Opera is one of the leading opera houses in the world. The members of the orchestra of the Wiener Staatsoper make up the Vienna Philharmonic Orchestra. @ kgq385en

**Marionettentheater (Marionette Theatre)**, Schloss Schönbrunn, Hofratstrakt 34, ☏ 8173247. The award-winning puppet theatre cultivates the tradition of artistic play with hand crafted puppets and, together with Mozart's music, provides princely entertainment. @ wry273en

**Naschmarkt**, Wienzeile, ☏ 400005430 ⊜ The largest fruit and vegetable market in Vienna, full of individuality and atmosphere, shows the lively antithesis to supermarkets and the encounter of many cultures. Saturday large flea market. @ lnh758en

**Hundertwasserhaus (Hundertwasser House)**, Kegelg. 37-39 ㉔ The building attracts visitors from all over the world because it bears the unmistakable signature of the Austrian artist Friedensreich Hundertwasser, who was known for his imaginative liveliness and individuality. @ gfn835en

**Margaretenhof**, Margaretenpl., 5. Bezirk (Wien). The architects Ferdinand Fellner and Hermann Helmer built this palace-like complex from 1884-1885, it is an early example of urban housing. @ dwk782en

**Parlament (Parliament)**, Dr.-Karl-Renner-Ring 3, ☏ 401102400, ⊘ Guided tours daily. In 1883, the Austrian Parliament was opened on Vienna's Ringstrasse. The construction under the direction of Theophil Hansen took 10 years and is in the style of Greek classicism. Until the outbreak of the First World War, the deputies of all countries and kingdoms of the Austrian half of the dual monarchy of Austria-Hungary met here. Today, the National Council and the Federal Council hold their sessions here. @ oyn148en

**Prater**, Riesenradpl. 2, ☏ 7292000 ㊐ Entertainment park with nostalgic rides, roller coasters, ghost trains, the Prater museum as well as the famous Ferris wheel from 1897. Recreation is offered by the Green Prater with its extensive meadows and forests as well as water areas. @ duk863en

**Spanische Hofreitschule (Spanish Riding School)**, Michaelerpl. 1, ☏ 53390310 ㊐ Visitors can gain an insight into the enchanting world of the Lipizzaners at a wide variety of events. One can regularly watch the morning work, take part in guided tours of the facility or enjoy the official presentations. @ ack331en

**Spittelberg**, in the 7th district. The district between Breite Gasse and Stiftgasse has model character for a revitalization with preservation of the historical (in this case Biedermeier) building substance and presents itself today as a "Beisl" and art district with flair. @ kni465en

✳️ **Urania**, Uraniastr. 1, ☎ 89174150000 ⓦ The Urania was built in 1910 as an educational building in neo-baroque style. Today it houses the adult education centre, an observatory, a cinema, a puppet theatre and a café-bar-restaurant. @ fnn776en

✳️ **Wiener Ringstraße**. After the former city fortification was removed in 1857-58, one of the most beautiful boulevards with buildings such as the Burgtheater, Kunsthistorisches Museum and Parliament was built on the site of Glacis. The liberal bourgeoisie with its palaces also set a monument here. @ mtu365en

🦌 **Tiergarten Schönbrunn (Schönbrunn Zoo)**, Maxingstr. 13b, palace park, ☎ 87792940 ⓦ One of the oldest zoos in the world with new ideas for animal husbandry is located in a baroque park environment. @ fqv153en

🦌 **Haus des Meeres (Aqua Terra Zoo)**, Fritz-Grünbaum-Pl. 1, ☎ 5871417 ⓦ The World War II flak tower now houses sharks, turtles, crocodiles, snakes and even monkeys. @ rtt675en

🦌 **Lainzer Tiergarten**, Hermesstr., 13. Bezirk (Wien), ☎ 400049200 ⓦ The extensive forest and nature reserve is home to numerous free-ranging wild animals such as deer, mouflon and wild boar. @ fhu454en

🦌 **Wüstenhaus Schönbrunn (Desert House)**, opposite the Palm House, ☎ 8779294500 ⓦ Flora and fauna native to desert areas from Central America to Madagascar. @ wmr514en

✴️ **Waldseilpark Kahlenberg (Kahlenberg Forest Rope Park)**, Josefsdorf 47, ☎ 3200476 ⏱ With obstacles such as rope bridges, wobbly nets, flying foxes, gnome courses and 150 exercises, the forest rope park offers the right challenge for every age and size. @ nar681en

🛁 **Therme Wien (Vienna thermal spa)**, Kurbadstr. 14, 10. Bezirk (Wien), ☎ 680099600, @ lpy738en

*Vienna! Monarchs called the city on the Danube their capital for more than seven centuries. It was the centre of an empire and today remains one of Europe's most important cultural centres. How can one briefly describe such a city without resorting to stilted clichés or omitting something important? One way, perhaps, is to look at the city's relationship to the river that feeds it.*

*Although Vienna lies on the banks of the Danube, which may even have been blue long ago, the city has no historic riverfront, no pleasant promenades along the water and little of a river city's character. Merely the Little Danube, a canal really, flows through the centre of the Austrian capital. In the 19th century Vienna sacrificed its direct links to the Danube by digging a ruler-straight canal to bypass the river's winding course and help regulate its flow.*

*Officials at the official opening of the canal in 1875 called it an Austrian engineering marvel. The small Wien River was also banished to a featureless man-made channel.*

*Are the city and the river irreconcilable opposites? The most recent attempt to manipulate the river and its landscape has, at least, brought the city's residents closer to the Danube. The broad flood plain along the straightened Danube, which for years had been a barren urban wasteland, was excavated for a new channel. The excavated material was piled in the centre, creating the long slim Donauinsel (Danube island) which has since become one of Vienna's most popular recreation areas.*

You have now reached the end of this cycling journey. We hope that you had an enjoyable and experience-rich cycling tour and are happy that you have chosen a bikeline-Cycling Guide to accompany you on your journey.

The bikeline-Team wishes you a safe and enjoyable return trip!

# Overnight accommodation

## Accommodation addresses

### Categories

- **i** Tourist-Information
- **H** Hotel, Inn
- **Hg** Hotel garni
- **B&B** Bed and Breakfast, Boarding House, Farm
- **Ho** Hostel
- **Mo** Motel
- **AH** Aparthotel, Holiday Flat (selection)
- **B** Bungalow
- **Hh** Hay hotel
- **S** Other
- **Youth hostel
- **Camp ground
- **Tent site (nature tent site)

We have not attempted to list every possible place where visitors can spend the night, and listings should not be construed as any kind of recommendation. Because we wish to expand this list and keep it up-to-date, we welcome any comments, additions or corrections you may have. There is no charge for a single-line entry, for lack of space we cannot guarantee one.

## Identification

| I | Price Range | less than € 25,– |
| II | Price Range | € 25,– to € 35,– |
| III | Price Range | € 35,– to € 50,– |
| IV | Price Range | € 50,– to € 70,– |
| V | Price Range | € 70,– to € 100,– |
| VI | Price Range | over € 100,– |

- o.F. no breakfast
- HP with breakfast and dinner
- only room with shared bathroom
- Bed+Bike Acommodation
- Cyklisté vítáni Acommodation
- 2.5 distance to the route in kilometres

## Prices

These categories are based on the price per person in a double room equipped with shower or bath, with breakfast. The indicated price categories correspond to the status of the survey or revision period and may differ from the actual prices. Price fluctuations are possible, especially during trade fairs, due to different room types and not least due to seasonal factors.

## Bike Workshops and Rental

- Bike workshop
- Bike rental
- E-Bike charging station
- E-Bike rental
- lockable parking facilities

## Distance

The blue number (2.5) at every accommodation shows the distance to the route in kilometres. Please note that this number refers to the linear distance, the difference in altitude and the actual distance covered is not included.

## Updates & corrections

You can obtain the latest corrections to the accommodation directory via the LiveUpdate at www.esterbauer.com. Please note that due to the pandemic and other crises, establishments have to close again and again and prices change regularly. These developments will accompany us for some years to come. The bikeline team is constantly trying to adjust and correct the data. However, we ask for your understanding if some information is no longer up-to-date. Our LiveUpdate will then help you.

# Passau to Linz along the north bank

## Passau (D)
Prefix 0851

[i] Tourist information, Rathauspl. 2, 396610 [0]

[i] Tourist information, Bahnhofstr. 28, 396610 [0]

[H] Burgwald, Salzweger Str. 9, 941690, OB, III [?]

[H] Cutellus, Kleine Messerg. 12, 49095204, 0160/94641829, IV [0]

[H] König, Untere Donaulände 1, 3850, IV-V [0]

[H] Morgentau, Bräug. 19, 49095599, IV-V [0]

[Hg] Passauer Wolf, Untere Donaulände 4, 931510, III-V [0]

[H] Goldenes Schiff, Unterer Sand 8, 34407, III-IV [0.5]

[Ho] Frau Dunschn, Ludwigstr. 18, Eingang zw. Buchh. Rupprecht u. Apotheke, 98853971, II [0.5]

[Jh] Jugendherberge Passau, Oberhaus 125, 493780, II-III [0]

[camping] Zeltplatz Passau, Halser Str. 34, 41457 [0.5]

[bike] Bikehaus Bikeambulanz, Bahnhofstr. 29, 9662570, 0151/12834224 [0]

[bike] Fahrrad-Klinik, Bräug. 10, 33411, 0170/3837651 [0]

[bike] Fahrradladen-Passau, Wittg. 9, 72226 [0]

[bike] Zweirad Seidel, Spitalhofstr. 83, 57813 [2]

[bike] Zweirad Würdinger, Äußere Spitalhofstr. 2, 6346 [2]

[bike] Zweirad-Center Zeller, Graneckerstr. 4, 56302 [2.5]

[bike] Bike Box, Obere Donaulände, parking lot Schanzlbrücke in front of the driveway, 34784. You will get the key opposite in the bicycle shop Passau. [0]

## Hals (Passau) (D)
Prefix: 0851

[H] Zur Triftsperre, Triftsperrstr. 15, 51162, III [2.5]

## Lindau (Passau) (D)
Prefix: 0851

[H] Aschenberger, Donaustr. 23, 42811, III [0]

## Kellberg (Thyrnau) (D)
Prefix: 08501

[i] Tourist-Information, St.-Blasius-Str. 10, 320 [2]

[H] Golf- und Landhotel Anetseder, Raßbach 8, 91313, IV-V [3]

[H] Lindenhof, Kurpromenade 12, 8080, IV [2]

[H] Kernmühle, Kernmühle 1, 567, III [0]

[H] Zum Kirchenwirt, St.-Blasius-Str. 1, 8116, III [1.5]

[B&B] Am König-Max-Stein, Wingersdorf 15, 486, I-II [1.5]

## Erlau (Obernzell) (D)
Prefix: 08591

[H][AH] Hotel Zur Post, Hauptstr. 22-24, 91490, III [0]

[H] Zum Edlhof, Edlhofstr. 10, 466, I I [0]

[B] Haus Erlautal, Erlautal 8, 912871, 0171/1096903, I-II [0.5]

## Obernzell (D)
Prefix: 08591

[i] Tourist Info, Marktpl. 42, 9116119 [0]

[H] Zum Freischütz, Bachstr. 7, 1863, II [0.5]

## Jochenstein (Untergriesbach) (D)
Prefix: 08591

[i] Tourist information, Marktpl. 24, Untergriesbach, 08593/9009-0 [3]

[H][camping] Kohlbachmühle, Kohlbachmühle 1, 320, II [0]

[H] Kornexl, Am Jochenstein 10, 1802, III [0]

## Engelhartszell
Prefix: 07717

[i] Tourist information, Marktpl. 61, 80550 [0.5]

[H] Zum Goldenen Schiff, Nibelungenstr. 2, 8009, IV [0.5]

[B&B] Restaurant-Pension Bernhard's, Maierhof 17, 8123, 0664/5948087, II [0.5]

[B] Aichinger Donaublick, Sauwaldstr. 122, 8172, 0664/4443865, II [1]

[B] Anita, Sauwaldstr. 15, 20053, CB, I [0.5]

[B] Beham, Marktstr. 25, 0664/3921189, I [0.5]

[B][AH] Hackner, Brunng. 250, 7140, 0699/81215137, II [0.5]

[B] Hufschmiede, Nibelungenstr. 11, 8059, 0680/2038643, II [0.5]

[AH] Huber, Nibelungenstr. 40, 8285, 0680/3013312, II [0.5]

[camping] Camping mit Schlafhaus, Nibelungenstr. 113, 805516, 0664/8708787 [0.5]

[bed] Donau(T)Raum AHOI, Nibelungen Str. 11, 805516, III [0.5]

[Be] Be Energised Gemeindeamt, Sauwaldstr. 20, 059/0006065 [0.5]

## Kramesau (Neustift im Mühlkreis)
Prefix: 07285

[H] Luger, Kramesau 4, Navieingabe: 4143 Neustift, 507, III-IV [0]

[B&B] Trautendorfer, Kramesau 5, 591, II [0]

## Niederranna (Hofkirchen im Mühlkreis)
Prefix: 07285

[i] Municipal office, Markt 8, Hofkirchen im Mühlkreis, 7011 [2]

[H] Draxler, Niederranna 3, 511, III-IV [0]

## Marsbach (Hofkirchen im Mühlkreis)
Prefix: 07285

[i] Municipal office, Markt 8, Hofkirchen im Mühlkreis, 7011 [2]

[B&B][AH] Eselgut Pühringer, Nr. 4, 293, 069911077711, OB, V [0]

## Freizell (Hofkirchen im Mühlkreis)

[i] Municipal office, Markt 8, Hofkirchen im Mühlkreis, 07285/7011 [2]

## Dorf (Niederkappel)
Prefix: 07286

[B&B][AH] Biohof Ramesedt, Dorf 10, 8116, OB, I [1]

## Au/Schlögen (Hofkirchen im Mühlkreis)
Prefix: 07286

B&B Zur Fährfrau, Au 1, (ggb. Schlögen), 07285/6317, II [0]

### Niederkappel
Prefix: 07286
- Municipal office, Hauptstr. 12, 8555 [2]

### Obermühl (Kirchberg ob der Donau)
Prefix: 07286
- Municipal office, Ortspl. 5, 07282/4601 [1]
- H Aumüller, Obermühl 13, 7216, III [0]
- H Bruckwirt, Graben 6, (in Kreuzung n. Altenfelden), 83210, HB, V [3]
- H Gierlinger, Grafenau 17, 7213, IV [0]

### Exlau (Kirchberg ob der Donau)
Prefix: 07232
- H Gasthof in der Exlau, Exlau 2, Neuhaus, 2907, III [0]

### Untermühl (Sankt Martin im Mühlkreis)
Prefix: 07232
- B&B Gasthof-Pension Ernst, Untermühl 4, 2919, IV [0]

### Oberlandshaag (Feldkirchen an der Donau)
Prefix: 07233
- H Faustschlössl, Oberlandshaag 72, 7402, 06643257204, V [0]
- B&B Fischerhof, Oberlandshaag 42, 7412, 0664/1610929, II [0]
- Kary, Aschacher Str. 134, 7407 [0]

### Unterlandshaag (Feldkirchen an der Donau)
- B&B AH Fingerneissl, Familie Rechberger-König, Unterlandshaag 60, 0664/3333307, III [0]

### Feldkirchen an der Donau
Prefix: 07233
- Tourism association, Hauptstr. 1, 7190 [0]
- AH Allerstorfer, Bergheimerstr. 5, 7207, 0699/11312204, II [0]

### Bad Mühllacken (Feldkirchen an der Donau)
Prefix: 07233
- B Rabeder, Bad Mühllacken 18, 6681, II [1.5]
- B Wolfsteiner-Lackner, Bad Mühllacken 60, 7281, 0664/8989929, I [2]

### Oberndorf (Feldkirchen an der Donau)
Prefix: 07233
- B&B Hengstschläger, Oberndorf 14, 6671, 0664/1636482 [1.5]

### Pesenbach (Feldkirchen an der Donau)
Prefix: 07233
- H Wirt in Pesenbach, Pesenbach 32, 7273, 0664/5190291, III [0.5]

### Freudenstein (Feldkirchen an der Donau)
- B&B Reiterhof Pfleger, Wagerleitnerstr. 8, 07233/6392, 0664/5041128, II-III [1]

### Weidet (Feldkirchen an der Donau)
Prefix: 07233
- B Leitner, Weidet 7, 7516, 0680/2360524, I [0.5]
- Campingplatz Puchner, Golfplatzstr. 21, close to the lakes, 0664/4824900 [1]

### Ottensheim
Prefix: 07234
- Tourist Information, Marktpl. 7, 8225530, 0699/10437643 [0]
- H Donauhof, Donaulände 9, An der Fähre, 83818, III [0]
- Hg Schwarzer Adler, Marktpl. 19, 82224, III [0]
- AH Fam. Fuchshuber, Stifterstr. 21, 82036, 0680/2434569, I [0.5]
- Camping Hofmühle, Höflein 20, (1,5 km westl.), 82418, 0699/11444906, 0699/12042770 [1]
- dasparkhotel, Rodlpark, OB [0]
- Intersport, Hostauerstr. 62-68, EKZ Donautreff, 83641 [0.5]
- Cafe Casagrande, Ledererg. 14, 82438, 0664/6509205 [0]

### Puchenau
Prefix: 0732
- B&B Kepplinger, Großambergstr. 17, 221759, 0699/10800085, II [0.5]

### Urfahr (Linz)
Prefix: 0732
- Hg Goldener Adler, Hauptstr. 56, 731147, V [0.5]

## Passau to Linz along the south bank

### Schärding
Prefix: 07712
- Cycling and guest service centre Alte Innbrücke, tourism association, Innbruckstr. 29, 43000 [13]
- H Biedermeier Hof, Passauer Str. 8, 30640, III [13]
- H Stiegenwirt, Schloßg. 2-6, 3070, IV [13]
- Hg Stadthotel Schärding, Kircheng. 19, 36130, V-VI [13]

### Passau (D)
Prefix: 0851
- Tourist information, Rathauspl. 2, 396610 [0]
- Tourist information, Bahnhofstr. 28, 396610 [0]
- H Burgwald, Salzweger Str. 9, 941690, OB, III [2.5]
- H Cultellus, Kleine Messerg. 12, 49095204, 0160/94641829, IV [0]
- H König, Untere Donaulände 1, 3850, IV-V [0]
- H Morgentau, Bräug. 19, 49095599, IV-V [0]
- Hg Passauer Wolf, Untere Donaulände 4, 931510, III-V [0]
- H Goldenes Schiff, Unterer Sand 8, 34407, III-IV [0.5]
- Ho Frau Dunschn, Ludwigstr. 18, Eingang zw. Buchh. Rupprecht u. Apotheke, 98853971, II [0.5]
- Jugendherberge Passau, Oberhaus 125, 493780, II-III [0.5]
- Zeltplatz Passau, Halser Str. 34, 41457 [1]
- Bikehaus Bikeambulanz, Bahnhofstr. 29, 9662570, 0151/12834224 [0]
- Fahrrad-Klinik, Bräug. 10, 33411, 0170/3837651 [0]

[cycle] Fahrradladen-Passau, Wittg. 9, 72226 0

[cycle] Zweirad Seidel, Spitalhofstr. 83, 57813 2

[cycle] Zweirad Würdinger, Äußere Spitalhofstr. 2, 6346 2

[cycle] Zweirad-Center Zeller, Graneckerstr. 4, 56302 2.5

[cycle] Bike Box, Obere Donaulände, parking lot Schanzlbrücke in front of the driveway, 34784. You will get the key opposite in the bicycle shop Passau. 0

### Innstadt (Passau) D
Prefix: 0851

[B&B] Vicus, Johann-Bergler-Str. 2, 931050, III-IV 0.5

[B&B] Vilsmeier, Lindental 28a, 36313, II-III 1

### Bayerisch Haibach (Passau) D
Prefix: 0851

[B&B] Gambrinus, Bayerisch Haibach 20, 2905, 0160/7991243, III 0

[B&B] Zur Freiheit, Wiener Str. 86, 4908491, 0151/28882064, I 0

### Freinberg
Prefix: 07713

[i] Tourism association Freinberg, Freinberg 4, 81020 1.5

[B&B] Topfit-Freizeitpark & Sexxeralm, Freinberg 74, 8494, II-III 2

### Hinding (Freinberg)
Prefix: 07713

[B&B] Blaas, Hinding 38, 8107, III 1

### Esternberg
Prefix: 07714

[i] Municipal office, Hauptstr. 33, 6655 1.5

[H] Hubinger, Hauptstr. 81, 6616 2

[B&B] Brabant, Lederfeldweg 1, 20312, 650/3120131, III 1.5

[cycle] Dullinger, Hauptstr. 52, 62000, 0664/2425935 2

### Kasten (Vichtenstein)
Prefix: 07714

[H] Klaffenböck, Kasten 15, 6505, III 0

[B&B] Donautal, Kasten 22, 63100, 0664/5641678, II 0

[camping] Campingplatz Kasten, Kasten Nr. 100, 8055, 0664/8784121 0

### Vichtenstein
Prefix: 07714

[i] Vichtenstein tourism association, Vichtenstein 70, 8055 1

### Engelhartszell
Prefix: 07717

[i] Tourist information, Marktpl. 61, 80550 0

[H] Zum Goldenen Schiff, Nibelungenstr. 2, 8009, IV 0

[B&B] Restaurant-Pension Bernhard's, Maierhof 17, 8123, 0664/5948087, II 0

[B] Aichinger Donaublick, Sauwaldstr. 122, 8172, 0664/4443865, II 0.5

[B] Anita, Sauwaldstr. 15, 20053, OB, I 0

[B] Beham, Marktstr. 25, 0664/3921189, I 0

[B] [AH] Hackner, Brunng. 250, 7140,

0699/81215137, II 0.5

[B] Hufschmiede, Nibelungenstr. 11, 8059, 0680/2038643, II 0

[AH] Huber, Nibelungenstr. 40, 8285, 0680/3013312, II 0

[camping] Camping mit Schlafhaus, Nibelungenstr. 113, 805516, 0664/8708787 0

[bed] Donau(T)Raum AHOI, Nibelunger Str. 11, 805516, III 0

[energy] Be Energised Gemeindeamt, Sauwaldstr. 20, 059/0006065 0

### Wesenufer (Waldkirchen am Wesen)
Prefix: 07718

[H] Seminarhotel Wesenufer, Wesenufer 1, 20090, III-V 0

[H] Schütz, Wesenufer 17, 7208, IV 0

[H] Zum Schiffmeister, Wesenufer 19, 0699/17385109, IV 0

[H] Zur blauen Donau, Vornwaldstr. 2, 7241, 0664/3432748, II 0

[B&B] Feiken, Wesenufer 65, 0664/3267470, II 0

### Schlögen (Haibach ob der Donau)
Prefix: 07279

[H] Donauschlinge, Schlögen 2, 8212, HB, IV-VI 0

[B&B] [camping] Freizeitanlage Schlögen, Mitterberg 3, 8241, III 0

### Inzell (Haibach ob der Donau)
Prefix: 07279

[H] Reisinger, Inzell 13, 8715, 8581, II 0

[B] Maria, Inzell 10, 8297, II 0

[camping] [B&B] Zum Hl. Nikolaus, Inzell 6, 8328, 0664/2347314, II 0

### Kobling (Haibach ob der Donau)
Prefix: 07279

[B&B] Idylle am Donauufer, Kobling 1, 0664/73493393, II 0

### Haibach ob der Donau
Prefix: 07279

[i] Municipal office, Kirchenpl. 4, 8235 1

[H] Hoamat, Hinterberg 9, 85485, V 1

[H] Mosthof 3erBerg, Berg 3, 85477, 0664/2635898, OB, II 1

[B&B] Silvia, Moos 2, 8522, 0660/6069676, III 2.5

[B&B] Fredl Z'linetshub, Linetshub 2, 8358 1

### Kaiserau (Aschach an der Donau)
Prefix: 07273

[H] [camping] Kaiserhof, Kaiserau 1, 0664/5313327, III 0

### Aschach an der Donau
Prefix: 07273

[i] Tourism association Aschach an der Donau, Kurzwernhartpl. 5, 6355, 0664/4082200 0

[H] Zur Sonne, Kurzwernhartpl. 5, 6308, III 0

[B&B] Hirsch, Reitingerstr. 13, 20585, 0664/88969417, III 0.5

[B&B] Kreta, Ritzberger Str. 7, 20502, 0688/64834287, III 0

[B&B] La Mamma, Stiftstr. 1, 0664/3135026,

III🛏 0

B&B Schloss Aschach, Harrachstr. 1, ☎ 7181, ☎ 0699/18181004, ☎ 0699/18181001, III-IV 0.5

B Haberna Maria, Grünauerstr. 14, ☎ 0681/10648285, II 0.5

🔧🚲 Radshop Fritz, Kurzwernhartpl. 11, ☎ 60388 0

🔧 Veloman Service, Schopperpl. 2, ☎ 20230 0

## Hartkirchen

Prefix: 07273

B Knogler, Schmiedstr. 6, ☎ 6454, II 1.5

B Simone Heinz, Haizingerstr. 7, ☎ 6453, ☎ 0664/9260442, II 1.5

B Wolkerstorfer, Haizing 23, ☎ 7397, ☎ 0676/4288660, ☎ 0676/6247804, I 🛏 2

B&B Gruber, Vornholz 7, ☎ 6651, ☎ 0664/3244578, I-II 🛏 1

## Pupping

Prefix: 07272

ℹ Tourist Office, Pupping 13, ☎ 2331 1.5

### Brandstatt (Pupping)

H Dieplinger, Brandstatt 4, ☎ 07272/2324, III-IV 0

B&B Haus Webinger, Brandstatt 1, ☎ 0676/5609748, II 0

## Eferding

Prefix: 07272

ℹ Tourism association Eferding, Stadtpl. 31, ☎ 5555-1711 0

H Brummeier, Stadtpl. 35, ☎ 2462, IV 0

H Kreuzmayr, Schmiedstr. 29, ☎ 4142, III🛏 0.5

🔧 Aichlseder Ulrike, Linzer Str. 19, ☎ 4313, ☎ 0676/7393330 0.5

### Fall (Wilhering)

Prefix: 07226

🏕 Camping Kaltenböck, Fallerstr. 28, ☎ 0676/895610120 0

## Wilhering

Prefix: 07226

ℹ Marktgemeindeamt, Linzer Str. 10, ☎ 2255 0

### Edramsberg (Wilhering)

B Wasmayer, Mühlbachstr. 35, ☎ 07226/2238, ☎ 0664/3862487 2

### Dörnbach (Wilhering)

H Fischer, Pfarrhofweg 2, ☎ 07221/88094, ☎ 0664/2038844, IV🛏 3.5

### St. Margarethen (Linz)

Prefix: 0732

H Rothmayr, St. Margarethen 17, ☎ 774849, III-IV 0

## Linz

Prefix: 0732

ℹ Tourist Information, Hauptpl. 1, Altes Rathaus, ☎ 70702009 0

H Arcotel Nike, Untere Donaulände 9, ☎ 76260, IV-VI 1

H City-Hotel, Schillerstr. 52, ☎ 652622, V 1

H Courtyard by Marriott, Europapl. 2, ☎ 69590, V 1.5

H Dom-Hotel, Baumbachstr. 17, ☎ 778441, IV-V 0.5

H Mama Muh, Graben 24, ☎ 772477, II-III🛏 0.5

H Montagehotel Business & City, Semmelweisstr. 70, ☎ 773201, IV 2

H Motel One, Hauptpl. 10-11, ☎ 2100110, V 0

H Prielmayerhof, Weissenwolffstr. 33, Kaplanhofviertel, ☎ 7741310, IV-V 1.5

H Schillerpark, Rainerstr. 2-4, Eingang: Schillerpl., ☎ 6950102, IV-VI 1

H Stadtoase Kolping, Gesellenhausstr. 5-7, ☎ 661690, III ☺ 1

H TWH Donauwelle, Am Winterhafen 13, ☎ 789990, IV-V 2

H Zum Schwarzen Bären, Herrenstr. 9-11, ☎ 772477, V 0.5

H ibis Linz City, Kärntner Str. 18-20, Bahnhofsnähe, ☎ 69401, V 1.5

H ibis Styles Linz, Wankmüllerhofstr. 37, Ecke Wolfgang-Paulistr., ☎ 347281, IV-V 3

Hg Wilder Mann, Goethestr. 14, (Bahnhofsnähe), ☎ 656078, III 1

B&B Antica Locanda, Mariahilfg. 1, ☎ 0650/6355869, III 0.5

🏠 Jugendgästehaus Linz, Stanglhofweg 3, ☎ 664434, III ☺ 1.5

🔧🚲 B7 Fahrradzentrum, Peter-Behrens-Pl. 9, at the tobacco factory, ☎ 681880 1.5

🔧 BikeFeeling, Bismarckstr. 14, ☎ 775116 1

V 0.5



### Urfahr (Linz)

Prefix: 0732

H Sommerhaus, Julius-Raab-Str. 10, ☎ 2457490, III-IV 1

Hg Goldener Adler, Hauptstr. 56, ☎ 731147, V🛏 0.5

🏠 Johannes Kepler Heim, Altenberger Str. 74, ☎ 244031, OB, II 1.5

🔧 Radsport Kiesl, Freistädterstr. 297, ☎ 750450 0.5

### Plesching (Steyregg)

Prefix: 0732

B DDr. Ömer Gottfried, Seeweg 1, ☎ 0676/4303943, OB, I 1

⛺ Pleschinger See, Seeweg 11, ☎ 245607, I 0

## Steyregg

Prefix: 0732

ℹ Municipal office, Weißenwolffstr. 3, ☎ 640155 0

B Födermayr Hanna, Stadtpl. 1, ☎ 640762, ☎ 0664/1848785, OB, II 0

B Wagner Franz, Windegg 5, ☎ 0664/1005626, OB, I 0.5

## Luftenberg an der Donau

B Paula Böcksteiner, Luftenbergstr. 132, ☎ 07237/3528, ☎ 0680/1204723 1.5

### Abwinden (Luftenberg an der Donau)

Prefix: 07237

H Lehenhof, Abwinden-Dorf 7, ☎ 27554, III [0]

B&B Stefanie Resanka, Abwinden-Dorf 227, ☎ 4530, II [0]

## Sankt Georgen an der Gusen
Prefix: 07237

i Municipal office, Marktpl. 12, ☎ 2255 [0.5]

## Langenstein
Prefix: 07237

i Municipal office, Hauptstr. 71, ☎ 2370 [0]

H Langenstein Ost, Hauptstr. 13, ☎ 5251, ☎ 0699/17555453, III [0]

B&B Pißenberger, Hauptstr. 3, ☎ 64370, ☎ 0664/2611648, II [0]

## Mauthausen
Prefix: 07238

i Tourist association Mauthausen, Vormarktstr. 3, ☎ 2243, ☎ 0676/3150151 [0]

H AH Gasthof Maly, Machlandstr. 1, ☎ 2249, ☎ 0699/10098068, III [0.5]

H Weindlhof, Kirchenweg 12, ☎ 2641, IV [0.5]

H Zur Traube, Heindlkai 15, ☎ 20230, ☎ 0664/5356285, III [0]

B&B Peterseil's Radl Zimmer, Reiferdorf 11, ☎ 2864, ☎ 0676/6803063, III [0]

B AH Froschauer-Erhart, Hinterholz 14, ☎ 4485, ☎ 0676/3166820, OB, I [1]

B&B AH Kurz, Reiferdorf 1, ☎ 3660, ☎ 0699/17205234, II [0]

B&B Mairhof zu Haidd, Haid 8, ☎ 2416, ☎ 0676/821252023, III [0.5]

## Au a. d. Donau (Naarn im Machlande)
Prefix: 07262

H Donauhotel Lettnerhof, Flößerweg 1, ☎ 57074, IV-V [0]

H AH Jägerwirt, Oberer Markt 24, ☎ 58514, III [0.5]

A B&B Campinganlage Au an der Donau, Hafenstr. 1, ☎ 53090, III [0]

## Naarn im Machlande
Prefix: 07262

i Municipal Office, Perger Str. 2, ☎ 582550 [1.5]

H Gasthof PIZZERIA Florian, Pergerstr. 4, ☎ 58274, ☎ 0664/73535402, II-III [1.5]

B Landhaus Hackner, Bäckerfeld 2, ☎ 53806, ☎ 0650/4155247, II [2]

## Mitterkirchen im Machland
Prefix: 07269

i Bycicle tourist information, Hütting 30, ☎ 30373, ☎ 0664/7361454 [0]

i Municipal office, Mitterkirchen 50, ☎ 82550, ☎ 0664/3841745 [0]

H Haberl, Mitterkirchen 18, ☎ 8423, III [0.5]

H Häuserer, Mitterkirchen 10, ☎ 8325 [0.5]

B&B Kraglhof, Mitterkirchen 26, ☎ 83130, III [0]

B&B Moser, Mitterkirchen 27, ☎ 8311, IV [0.5]

## Baumgartenberg
Prefix: 07269

i Municipial office, Baumgartenberg 85, ☎ 2550 [0]

B Lettner, Mühlberg 1, ☎ 7195, ☎ 0664/5158584 [1]

B Zickerhofer, Steindl 101, ☎ 410, ☎ 0699/88804120 [1]

Kaindl, Baumgartenberg 40, ☎ 221 [0]

## Klam
Prefix: 07269

i Municipal office, Klam 43, ☎ 7255 [0]

H Kirchenwirt, Klam 1, ☎ 7206, III-IV [0]

## Herdmann (Grein a. d. Donau)
Prefix: 07268

AH Schacherhof, Herdmann 5, ☎ 6601, ☎ 0660/6552163, II-III [1]

B&B Wurzergut, Herdmann 10, ☎ 456, I [1]

## Grein a. d. Donau
Prefix: 07268

i Tourist association, Stadtpl. 5, ☎ 7055 [0]

H Goldenes Kreuz, Stadtpl. 8, ☎ 3160, IV [0]

H Zur Traube, Greinburgstr. 6, ☎ 312, III [0]

B Eder, Jubiläumstr. 38, ☎ 410, ☎ 0664/2422807 [0.5]

B AH Haus Kamleitner, Wienerweg 47, ☎ 7975, ☎ 0677/63547533, II [0.5]

B Prinz, Brucknerstr. 11, ☎ 7918, II [0.5]

A Camping Grein, Campingplatz 1, ☎ 21230, ☎ 0699/19039010 [0]

Grell, Kreuzner Str. 1, ☎ 230 [0]

## Struden (Sankt Nikola an der Donau)
Prefix: 07268

B&B Wörthbauer, Struden 26, ☎ 8025, ☎ 0650/3070259 [0]

## Sankt Nikola an der Donau

i Municipal office, St. Nikola 16, ☎ 07268/8155 [0]

AH Apartment St. Nikola, An der Donau 34, ☎ 0664/9267570, IV [0]

## Sarmingstein (Sankt Nikola an der Donau)
Prefix: 07268

B&B Strudengauhof, Sarmingstein 13, ☎ 8302, II [0]

## Ysperdorf (Hofamt Priel)
Prefix: 07414

H Donaublick, Ysperdorf 3, ☎ 7228, ☎ 0699/16655441, III [0]

## Weins

H Hinterleithner, Weinserstr. 95, ☎ 07414/7203, III [0]

## Harland (Hofamt Priel)
Prefix: 07412

B&B Porranzl, Harland 6, ☎ 55484, III [2]

## Hofamt Priel

i Municipal office, Dorfpl. 1, ☎ 07412/524210 [0.5]

H Naglhof, Knogl 7, ☎ 07412/52373, III [0.5]

## Persenbeug
Prefix: 07412

i Municipal office, Rathauspl. 1, ☎ 52206 [0]

H Böhm, Hauptstr. 16, ☎ 58930, III [0]

B Köck, Donaustr. 34, ☎ 52843, ☎ 0664/8974782, I [1]

B Slawitscheck, Nibelungenstr. 62, ☎ 58955, I [1]

## Hagsdorf (Persenbeug)

B AH Leeb, Hagsdorf 19, ☎ 0664/73554849, I [0]

### Metzling (Persenbeug)
Prefix: 07412
- [H] Die Donaurast, Wachaustr. 28, ☎ 52438, IV [0]
- [H] Zum goldenen Groschen, Wachaustr. 57, ☎ 52443, I [0]

### Marbach an der Donau
Prefix: 07413
- [i] Municipal office, Marktstr. 28, ☎ 7045 [0]
- [H] Wachauerhof, Donaustr. 54, ☎ 7035, IV [0]
- [H] Gasthof Haselberger, Donaustr. 70, ☎ 355, III-IV [0]
- [H] Zur Schönen Wienerin, Marktstr. 1, ☎ 7077, III-IV [0]
- [B] Loidhold, Marktstr. 40, ☎ 343, ☎ 0660/4892492, III [0]
- [A][AH] Camping Marbach, Campingweg 2, ☎ 20733, ☎ 0664/73559125 [0]
- [🔧][🚲] Bikeshop-Steindl, Marktstr. 32, ☎ 0680/2086908 [0]

### Maria Taferl
Prefix: 07413
- [i] Municipal office, Nr. 35, ☎ 7040 [0]
- [H] Rose, Hauptstr. 20, ☎ 304, IV [0]
- [H] Schachner, Nr. 24, ☎ 6355, HB, VI [0]
- [B&B] Cafe Maria-Theresia, Nr. 9, ☎ 7033 [0]
- [B] Rameder-Hackl, Nr. 25, ☎ 7039 [0]

### Artstetten-Pöbring
Prefix: 07413
- [i] Municipal office, Schlossstr. 1, ☎ 8235 [0]
- [H] Hirsch, Pöbring 22, ☎ 8393 [2]

- [H] Schlossgasthof, Schlossstr. 2, ☎ 8303, III [0]
- [B][AH] Blumentalhof, Ziegelstadl 3, ☎ 8289, ☎ 0676/4854401, II [0]
- [B][AH] Koch, Am Jakobsweg 11, ☎ 8902 [0]
- [B&B] Gabis Bauernhof, Hart 20, ☎ 8485, ☎ 0676/4820940, II [1.5]

### Leiben
Prefix: 02752
- [i] Municipal office, Hauptstr. 34, ☎ 70042 [0]
- [H] Hochstöger, Hauptstr. 38, ☎ 712522, ☎ 0664/2533106 [0]
- [B&B][AH] Mayerhof, Aichau 4, ☎ 71897, ☎ 0650/4616433, II [1.5]

### Klein-Pöchlarn
Prefix: 07413
- [i] Municipal office, Artstettner Str. 7, ☎ 8300 [0]
- [B&B] Kammerer, Linzer Str. 8, ☎ 8297, II-III [0]
- [B&B] Paradiesgartl, Kremser Str. 6, ☎ 8224, ☎ 0664/2254467, II [0]
- [B&B] Schaumüller/Pieber, Zur Fähre 6, ☎ 8361, ☎ 0664/73684534, II [0]

### Lehen (Leiben)
Prefix: 02752
- [H] Dürregger, Ebersdorf 4, ☎ 71415, III [0]
- [H] Gruber, Donaublick 6, ☎ 71225, III [0]
- [B&B] Gästehaus Wachau, Wachaustr. 1, Ebersdorf, ☎ 0676/7035943, II-III [0]

### Urfahr (Leiben)
Prefix: 02752
- [B&B][AH] Cottage Number 9, Urfahr 9, ☎ 02752/72252, ☎ 0664/5371240, III [0]

### Weitenegg (Leiben)
Prefix: 02752
- [H] Gruber, Weitenegg 10, ☎ 70031, IV [0]

### St. Georgen (Emmersdorf a. d. Donau)
- [B&B] Wintesperger, St. Georgen 4, ☎ 02752/71726, ☎ 0664/2786452, III-IV [0.5]

### Luberegg (Emmersdorf a. d. Donau)
Prefix: 02752
- [H] Landhotel Wachau, Luberegg 20, ☎ 72572, V-VI [0]

### Emmersdorf a. d. Donau
Prefix: 02752
- [i] Tourist infopoint, Beim Kreisverkehr, close to roundabout, ☎ 70010 [0]
- [i] Municipal office, Nr. 22, ☎ 71469 [0]
- [B] Haus Sundl, Rote-Kreuz-Str. 18, ☎ 71419, ☎ 0664/3943765, III [0.5]
- [B&B] Pemmer, Hofamt 24, ☎ 71291, ☎ 0680/4063271, II [0.5]
- [A] Donaucamping, Donaulände 1, ☎ 71707, ☎ 0676/6706652 [0]
- [🚲] nextbike-Station, Nr. 540/22, at the roundabout and tourist info, ☎ 02742/229901 [0]

## Linz to Melk along the south bank

### Linz
Prefix: 0732
- [i] Tourist Information, Hauptpl. 1, Altes Rathaus, ☎ 70702009 [0]

- [H] Arcotel Nike, Untere Donaulände 9, ☎ 76260, IV-VI [0.5]
- [H] City-Hotel, Schillerstr. 52, ☎ 652622, V [1]
- [H] Courtyard by Marriott, Europapl. 2, ☎ 69590, V [1.5]
- [H] Dom-Hotel, Baumbachstr. 17, ☎ 778441, IV-V [0.5]
- [H] Mama Muh, Graben 24, ☎ 772477, II-III [0.5]
- [H] Montagehotel Business & City, Semmelweisstr. 70, ☎ 773201, IV [2]
- [H] Motel One, Hauptpl. 10-11, ☎ 2100110, V [0]
- [H] Prielmayerhof, Weissenwollfstr. 33, Kaplanhofviertel, ☎ 7741310, IV-V [1.5]
- [H] Schillerpark, Rainerstr. 2-4, Eingang: Schillerpl., ☎ 6950102, IV-VI [1]
- [H] Stadtoase Kolping, Gesellenhausstr. 5-7, ☎ 661690, III [1]
- [H] TWH Donauwelle, Am Winterhafen 13, ☎ 789990, IV-V [0.5]
- [H] Zum Schwarzen Bären, Herrenstr. 9-11, ☎ 772477, V [0.5]
- [H] ibis Linz City, Kärntner Str. 18-20, Bahnhofsnähe, ☎ 69401, V [1.5]
- [H] ibis Styles Linz, Wankmüllerhofstr. 37, Ecke Wolfgang-Paulistr., ☎ 347281, IV-V [3]
- [Hg] Wilder Mann, Goethestr. 14, (Bahnhofsnähe), ☎ 656078, III [1]
- [B&B] Antica Locanda, Mariahilfg. 1, ☎ 0650/6355869, III [0.5]
- [🏠] Jugendgästehaus Linz, Stanglhofweg 3, ☎ 664434, III [2]
- [🔧][🚲] B7 Fahrradzentrum, Peter-Behrens-Pl. 9,

at the tobacco factory, ☎ 681880 [1]
🚲 Bike-Feeling, Bismarckstr. 14, ☎ 775116 [1]

## Ausee (Luftenberg an der Donau)
Prefix: 07223

[A] Ferien- und Campingdorf Au-See, Ausee Str., Alter Schmidberg 2, ☎ 0664/4035967, ☎ 0664/88188684 [1]

[A] [Ht] Krebshaus, Auseestr., ☎ 81802, ☎ 0664/4035967, II 0.5

## Pichling (Linz)
Prefix: 0732

[H] Zum Hauermandl, Oidener Str. 98, ☎ 320213, IV 3.5

[A] Pichlinger See, Wiener Str. 937, ☎ 305314 3

## Raffelstetten (Asten)

[B&B] Raffelstettnerhof, König-Ludwig-Str. 11, ☎ 07224/68154 1.5

## Bruck bei Tödling (St. Florian)

[AH] Ebner, Bruck bei Tödling 2, ☎ 0650/3263700, ☎ 0650/6457075, I-II 2.5

## Asten
Prefix: 07224

[i] Municipal office, Marktpl. 2, ☎ 663810 0.5

[H] Stögmüller, Wienerstr. 13, ☎ 66197, ☎ 0664/4336326, III 0.5

[H] Zum Goldenen Schiff, Wienerstr. 14, ☎ 66122, ☎ 0664/1263848 0.5

[B&B] Zum Löwen, Bahnhofstr. 4, ☎ 0676/3363596, III [1]

[B] [AH] Dorninger, Wienerstr. 10, ☎ 0664 4195244, ☎ 0664/6503181, OB, III 0

[B] Herbert Häntschel, Einsiedlstr. 22b, ☎ 0664/2040990, I 0.5

## St. Florian
Prefix: 07224

[i] Municipal office, Leopold-Kotzmann-Str. 1, ☎ 42550 0

[H] Florianerhof, Marktpl. 12-13, ☎ 42540, ☎ 0664/12236, IV 😊 0

[H] Erzh. Franz Ferdinand, Marktpl. 12-13, ☎ 42540, ☎ 0664/1223673, IV 😊 0

[H] Pfistermüller, Am Bäckerberg 1, ☎ 4276, ☎ 0664/9114290, III 0.5

[H] Zur Kanne, Marktpl. 7, ☎ 4288, IV 0

[B&B] Gästehaus Stift, Stiftstr. 1, ☎ 890213, IV 0.5

## Enns
Prefix: 07223

[i] Tourist information, Hauptpl. 19, ☎ 82777 0.5

[H] Zum Goldenen Schiff, Hauptpl. 23, ☎ 86086, IV 0.5

[H] Backhendlstation Ennserpfandlstube, Mauthausner Str. 37, ☎ 83875, ☎ 0660/7729441, III 0

[B&B] Wall, Mauthausner Str. 11, ☎ 82532, II-III 0.5

[B] Berndl, Stiegeng. 3, ☎ 82278, ☎ 0664/9787489, OB, I 0.5

[B] Horvatits, Bahnhofweg 16, ☎ 85317, II 0

## Ennsdorf
Prefix: 07223

[H] Stöckler Zum Grünen Baum, Wienerstr. 5, ☎ 82600, ☎ 0650/4447844, III 0

[B] Schmidthaler, Sperlingg. 9, ☎ 81186,

☎ 0676/5246244, II 2

## Pyburg (Ennsdorf)

[B] Passenbrunner, Weidenweg 5, ☎ 0699/10961155, OB, I 0.5

## St. Pantaleon-Erla
Prefix: 07435

[i] Municipal office, Ringstr. 13, ☎ 7271 0

[H] Winklehner, Ringstr. 14, ☎ 7584, III 0

[B] Gmeiner, Klein Erla 59, ☎ 7235 2.5

## Wallsee-Sindelburg
Prefix: 07433

[i] Municipal office, Marktpl. 2, ☎ 22160 0

[H] Grünling, Marktpl. 7, ☎ 2231, III 0

[H] Hehenberger, Sindelburgerstr. 1, ☎ 2207, III 0.5

[H] Sengstbratl, Marktpl. 21, ☎ 2203, ☎ 0664/3891332, III 😊 0

[H] Wallseerhof, Alte Schulstr. 12, ☎ 2223, III 0

🔧 Glaninger, St.Severinstr. 6, ☎ 22130 0

## Ardagger
Prefix: 07479

[H] Zur Donaubrücke, Tiefenbach 1, (Donaubrücke), ☎ 6119, III-IV 0

## Ardagger Markt (Ardagger)
Prefix: 07479

[i] Ardagger municipal office, Markt 55, ☎ 7312 0

[H] Schiffsmeisterhaus, Ardagger Markt 60, ☎ 6318, ☎ 0664/3357400, III 0

[B] Hölzl, Markt 76, ☎ 6618, ☎ 0681/81829591, I 0

[AH] Apartment Ardagger, Markt 62, ☎ 6318, ☎ 0664/3357400, III 0

## Ardagger Stift (Ardagger)
Prefix: 07479

[H] Langasthof Winter, Stift 3, ☎ 65650, V 0

[B&B] Baumgartenhof, Stift 10, ☎ 7393, ☎ 0664/1741313, II 0

## Hößgang (Neustadtl an der Donau)
Prefix: 07471

[i] Municipal office, Marktstr. 16, ☎ 22400 4

## Freyenstein (Neustadtl an der Donau)
Prefix: 07471

[H] Ziseritsch, Freyenstein 8, ☎ 2272, ☎ 0660/3461618, I 0

## Willersbach (Neustadtl an der Donau)

[H] [A] Krenn, Willersbach 40, ☎ 07412/52678, ☎ 0664/4855324, III 0

## Ybbs an der Donau
Prefix: 07412

[i] Info Center Nibelungengau, Stauwerkstr. 86, ☎ 55233 0

[H] Asia Wok Ybbshof, Stauwerkstr. 71, ☎ 53404, III 0

[H] Donau Lodge, Wiener Str. 10, ☎ 54334, V 😊 0

[Mo] Wohnen beim Bäcker, Stauwerkstr. 85, ☎ 5555515, OB, III 0

[H] Babenbergerhof, Wiener Str. 10, ☎ 54334, IV 😊 0

[H] Mang, Herreng. 8, ☎ 20077, III-IV 0

[B&B] Lindenhof, Stauwerkstr. 45,

☎ 0677/63887772, III⊕ 0.5
[AH] Mathilde, Kircheng. 11, ☎ 0676/3401591 0
[bike] Posh Cycling, Stauwerkstr. 22, ☎ 0664/1516946 0.5

### Sarling (Ybbs an der Donau)
Prefix: 07412
[H] Kaiser, Sarlingstr. 17, ☎ 56220, III 0.5
[B&B] Haselberger Helga, Bodenfeldstr. 4, ☎ 0650/2402702, III 0.5

### Krummnußbaum
Prefix: 02757
[i] Municipal office, Rathausstr. 8, ☎ 2403 0.5
[H] Nusserl, Hauptstr. 36, ☎ 2331, ☎ 0676/5430099, II⊕ 0.5
[B&B] [AH] Kloimüller, Hauptstr. 9, ☎ 2525, ☎ 0676/5104304, I-II 0.5

### Pöchlarn
Prefix: 02757
[i] Town office, Kirchenpl. 1, ☎ 2310 0
[H] Nibelungenmotel, Mankerstr. 54a, Check in: Gasthaus Gramel (gegenüber), ☎ 21112, ☎ 4873, III⊕ I
[B&B] Haus Barbara, Wiener Str. 4, ☎ 2321, ☎ 0660/1525392, III⊕ 0
[B] Wagner, Wiener Str. 33, ☎ 0660/4877118, ☎ 0676/6405783, OB, II 0
[B] Waldbauer, Wienerstr. 60a, ☎ 7395, ☎ 8553, OB, II 0.5
[camp] [NF] Naturfreundehaus-Lagerquartier, Schiffhausweg 4, ☎ 0650/6835820 0
[camp] Union Ruderverein, Regensburgerstr. 16, ☎ 3197, ☎ 0676/7534860, I 0
[bike] Fahrrad Pichler, Rechenstr. 1, ☎ 2456 0.5

### Melk
Prefix: 02752
[i] Info centre, Kremser Str. 5, ☎ 51160 0
[H] Zum Fürsten, Rathauspl. 3, ☎ 52343, III-IV 0
[B&B] Café Central, Hauptpl. 10, ☎ 52343, ☎ 0664/88469101, III 0
[Youth hostel] Junges Hotel Melk, Abt Karl-Str. 42, ☎ 52681, II 0.5
[camp] Campingplatz der Stadt Melk, Kolomaniau 3, ☎ 0676/8447156540 0

## Emmersdorf to Vienna along the north bank

### Emmersdorf a. d. Donau
Prefix: 02752
[i] Tourist infopoint, Beim Kreisverkehr, close to roundabout, ☎ 70010 0
[i] Municipal office, Nr. 22, ☎ 71469 0.5
[B] Haus Sundl, Rote-Kreuz-Str. 18, ☎ 71419, ☎ 0664/3943765, III I
[B&B] Pemmer, Hofamt 24, ☎ 71291, ☎ 0680/4063271, II 0.5
[camp] Donaucamping, Donaulände 1, ☎ 71707, ☎ 0676/6706652 0.5
[bike] nextbike-Station, Nr. 540/22, at the roundabout and tourist info, ☎ 02742/229901 0

### Aggsbach Markt
Prefix: 02712
[i] Municipal office, Aggsbach 48, ☎ 214 0
[B&B] [AH] Anna, Aggsbach-Markt 24, ☎ 253, ☎ 0680/2147724 0.5
[B] Landhaus Wachau, Aggsbach Markt 86, ☎ 0660/7343117, II 0.5
[AH] Gerstbauer, Aggsbach-Markt 19, ☎ 384, ☎ 0650/7278900, II 0.5
[bike] nextbike-Station, Nr. 170, ☎ 02742/229901 0

### Groisbach (Aggsbach Markt)
Prefix: 02712
[B] Gästehaus Wilhelm, Groisbach 20, ☎ 557, II 0
[B] Weingut Herlinde, Groisbach 30, ☎ 551 ⊕ 0
[AH] Wilhelm, Groisbach 4, ☎ 557, ☎ 0680/2147724 0

### Willendorf (Aggsbach Markt)
Prefix: 02712
[H] Gasthof zur Venus, Willendorf 36, ☎ 202020, ☎ 0676/7311822, III 0
[B&B] Schrutz, Willendorf 63, ☎ 556 0

### Schwallenbach (Spitz a. d. Donau)
Prefix: 02713
[B&B] [AH] Gästehaus Schütz, Schwallenbach 31, ☎ 2174, ☎ 0676/7879541, III⊕ 0

### Spitz a. d. Donau
Prefix: 02713
[i] Tourist organisation of the Danube in Lower Austria, Schlossg. 3, ☎ 30060-60 0.5
[i] Tourist Info, Mitterg. 3a, ☎ 2363 0
[H] Boutiquehotel Weinspitz, In der Spitz 3, ☎ 2644, V 0.5
[H] Weinhotel Wachau, Ottenschlägerstr. 30, ☎ 2254, IV-V ☺ 0.5
[B&B] Café Bruckner, Hauptstr. 9, ☎ 2329, III 0
[B&B] Donauschlössel, Donaulände 3, ☎ 0664/9156901, III 0.5
[B&B] Gästehaus Datzinger, Rote Torg. 13a, ☎ 2493, ☎ 0664/73203767, III-IV 0.5
[B&B] [AH] Weingut Rixinger, Gut am Steg 8, ☎ 2304, ☎ 0676/9656855, III 1.5
[B&B] Weingut Strawanzer, In der Spitz 3, ☎ 2644, IV 0.5
[B] Gästehaus Martin, Ottenschlagerstr. 34, ☎ 0676/5635982, IV I
[B] Weingut Gebetsberger, Hauptstr. 34, ☎ 2096, ☎ 2660, ☎ 0664/2337608, II-III 0
[bike] Kaufhaus Gurtner, Hauptstr. 26, ☎ 2317 0

### St. Michael (Weißenkirchen in der Wachau)
Prefix: 02713
[B] Gästehau Huber, St. Michael 10, ☎ 2282, ☎ 0664/73575327 0
[B] [AH] Gästehaus zur Wehrkirche, St. Michael 3, ☎ 72919, ☎ 0650/3724410, III 0

### Wösendorf
Prefix: 02715
[B&B] Gästehaus Denk, Winklg. 133, ☎ 0680/3073810, IV 0
[B&B] Weinbau Wagner, Hauptstr. 90, ☎ 2336, ☎ 0650/2336000, II 0
[B&B] [AH] Weinbau Weidenauer, Kellerg. 92, ☎ 72864, ☎ 0664/1423948, III 0.5
[B] Machherndl, Hauptstr. 105, ☎ 2402, I⊕ 0
[B] Urlaub bei Seppi, Winklg. 50, ☎ 0676/5495993, II 0

(B) Weingärtnerei Lengsteiner, Winklg. 53, ☎ 2224, III [0]

(KFZ) KFZ Machherndl, Bachg. 19, ☎ 2392 [0]

## Joching (Weißenkirchen in der Wachau)
Prefix 02715

(H) Weingut Holzapfel, Prandtauerpl. 36, ☎ 2310, VI [0]

(B) Gästehaus Ebner, Weinbergstr. 23, ☎ 0664/4409038, III [0]

(B) Landhaus Smöch, Nr. 55, ☎ 2839, ☎ 0664/3819863, IV-V [0]

(B)(AH) Weinbau-Gästezimmer Jamek, Joching 33, ☎ 2596, II [0]

## Weißenkirchen in der Wachau
Prefix: 02715

(i) Tourist-Info, Wachaustr. 242, ☎ 2600 [0.5]

(i) Municipal office, Rathauspl. 32, ☎ 2232 [0]

(H)(AH) Donauwirt, Wachaustr. 47, ☎ 2247, V [0]

(Hg) Donauhof, Donaug. 298, ☎ 2353, IV-V [0]

(Hg) Weinquadrat, Landstr. 238, ☎ 20008, V [0]

(B&B)(AH) Gästehaus Schmelz, Obere Bachg. 79, ☎ 2388, ☎ 0699/19074609, IV-V [0]

(B) Lehensteiner Weinbau & Gästezimmer, Kremser Str. 7, ☎ 2284, ☎ 0664/5732880, III-IV [0]

(B&B) Freisingerhof, Freisingerpl. 55, ☎ 2320, ☎ 0664/3727298 [0]

(Radservice) Radservice-Box, Wachaustr. 242, ☎ 2600. At the infopoint you will find a Servicebox for your bicycle with tools & bicycle hoses. [0.5]

## Dürnstein
Prefix: 02711

(i) Municipal office, Dürnstein 25, ☎ 219 [0]

(i) Tourist office, Dürnstein 132, ☎ 200 [0]

(H) Gartenhotel & Weingut Pfeffel, Zur Himmelsstiege 122, ☎ 206, V-VI [0]

(H) Relais & Châteaux Hotel Schloss Dürnstein, Dürnstein 2, ☎ 212, VI [0]

(H) Richard Löwenherz, Dürnstein 8, ☎ 222, VI [0]

(H) Sänger Blondel, Dürnstein 64, ☎ 253, IV-V [0]

(B) Weixelbaum, Dürnstein 52, ☎ 422, ☎ 0699/11378255, III [0]

(B&B) Rolea, Talgraben 115, ☎ 20407, ☎ 0660/3431100, III [0]

(B&B)(AH) Winzerhof Stöger, Dürnstein 57, ☎ 396, IV [0]

## Oberloiben (Dürnstein)
Prefix: 02732

(B&B) Doppler, Oberloiben 47, ☎ 73711, ☎ 0664/73756485, II [0]

(B&B) Leonhartsberger, Oberloiben 3, ☎ 84398, ☎ 0660/1559233, IV [0]

(B&B) Schweighofer, Oberloiben 11, ☎ 84337, III [0]

(B&B) Winzerhof Mörtinger, Oberloiben 20, ☎ 76152, II [0]

## Unterloiben (Dürnstein)
Prefix: 02732

(B) Scheibenpflug, Unterloiben 58, ☎ 72411, ☎ 0664/4348406, I [0]

(B&B) Dinstlhof, Unterloiben 6, ☎ 70600, III [0]

## Stein (Krems a. d. Donau)
Prefix: 02732

(i) Tourist Information, Museumspl. 5, ☎ 908010 [0]

(i) Shipping and World Heritage Centre, Welterbepl. 1, ☎ 78282 [0]

(B&B) Einzinger, Steiner Landstr. 82, ☎ 82316, III [0]

(B) Stasny, Steiner Landstr. 22, ☎ 82843, ☎ 0676/7700236, III [0]

(AH) Fiala, Reisperbachtalstr. 24, ☎ 77531, ☎ 0664/73252532, II-III [0.5]

(disabled) ÖAMTC Donaupark-Camping, Yachthafenstr. 19, Stein, ☎ 84455 [0.5]

(Rad) Rund um's Rad, Steiner Landstr. 103, ☎ 71071 [0]

## Egelsee (Krems a. d. Donau)
Prefix: 02732

(H) Lechner, Sandlstr. 11, ☎ 41201, II [2.5]

## Krems a. d. Donau
Prefix: 02732

(i) Tourist Info Wachau, Körnermarkt 14, ☎ 82676 [0]

(H) Alte Post, Obere Landstr. 32, ☎ 82276, III-IV [0]

(H) Klinglhuber, Wiener Str. 10, (Eingang vis à vis Hohensteinstr. 5), ☎ 86960, II-V [0]

(H) Parkhotel Krems, Edmund-Hofbauer-Str. 19, ☎ 0660/2103161, IV [0]

(H) Steigenberger Hotel and Spa, Am Goldberg 2, ☎ 71010, V-VI [0.5]

(H) Unter den Linden, Schillerstr. 5, ☎ 82115, IV-V [0]

(H) arte Hotel Krems, Dr. Karl Dorrek-Str. 23, ☎ 71123, ☎ 80, V [0.5]

(B&B) Weingut Hutter, Weinzierlbergstr. 10, ☎ 82006, V [1]

(icon) Kolping Campus Krems, Alauntalstr. 95 u. 97, ☎ 83541, III [0.5]

(icon) Radfahrer-Jugendherberge Krems, Ringstr. 77, ☎ 83452, ☎ 0664/6530615, OB, II [0]

(Rad) Radstudio Krems, Südtirolerpl. 4, ☎ 81880 [0]

(Rad) Zweirad Aichinger, Hohensteinstr. 22a, ☎ 82876 [0]

## Rohrendorf bei Krems
Prefix: 02732

(B&B) Krappel, Hans Heppenheimerstr. 8, ☎ 72181, ☎ 0676/3304244, IV [2.5]

(B&B)(AH) Trachsler, Weidg. 2, ☎ 81795, ☎ 0664/3605666, III [1.5]

(B&B) Wein-Genuss, Untere Hauptstr. 53, ☎ 796860, ☎ 0676/6256022, V [1.5]

(B&B)(AH) Weingut & Gästehaus Rosenberger, Leiserg. 29, ☎ 83843, IV [1.5]

(B&B)(AH) Weingut Weber, Untere Hauptstr. 52, ☎ 84452, III [2]

(B&B) Schmankerl und Gast, Obere Hauptstr. 38, Navi: Oberer Mitterweg 31, ☎ 0664/2085998, IV [1.5]

(B&B) Winzerhof Bogner, Obere Hauptstr. 24, ☎ 84460, III [1.5]

## Altenwörth (Kirchberg am Wagram)
Prefix: 02279

Tourist Office, Hauptstr. 4, 0681/10277829 0

Kainberger, Sigmarstr. 22, 3695 0

Weinbauernhof Waltner, Sigmarstr. 23, 0676/6775102, III 0

## Zwentendorf an der Donau

Prefix: 02277

Municipal office, Rathauspl. 4, 2209 0

Jeschko, Barbarag. 13, 0650/8418275, II 0.5

Keiblinger, Ing.-August-Kargl-Str. 21, 2271, 2027, I 0.5

Pawelka, Ing. August-Kargl-Str. 1, 2747, 0699/12086123, II 0

Zelenka, Moosbierbaumer Str. 7, 2931, 0650/9848810, III 0.5

Campingplatz, Pappelalllee 1, 220913 0.5

## Atzenbrugg

Diamond Country Club, Am Golfplatz 1, 02275/20075, IV-V 3.5

## Erpersdorf (Zwentendorf an der Donau)

Prefix: 02277

Lutz, Allee 23a, 2314, I 0.5

## Pischelsdorf (Zwentendorf an der Donau)

Prefix: 02277

Daniela, Pischeldorf 33, 2484, II 0.5

Haus Marianne, Pischelsdorf 37, 2554, 0664/5323649, II 0.5

Marschall, Pischelsdorf 44, 0676/4202313, II 0.5

## Langenschönbichl

Prefix: 02272

Theresa, Sonnenstr. 27, 0676/5322332, III 0.5

Gästehaus Lager, Hauptstr. 41, 7338, 0680/2113078 0

## Tulln an der Donau

Prefix: 02272

Tourist Info, Minoritenpl. 2, 67566-0 0

Kirchenblick, Seilerg. 11, 0664/9688717, III 0.5

Renate, Langenlebarner Str. 92, 65077, 0664/5335019, II 1

Junges Hotel Tulln, Marc Aurel Park 1, 651650, II 0

Donaupark Camping, Donaulände 76, 6520013821 0.5

2-Rad Wegl, Jasomirgottg. 4-6, 62695 0.5

Forstinger, Kaplanstr. 12, 059101/9020 1.5

Rad-Service-Stationen, Hauptbahnhof 1

Radsport Voch, Rudolfstr. 5a, 62278 0.5

more than bike, Bahnhofstr. 6, 0660/6229827 0.5

nextbike-Station, 02742/229901 1

## Stockerau

Prefix: 02266

Municipal office, Rathauspl. 1, 69518 0

City-Hotel, Hauptstr. 49, 62930, V 0.5

Drei Königshof, Hauptstr. 29-31, 627880, IV-V 0.5

Kaiserrast, Donaukraftwerkstr. 1, 68000, III-IV 1

Zum weißen Rössel, Josef Wolfikstr. 36, 62617 0.5

Forstinger, Rudolf-Hirsch-Str. 3, 059101/9035 2

Pink Stockerau, Hauptstr. 30, 62434 0.5

Sportmike, Sparkassapl. 2, 72626, 0699/11694411 0.5

Zweirad Spazierer, Bahnhofstr. 11, 62840 0.5

## Korneuburg

Prefix: 02262

Municipal office, Hauptpl. 39, 770 0.5

Zur Sonne, Laaer Str. 12, 0650/4010698, IV 0

Ökotel, Kaiserallee 31, Bisamberg, 0594/59410, III 1

Michlfarm, Zum Scheibenstand 11, 068110617283, OB, III 0

Ullmann, Klein-Engersdorfer Hauptstr. 25, Bisamberg, 0664/7879254 3.5

Gutmann, Eisenbahng. 4, 0664/2004806 0.5

## Wien (Vienna)

Prefix: 01

Tourist information, Albertinapl./Maysederg., 1. Bezirk (Wien), 24555 0.5

## Wien/1. Bezirk

Prefix: 01

Tourist information, Albertinapl./Maysederg., 24555 0.5

Tourist information, Albertinapl./Maysederg., 24555 0.5

Austria, Am Fleischmarkt 20, Wolfeng. 3, 51523, II-V 0.5

https://www.hotel-tigra.at/en/, Tiefer Graben 14-20, 53396410, IV-V 0.5

Domizil, Schulerstr. 14, 5133199, IV-V 0.5

Starlight Suiten Renngasse, Renng. 13, 5339989, V-VI 0.5

Arenberg Boutique Hotel Zentrum, Stubenring 2, 51252910, V-VI 0

Neuer Markt, Seilerg. 9, 5122316, III-V 0.5

Sacher Apartments, Rotenturmstr. 1-3, 7. Stock, 5333238, 0676/4451658, OB, IV-V 0

Pedal Power Vienna, Bösendorferstr. 5, 7297234 0

Radhaus Singer, Reichsratsstr. 13, 4062143 0.5

Trek Bicycle Vienna, Hegelg. 19, 5130514 0

Vienna Explorer, Franz-Josefs-Kai 45, 8909682 0

## Wien/2. Bezirk

Prefix: 01

Kunsthof, Mühlfeldg. 13, 2143178, III-IV 0.5

Odeon, Weintraubeng. 31, 2142362, 0650/4720732, IV 0.5

Stefanie, Taborstr. 12, 211500, V 0.5

Wilhelmshof, Kleine Stadtgutg. 4, 21455210, IV-V 0.5

Peter Vesecky, Böcklinstr. 64, 7289311 1.5

🔧 Sator Bike Shop, Böcklinstr. 104, ☏ 7289136 ②

## Wien/3. Bezirk
Prefix: 01

Ⓗ Garten- & Kunsthotel Gabriel, Landstraßer Hauptstr. 165, ☏ 7123205, III-IV ②

Ⓗ Mercure Grand Hotel Biedermeier Wien, Landstraßer Hauptstr. 28, ☏ 716710, V-VI ①

Ⓗ Vienna Sporthotel, Baumg. 83, ☏ 79882010, IV-V 2.5

B&B Kiki Rooms, Landstraßer Hauptstr. 33, ☏ 7121068, III ①

## Wien/4. Bezirk
Prefix: 01

Ⓗ Beim Theresianum, Favoritenstr. 52, ☏ 5051606, V 0.5

Ⓗ Carlton Opera, Schikanederg. 4, ☏ 5875302, III-VI 0.5

Ⓗ Johann Strauss, Favoritenstr. 12, ☏ 5057624, IV-VI 0.5

Ⓗ Kaiserhof Wien, Frankenbergg. 10, ☏ 4170963, V-VI 0.5

Ⓗ Sommerhotel Wieden, Schelleing. 36, ☏ 50152100, IV. open from July to September 0.5

🔧 2rad-shop Gerhardt, Wiedner Hauptstr. 55, ☏ 0676/6850715 0.5

🔧 ARGUS Shop, Frankenbergg. 11, ☏ 9195019 0.5

## Wien/5. Bezirk
Prefix: 01

Ⓗ Austria Trend Hotel Ananas, Rechte Wienzeile 93-95, Eingang Sonnenhofg. 8-10, ☏ 54620901, III-V 1.5

Ⓗ Holiday Inn Wien City, Margaretenstr. 53, ☏ 58850, IV-V ①

Ⓗ Ibis Wien City, Schönbrunner Str. 92, ☏ 590070, III-IV ②

ⒶⒽ Residenz Johann-Strauß, Einsiedlerg. 19, ☏ 5441351, ☏ 0676/5378816, II-V ②

🔧 MITICO Bikes Vienna, Margaretenstr. 107, ☏ 9072087 1.5

🔧 die radwerkstatt, Margaretengürtel 134, ☏ 5443801 ②

## Wien/6. Bezirk
Prefix: 01

Ⓗ Terminus, Fillgraderg. 4, ☏ 58773860, III-IV 0.5

🏛 Kolpinghaus Wien Zentral, Gumpendorferstr. 39, ☏ 58756310, II-IV ①

🏛 Westend City Hostel, Fügerg. 3, ☏ 5976729, III ②

🔧 Bicycle Company, Getreidemarkt 1, ☏ 8901028 0.5

🔧 Fahrrad+Skii, Linke Wienzeile 124/128, ☏ 5978288, ☏ 0664/1004659 1.5

🔧 IG Fahrrad, Otto Bauer G. 16, ☏ 5235113, ☏ 0650/3346723 1.5

🔧 Radsport Niesner, Schmalzhofg. 10, ☏ 5970477, ☏ 0664/1810921 1.5

## Wien/7. Bezirk
Prefix: 01

Ⓗ K & K Maria Theresia, Kirchbergg. 6, ☏ 52123, IV-V 0.5

B&B Atrium, Burgg. 118, ☏ 0664/3436212, III-IV 1.5

B&B Columbia, Kochg. 9, ☏ 4056757, II ①

B&B Dormium, Kandlg. 35/7, ☏ 5267340, ☏ 0681/10395390, IV 1.5

🏠 JH, Myrtheng. 7, Neustiftg. 85, ☏ 5236316, I ①

🔧 Radplatz, Kaiserstr. 106, ☏ 9612610 1.5

## Wien/8. Bezirk
Prefix: 01

B&B Zipser, Lange G. 49, ☏ 404540, III-V ①

## Wien/9. Bezirk
Prefix: 01

Ⓗ Bleckmann, Währinger Str. 15, ☏ 4080899, III 0.5

Ⓗ Gala, Viriotg. 5, ☏ 310083711, III ②

Ⓗ Harmonie, Harmonieg. 5-7, ☏ 3175604, V ①

Ⓗ Mozart, Nordbergstr. 4, ☏ 3171537, III-V ①

🔧 Arizona Bike, Nußdorfer Str. 3/3, ☏ 0680/1161575 1.5

🔧 Bikers, Spittelauer Lände 12, bei P+R Spittelau, ☏ 2764960 ②

🔧 Mountainbiker, Währinger Gürte 146/150, ☏ 4707186 ②

## Wien/10. Bezirk
Prefix: 01

Ⓗ Zeitgeist Vienna, Sonnwendg. 15, ☏ 902650, V-VI 0.5

B&B Arnes, Quellenstr. 120, ☏ 0699/13040580, OB, II-III 1.5

## Wien/15. Bezirk
Prefix: 01

Ⓗ Boutiquehotel Stadthalle, Hackeng. 20, (Westbhf), ☏ 9824272, V ②

Ⓗ Lucia, Hütteldorfer Str. 79, ☏ 7865272, IV-V ③

Ⓗ Westbahn, Pelzg. 1, ☏ 9821480, V ②

B&B Fünfhaus, Sperrg. 12, ☏ 8923545, III 2.5

Ⓗⓞ Ruthensteiner, Robert-Hamerlingg. 24, ☏ 8934202, OB, I-III 2.5

## Wien/19. Bezirk
Prefix: 01

Ⓗ Derag Livinghotel Kaiser Franz Joseph, Sieveringer Str. 4, ☏ 3207355, ☏ 329000, IV 2.5

Ⓗ Müllner, Grinziger Allee 30, ☏ 32084530, OB, III 2.5

🔧 Donau Fritzi, Heiligenstädterstr. 180, Donaupromenade am Radweg, ☏ 3704598 0.5

## Wien/20. Bezirk
Prefix: 01

🏛 Jugendgästehaus, Adalbert Stifter Str. 73, ☏ 3328294, I ①

🔧 Fahrrad Trappl, Leystr. 75, ☏ 3300696 ①

## Wien/21. Bezirk
Prefix: 01

B&B Fuchs, Jedlersdorfer Pl. 29, ☏ 0664/3023855, IV 3.5

ⒶⒽ Vivo, Freytagg. 25-27, ☏ 3561919, OB, II-IV 1.5

🔧 Aschauers Radverleih Donauinsel, Donauinsel 2, Parkplatz Floridsdorfer

Brücke, ☎ 2788698 **0**
🏊 Dorfinger, Galvanig. 19, ☎ 2711447,
☎ 0676/9501222 **1.5**

# Melk to Vienna along the south bank

## Melk
Prefix: 02752
ℹ️ Info centre, Kremser Str. 5, ☎ 51160 **0**
Ⓗ Zum Fürsten, Rathauspl. 3, ☎ 52343, III-IV **0.5**
Ⓑ Café Central, Hauptpl. 10, ☎ 52343,
☎ 0664/88469101, III **0**
🏛 Junges Hotel Melk, Abt Karl-Str. 42, ☎ 52681,
II **1**
⛺ Campingplatz der Stadt Melk, Kolomaniau 3,
☎ 0676/8447156540 **0.5**

## Schönbühel (Schönbühel-Aggsbach)
Prefix: 02752
ℹ️ Municipal office, Nr.48, ☎ 8619 **0**
Ⓗ ⛺ Stumpfer, Melker Str. 1, ☎ 8510, IV **0**
Ⓐ Ⓗ Jausenstation beim Schloss, Schönbühel 42,
☎ 0664/2521424, III **0**

## Aggsbach-Dorf (Schönbühel-Aggsbach)
Prefix: 02753
ℹ️ Municipal office, Nr. 48, ☎ 8269 **0**
Ⓗ Residenz Wachau, Aggsbach Dorf 19,
☎ 8221, V-VI **0**
Ⓑ Domingo, Aggsbach Dorf 129, ☎ 8353, II **0**
Ⓑ Haidn, Aggsbach Dorf 100, ☎ 8277,
☎ 0676/6717161, III **0**
Ⓑ Reisinger, Aggsbach Dorf 20, ☎ 8372,

☎ 0664/4314170, II **0**

## Aggstein (Schönbühel-Aggsbach)
Prefix: 02753
Ⓑ Radlerhof Kienesberger, Aggstein 8, ☎ 8455,
☎ 0676/7777060, III **0**

## Oberarnsdorf (Mitterarnsdorf)
Prefix: 02714
ℹ️ Municipal office, Rossatz 29, Rossatz (Mitterarnsdorf), ☎ 6217 **0.5**
Ⓑ Weingut Hick, Oberarnsdorf 58, ☎ 8214,
III **0.5**
Ⓑ Wessner, Oberarnsdorf 61, ☎ 8480, I-II **0.5**

## Hofarnsdorf (Mitterarnsdorf)
Prefix: 02714
Ⓗ Zur Wachau, Mitterarnsdorf 55, ☎ 8217,
☎ 0676/9504064, IV **0.5**
Ⓑ Auer, Hofarnsdorf 31, ☎ 0680/2080045,
III **0.5**
Ⓑ Fuchsbauer, Hofarnsdorf 20, ☎ 8358,
☎ 0664/7884563 **0.5**

## Bacharnsdorf (Mitterarnsdorf)
Ⓑ Ⓐ Weinbau & Gästezimmer Pammer,
Bacharnsdorf 18, ☎ 02714/6545,
☎ 0664/4205369, II **0**

## Rührsdorf (Mitterarnsdorf)
Prefix: 02714
Ⓑ Weingut Polz, Rührsdorf 22, ☎ 6326,
☎ 0664/4320426, ☎ 0664/1806128, II **0**

## Rossatz (Mitterarnsdorf)
Prefix: 02714

ℹ️ Municipal office, Rossatz 29, ☎ 6217 **0.5**
Ⓗ Rossatz 8, Rossatz 8, ☎ 58337,
☎ 0660/5324699, III-VI **0.5**
Ⓑ Ⓐ Haus Annemarie, Rossatz 164, ☎ 6261,
☎ 0664/5047874, III **0.5**
Ⓑ Landhaus Rossatz, Rossatz 172, ☎ 6362,
☎ 0676/9214141, II **0.5**
Ⓑ Subenhof, Rossatz 16, ☎ 6252,
☎ 0664/3519590 **0.5**
Ⓑ Wendler, Rossatz 66, ☎ 6542 **0.5**

## Rossatzbach (Mitterarnsdorf)
Prefix: 02714
Ⓑ Gästehaus Weidenauer, Rossatzbach 46,
☎ 6580, ☎ 0664/4002689, III **0**
⛺ Wachauamping Rossatz, Rossatzbach 21,
☎ 6217, ☎ 0676/848814800 **0**

## Hundsheim (Mautern a. d. Donau)
Prefix: 02732
Ⓑ Ⓐ Haus Schweigl, Hundsheim 20, ☎ 85750,
☎ 0650/4304640, II **0**
Ⓑ Winzerhof Eder, Hundsheim 7, ☎ 74949,
☎ 0676/6558700 **0**

## Mauternbach (Mautern a. d. Donau)
Prefix: 02732
Ⓑ Ⓐ Weinhof am Römerweg, Mauternbach 11,
☎ 72848, ☎ 0676/3511490, II **0.5**
Ⓑ Gerlinde, Mauternbach 30, ☎ 86211,
☎ 0664/1116908, ☎ 0676/3515632 **0.5**

## Mautern a. d. Donau
Prefix: 02732
ℹ️ Town office, Rathauspl. 1, ☎ 83151 **0**

Ⓗ Landhaus Bacher, Südtirolerpl. 2, ☎ 82937,
V-VI **0**
Ⓗ Wirtshaus Hofer, Südtirolerpl. 3,
☎ 0664/73931100, III **0**
Ⓑ Nikolaihof, Kainzstr. 14, ☎ 0676/4331828,
IV **0.5**
Ⓑ Severinhof, Frauenhofg. 12, ☎ 84643,
☎ 0664/5792649, II **0**
Ⓑ Brauneis, Grüner Weg 37, ☎ 85188,
☎ 0650/9917591, III **0**
🚲 nextbike-Station, Schloßg. 8, Parkplatz der
Römerhalle, ☎ 02742/229901 **0**

## Palt (Furth bei Göttweig)
Prefix: 02732
Ⓗ MALAT Weingut und Hotel, Hafnerstr. 12,
☎ 82934, VI **0**
Ⓗ Weinresidenz Sonnleitner, Zeughausg. 239,
☎ 70446, V-VI **0**
Ⓑ Brandl-Göstl, Rudolf Müllauerstr. 455,
☎ 0699/10529633, III **0.5**
Ⓑ Wein- u. Gästehof Edlinger, Lindeng. 22,
☎ 77622, ☎ 0664/3445998, III **0**

## Furth bei Göttweig
Prefix: 02732
ℹ️ Municipal office, Obere Landstr. 65,
☎ 846220 **0**
Ⓗ Zur Goldenen Krone, Untere Landstr. 1,
☎ 84666, ☎ 0650/2772573, V **0**
Ⓑ Mülbe, Linke Bachzeile 41, ☎ 0676/7055739,
II **0**
Ⓑ Schwarzhapl-Ramler, Landwidweg 394,

C 75763, II 0.5

### Stift Göttweig (Furth bei Göttweig)
Prefix: 02732
B Benediktinerstift Göttweig, Stift Göttweig 1,
C 855810, IV 0

### Klein-Wien (Furth bei Göttweig)
Prefix: 02736
H Landgasthof Schickh-Salzer, Avastr. 2,
C 7218, III 0.5

### Thallern (Krems a. d. Donau)
Prefix: 02739
B Beranek, Thallerner Hauptstr. 75, C 2065,
C 0664/73640672, I 0

### Oberfucha (Furth bei Göttweig)
Prefix: 02739
B&B Parzer, Furthnersteig 55, C 24145, III 1

### Angern (Krems a. d. Donau)
Prefix: 02739
B&B AH Weinhof Aufreiter, Dorfstr. 34, C 2205, III-
IV 0
B Weinhof Maier, Dorfstr. 17, C 0676/3875350,
C 0676/4737132, IV 0

### Hollenburg (Krems a. d. Donau)
Prefix: 02739
B Hochleitner, Römerstr. 19, C 2168,
C 0664/73456181 0

### Wagram o. d. Traisen (Traismauer)
Prefix: 02783
H Landgasthof Huber Zum schwarzen Adler,
Wachaustr. 43, C 8481, III 2

---

AH Winzerhaus Schöller, Wagramerstr. 10,
C 535, C 0664/4266261, III-V 2.5
Zweirad Schwab, Wachaustr.9, C 6320 2

### St. Georgen a. d. Traisen (Traismauer)
Prefix: 02783
B&B Weingut Haimel, St. Georgener G. 5,
C 0664/8226477, IV 1
B Schopper, Kremser Str. 84, C 8885,
C 0650/2513150 1

### Traismauer
Prefix: 02783
i Tourist information, Hauptpl. 1, C 8555 0
Hg Zum Schwan, Wiener Str. 12, C 6236, III-
IV 0.5
H Aprico, In der Traisenau 1, C 0680/1541486,
IV 0
H Nibelungenhof, Wiener Str. 23, C 6349,
C 0676/4004645, IV-II 0.5
B Schreiblehner, Untere Siebenbrunneng. 15,
C 7471, C 0650/4639135 0.5
B&B Bed, Bike and Breakfast, Wienerstr. 4,
C 0664/8330030, IV 0.5

### Stollhofen (Traismauer)
Prefix: 02783
B Kaiblinger, Kriemhildstr. 6, C 6391,
C 0664/4929012 0.5
B Maissner, Friedhofstr. 3, C 6814,
C 0650/6589830 1
B Muck, Schwemmg. 2a, C 0676/9409020 1

### Zwentendorf an der Donau
Prefix: 02277

---

i Municipal office, Rathauspl. 4, C 2209 0
B&B Jeschko, Barbarag. 13, C 0650/8418275,
II 0.5
B Keiblinger, Ing.-August-Kargl-Str. 21, C 2271,
C 2027, I 0.5
B Pawelka, Ing. August-Kargl-Str. 1, C 2747,
C 0699/12086123, II 0
B Zelenka, Moosbierbaumer Str. 7, C 2931,
C 0650/9848810, III 0.5
A Campingplatz, Pappelalllee 1, C 220913 0.5

### Erpersdorf (Zwentendorf an der Donau)
Prefix: 02277
B Lutz, Allee 23a, C 2314, I 0.5

### Pischelsdorf (Zwentendorf an der Donau)
Prefix: 02277
B Daniela, Pischeldorf 33, C 2484, II 0.5
B Haus Marianne, Pischelsdorf 37, C 2554,
C 0664/5323649, II 0.5
B AH Marschall, Pischelsdorf 44,
C 0676/4202313, II 0.5

### Langenschönbichl
Prefix: 02272
B&B Theresa, Sonnenstr. 27, C 0676/5322332,
III 0.5
B Gästehaus Lager, Hauptstr. 41, C 7338,
C 0680/2113078 0

### Tulln an der Donau
Prefix: 02272
i Tourist Info, Minoritenpl. 2, C 67566-0 0
B&B Kirchenblick, Seilerg. 11, C 0664/9688717, III
0.5

---

B&B Renate, Langenlebarner Str. 92, C 65077,
C 0664/5335019, II 0.5
Hh Junges Hotel Tulln, Marc Aurel Park 1,
C 651650, II 0
A Donaupark Camping, Donaulände 76,
C 6520013821 0
2-Rad Wegl, Jasomirgottg. 4-6, C 62695 0.5
Forstinger, Kaplanstr. 12, C 059101/9020 1
Rad-Service-Stationen, Hauptbahnhof 1
Radsport Voch, Rudolfstr. 5a, C 62278 0.5
more than bike, Bahnhofstr. 6,
C 0660/6229827 0.5
nextbike-Station, C 02742/229901 1

### Langenlebarn
Prefix: 02272
H Buchingers Donauhotel, Wiener Str. 5,
C 62527, II 0
B Berger-Raab, Wiener Str. 43,
C 0664/5343176 0

### Muckendorf (Muckendorf-Wipfing)
Prefix: 02242
i Municipal office, Bahnstr. 3, C 70214 1
H Zum Wolf in der Au, Tullner Str. 1, C 70223,
C 0664/4026185 0.5

### Greifenstein
Prefix: 02242
i Municipal office, Altg. 30, St. Andrä-
Wördern, C 31300 2
B Sappert, Hadersfelderstr. 3, C 32828, OB, I 0
B AH Villa Neuwirth, Hadersfelderstr. 11,
C 33589, C 0676/5143590, II-III 0

[AH] Alte Post, Hauptstr. 25, ☎ 0699/10981383, III ⌨ 0

## Höflein (Klosterneuburg)

Prefix: 02243

[H] Roter Hahn, Hauptstr. 117, ☎ 0660/6666630, III 0.5

[H] Zum Goldenen Anker, Hauptstr. 143, ☎ 80134, II 0.5

## Kritzendorf (Klosterneuburg)

Prefix: 02243

[B&B] Pension Huber, Hauptstr. 90- 92, ☎ 33884, ☎ 0664/1616331, III-IV 0

[AH] Hauerhof 99, Hauptstr. 99, ☎ 0676/4305979, III-IV ⌨ 0.5

## Klosterneuburg

Prefix: 02243

[i] Klosterneuburg tourism, In der Au 2-4, Freizeitzentrum Happyland, ☎ 32038 0.5

[H] Anker, Niedermarkt 5, ☎ 32134, III ☺ 0

[H] Hotel Schrannenhof, Niedermarkt 17-19, ☎ 32072, IV ☺ 0

[Hg] Appartements Andrea, Medekstr. 15, ☎ 06763538035, OB, IV ☺ 0.5

[Hg] Hotel-Pension Goldenberg, Kierlinger Str. 94b, ☎ 26090, OB, II-III 1.5

[B&B] Hotel-Pension Alte Mühle, Mühleng. 36, ☎ 37788, III ☺ 0.5

[B] Sonne, Waisenhausg. 12, ☎ 0664/5057669, III 0.5

[▲] Donaupark Camping, In der Au 1, ☎ 25877 0

## Weidling

[B] Villa Kreuthhof - Appartements, Reicherg. 1, ☎ 0676/3169818, IV 2.5

## Wien (Vienna)

Prefix: 01

[i] Tourist information, Albertinapl./Maysederg., 1. Bezirk (Wien), ☎ 24555 0.5

# Geographical Index

Page numbers from page 166 refer to the list of accommodations


## A

| | |
|---|---|
| Abwinden | 64, 170 |
| Aggsbach-Dorf | 139, 178 |
| Aggsbach Markt | 109, 174 |
| Aggstein | 140, 178 |
| Albern | 68 |
| Altenwörth | 124, 175 |
| Angern | 146, 179 |
| Ardagger | 173 |
| Ardagger Markt | 96, 173 |
| Ardagger Stift | 96, 173 |
| Artstetten-Pöbring | 78, 172 |
| Aschach an der Donau | 48, 169 |
| Asten | 86, 173 |
| Atzenbrugg | 176 |
| Au a. d. Donau | 68, 171 |
| Au/Schlögen | 26, 167 |
| Ausee | 85, 173 |

## B

| | |
|---|---|
| Bacharnsdorf | 141, 178 |
| Bad Mühllacken | 168 |
| Baumgartenberg | 70, 171 |
| Bayerisch Haibach | 169 |
| Brandstatt | 51, 170 |
| Bruck bei Tödling | 173 |

## D

| | |
|---|---|
| Dorf | 26, 167 |
| Dornach | 70 |
| Dörnbach | 170 |
| Dürnstein | 114, 175 |

## E

| | |
|---|---|
| Edramsberg | 170 |
| Eferding | 51, 170 |
| Egelsee | 175 |
| Eizendorf | 70 |
| Emmersdorf a. d. Donau | 80, 172, 174 |
| Engelhartszell | 22, 42, 167, 169 |
| Enghagen | 88 |
| Enns | 88, 90, 173 |
| Ennsdorf | 173 |
| Erlau | 20, 167 |
| Erpersdorf | 176, 179 |
| Esternberg | 42, 169 |
| Exlau | 168 |

## F

| | |
|---|---|
| Fall | 52, 170 |
| Feldkirchen an der Donau | 30, 168 |
| Freinberg | 169 |
| Freizeithafen Ardagger | 96 |
| Freizell | 26, 167 |
| Freudenstein | 168 |
| Freyenstein | 98, 173 |
| Furth bei Göttweig | 144, 178 |

## G

| | |
|---|---|
| Goldwörth | 31 |
| Gottsdorf | 77 |
| Grafenau | 27 |
| Greifenstein | 152, 179 |
| Grein a. d. Donau | 72, 171 |
| Grimsing | 109 |
| Groisbach | 109, 174 |
| Gusen | 64 |

## H

| | |
|---|---|
| Hagenau | 34 |
| Hagsdorf | 76, 171 |
| Haibach ob der Donau | 48, 169 |
| Hals | 167 |